Religion in Modern English Drama

✳✳✳✳✳✳✳✳✳✳✳✳✳✳✳✳✳✳✳✳✳✳✳✳✳✳✳✳✳✳✳✳✳✳✳

by

GERALD WEALES

GREENWOOD PRESS, PUBLISHERS
WESTPORT, CONNECTICUT

Library of Congress Cataloging in Publication Data

Weales, Gerald Clifford, 1925-
    Religion in modern English drama.

    Reprint of the ed. published by University of
Pennsylvania Press, Philadelphia.
    Bibliography: p.
    Includes index.
    1. English drama--20th century--History and
criticism. 2. Christian drama, English--History and
criticism. 3. Religion in drama. I. Title.
[PR739.R4W4 1976]   822'.9' 10931   75-45367
ISBN 0-8371-8735-4

Originally published in the United States in 1961 by University
of Pennsylvania Press, Philadelphia

Reprinted with the permission of University of Pennsylvania
Press

Reprinted in 1976 by Greenwood Press,
a division of Williamhouse-Regency Inc.

Library of Congress Catalog Card Number 75-45367

ISBN 0-8371-8735-4

Printed in the United States of America

For

MOTHER and DAD

Acknowledgments

Acknowledgment is made to the following for permission to quote from copyright material:

From the opera *The Rake's Progress*, music by Igor Stravinsky, libretto by W. H. Auden and Chester Kallman, copyright 1951 by Boosey & Hawkes, Inc., used by permission.

From *Old Testament Plays*, by Laurence Housman, by permission of Jonathan Cape, Ltd.

From *A Comedy of Good and Evil*, 1924, Richard Hughes, by permission of A. Watkins, Inc., and Chatto and Windus, Ltd.

From "The Love Song of J. Alfred Prufrock" and "Sweeney Among the Nightingales" from *Collected Poems*, 1909-1935, by T. S. Eliot, copyright, 1936, by Harcourt, Brace and Company, Inc.; "East Coker," "Burnt Norton" and "The Dry Salvages," from *Four Quartets*, copyright, 1943, by T. S. Eliot; *Murder in the Cathedral*, by T. S. Eliot, copyright, 1935, by Harcourt, Brace; *The Family Reunion*, copyright, 1939, by T. S. Eliot; *The Cocktail Party*, copyright, 1950, by T. S. Eliot; *The Confidential Clerk*, copyright, 1954, by T. S. Eliot; *The Rock*, by T. S. Eliot, copyright, 1934, by Harcourt, Brace —all by permission of Harcourt, Brace. From *On Poetry and Poets*, copyright 1951, 1957 by T. S. Eliot, by permission of the publishers,

Farrar, Straus and Cudahy. From *The Use of Poetry and the Use of Criticism* and *Poetry and Drama*, by T. S. Eliot, by permission of Harvard University Press. From all these works of T. S. Eliot, by permission of Faber and Faber, Ltd.

From *The Shadow Factory* and *Henry Bly and Other Plays*, by Anne Ridler, by permission of Faber and Faber, Ltd.

From *This Way to the Tomb*, by Ronald Duncan, by permission of Faber and Faber, Ltd. From *Stratton* and *Death of Satan*, by Ronald Duncan, by permission of David Higham Associates Ltd.

From *Seed of Adam and Other Plays, The Image of the City, Three Plays, Cranmer of Canterbury* and *Judgement at Chelmsford*, by Charles Williams, by permission of Oxford University Press. From *The Descent of the Dove,* by Charles Williams, and *All Hallow's Eve*, by Charles Williams, copyright 1948 by Pelligrini & Cudahy, by permission of the publishers Farrar, Straus and Cudahy: also by permission of David Higham Associates Ltd.

From *The Man Born to Be King*, by Dorothy L. Sayers, copyright by Harper & Brothers, used by permission; also by permission of David Higham Associates Ltd.

From *The Burning Glass*, by Charles Morgan, by permission of Macmillan & Company, Ltd., and St. Martin's Press, Inc.

From *The Trial of Jesus* and *The Coming of Christ,* by John Masefield, by permission of the Macmillan Company, the Society of Authors, and Dr. John Masefield, O.M.

From *Saints and Sinners*, by Henry Arthur Jones, and *The Life and Letters of Henry Arthur Jones,* by Doris Arthur Jones, by permission of the Macmillan Company.

From *David*, by D. H. Lawrence, from *Religious Drama* 1, copyright 1957, by Meridian Books, Inc., by permission of Meridian.

From *A Sleep of Prisoners, The Firstborn, Thor, with Angels, The Lady's Not for Burning* and *The Dark Is Light Enough,* by Christopher Fry, by permission of Oxford University Press. From *The Boy with a Cart*, by Christopher Fry, by permission of Oxford University Press, Inc., and Frederick Muller, Ltd. From *An Experience of Critics,* by Christopher Fry, by permission of Perpetua, Ltd. Also by permission of Leah Salisbury, Inc.

From *The Plays of J. B. Priestley* and the "Author's Note for this Edition" from *Three Time-Plays*, by J. B. Priestley, by permission of A. D. Peters.

From *The Living Room* and *The Potting Shed*, by Graham Greene, by permission of The Viking Press, William Heinemann, Ltd., and Laurence Pollinger, Ltd.

From *Magic*, by G. K. Chesterton, copyright renewed 1941, by permission of G. P. Putnam's Sons.

From *Three Plays*, by Harley Granville Barker, by permission of Field Roscoe & Co.

From *A Well-Remembered Voice, Dear Brutus* and *The Boy David*, by J. M. Barrie, by permission of Charles Scribner's Sons and Hodder and Stoughton, Ltd., From the Introduction by Harley Granville-Barker to *The Boy David*, by permission of Charles Scribner's Sons. The quotations from the plays of James M. Barrie and from the Introduction by Harley Granville-Barker to *The Boy David* are fully protected by copyright and may not be used in any manner without the permission of Charles Scribner's Sons.

From *Christ in the Concrete City*, by Philip Turner, by permission of the Religious Drama Society and the S.P.C.K.

From *Holy Family* and *The Prodigal Son*, by R. H. Ward, by permission of the Religious Drama Society, the S.P.C.K. and the author. From *The Destiny of Man* and *Faust in Hell*, by R. H. Ward, by permission of the author.

From the works of George Bernard Shaw, by permission of the Public Trustee and the Society of Authors.

From *Man and Literature,* by Norman Nicholson, by permission of the Student Christian Movement Press Ltd.

From *Two Plays and a Preface*, by Nigel Dennis, by permission of Vanguard Press, Inc., and Weidenfeld & Nicolson, Ltd.

If piety can't act, Father, piety ought not to be in a play.

Judgement at Chelmsford
Charles Williams

Preface

So many people offered me advice and admonition, comfort and criticism while this book was in preparation that I cannot list them all here. To anyone who found a missing footnote for me, held copy while I read proof, made suggestions that led me astray or simply stood aside, smiling fondly, while I went at it, thank you. A few who did more than a little should be thanked formally: Miss Nora Magid, who reluctantly read the manuscript in so many forms; Mr. E. Martin Browne, who directed me to a few playwrights I might have missed and who caught some factual errors which might otherwise have found their way into final copy; Professors Eric Bentley and S. F. Johnson of Columbia, who, in the line of duty, read the manuscript in its first form; Miss Carol Worley, who helped with the typing.

G. W.

Philadelphia
April, 1960

Introduction

The successful production of religious plays, those of T. S. Eliot and Christopher Fry, on the English commercial stage in the years since World War II is not an isolated phenomenon in the history of modern English drama. I hope to show in this study that Eliot and Fry are related to two distinguishable streams of English drama and that their success, accepting always their obvious dramatic abilities, rests in part on the confluence of those two streams. The two playwrights belong in a line that runs back as far as Henry Arthur Jones, whose *Saints and Sinners* (1884) is here used as the first play in an examination of the uses of religion on the commercial stage. At the same time, the immediate roots of Eliot and Fry as dramatists lie in the semiprofessional church drama movement which begins in modern times roughly with William Poel's revival of *Everyman* (1901). The followers of Jones have made the discussion and presentation of religion acceptable to the commercial stage, and the movement that followed Poel's revival has set up a climate in which the religious playwright is assured that his treatment of his own religious concerns will be regarded as more than a dramatic contrivance.

In Part One of this study I examine the ways in which religion has been used on the commercial stage. In Part Two I trace the history of the church drama movement. In Part Three I discuss religious drama since World War II, bringing the separate concerns of Part One and Part Two up to date and at the same time focusing on Eliot and Fry and their followers, who have moved comfortably between the commercial and the church theater. I have tried to strike a balance between the two possible approaches to such material—the presentation of typical playwrights and the cataloguing of plays in volume. The essay is certainly not exhaustive, but it does include discussion of a great number of plays in an attempt to present an accurate account of what has gone on in England at the meeting of religion and drama.

To keep the study within bounds, somewhat arbitrary decisions had to be made about what material was to be covered. The expression *English drama* is used here to mean drama in England and is not extended to include either the American or the Irish playwrights. This double exclusion does not presuppose that there would be no value in a similar study of the Americans or the Irish. The presence or the absence of individual playwrights may be open to question, but there is logic of a sort in all the decisions. W. B. Yeats and Sean O'Casey were reluctantly passed over because their presence would have opened the door to a consideration of Irish drama as a whole. On the other hand, Bernard Shaw and St. John Ervine are included. Shaw obviously belongs in any study of English drama, and Ervine is present because, unlike O'Casey, his transplantation to England turned him into a playwright whose work is indistinguishable from that of any number of English commercial dramatists. The occasional Scot (James Bridie), Welshman (J. O. Francis, Richard Hughes), and Manxman (Hall Caine) are possible because—even recognizing that there has been a fitful Scottish dramatic movement during the century—they do not bring a national drama that would demand consideration.

The implications of any study of religious drama are endless. As there are geographical limits in this book, so too there is a necessary thematic limitation. Religious drama in modern England could be studied in relation to a whole social phenomenon, the supposed religious revival, but such a study is present here only by implication in the chapters on the historical growth of the church drama movement and in the examination of the particular spiritual concerns of some of the leading religious playwrights. The relationship between medieval religious drama in England and the modern revival might also be a subject for extensive discussion. Although workers in church drama, such as E. Martin Browne in his pamphlet *Religious Drama*, look back to the medieval relationship of church and stage with some sense of continuity, the line between the ancient and modern moralities is not clear enough to make a detailed relative study valuable in the context of this book. The subject is treated here only in discussing the extent to which staged revivals of early religious plays, following Poel's *Everyman*, led to the writing of new plays and in describing the specific borrowings that individual playwrights made in following medieval models. Although many of the playwrights under consideration have drawn on their continental, particularly French, forebears, the relationship of the English dramatists to those in the rest of Europe is only glancingly present here. I am primarily concerned to show that there are two English traditions within this century, to either or both of which any English writer of religious plays has an important relationship. I do not mean that religious drama in England is an hermetically sealed product with *Saints and Sinners* at one end and the latest religious play at the other. The emphasis is essentially a practical, working convenience and not a qualitative or philosophic insistence.

The use of the word *religion* in this essay also needs clarification. It is generally used to imply some concept of God, usually that of an established church or belief. Although political or philosophical faith can have the emotional intensity of religious belief, such kinds of faith are not under discussion here, except with playwrights, like Bernard Shaw and James Bridie, who make extensive use of conventional religious terminology (often unconventionally) in the presentation of their ideas. Many of the plays examined are not religious in any sense, but they are here because they carry the socially recognizable marks of religion in England —the church, the clergyman, the Bible, the invocation of God.

Primarily the study is concerned with Christian drama. Even

those playwrights who present, dramatically or argumentatively, some idea of personal religion are likely to use Christian ideas in their presentations. For that reason and for the sake of definition, some workable designation for the word *Christian* had to be found. Although the many Christian sects have never agreed on such a definition, for the sake of this book a Christian is one who believes in the incarnation, crucifixion, and resurrection of Christ as historical and spiritual facts. Such a definition is intentionally limiting. It is useful to me as I attempt to explain the nature of the individual beliefs that are presented in this study. At no point is religion, faith or belief used to mean Christianity, except when a playwright is identified as a believing Christian.

I am passing no judgment on the belief of any of the playwrights. In some cases, the sincerity of playwrights has been questioned where use of religion is a stage gimmick and no more. In others, the social implications of certain beliefs have been discussed. For the most part, an attempt has been made to define the nature of a playwright's belief whenever the playright is of more than passing interest. The critical evaluation of the plays, of the presentation of the dramatic ideas, is not intended as an evaluation of the ideas as such. Although such an evaluation might be useful, it would be fatal to an attempt to describe the growth of religious drama in England during this century. The believing Christian might confuse faith and dramaturgy; the believing atheist might do the same. I have no axe to grind. This study is neither Christian nor non-Christian apologetics. A religious idea, a Christian idea, like any other idea, can be an impetus to drama. This book is an account of the plays that have arisen from that impetus during this century.

Contents

Chapter

INTRODUCTION

PART ONE: COMMERCIAL DRAMA

I	THE LEGACY OF HENRY ARTHUR JONES	3
II	BARRETT, THE BIBLE AND THE BIG SHOWS	24
III	SENTIMENTAL SUPERNATURALISM	38
IV	A DOCTRINE OF SUBSTITUTION	51

PART TWO: CHURCH DRAMA

V	UP FROM EVERYMAN	93
VI	CANTERBURY, CHICHESTER AND THE RELIGIOUS DRAMA SOCIETY	107
VII	LAURENCE HOUSMAN AND JOHN MASEFIELD	122
VIII	CHARLES WILLIAMS AND DOROTHY SAYERS	142

PART THREE: THE POST-WAR YEARS

IX	T. S. ELIOT AND CHRISTOPHER FRY	183
X	THE MERCURY POETS	226
XI	COMMERCIAL DRAMA: A REPRISE	243
XII	THE CHURCH CIRCUIT	255
XIII	THE DIVISION AND THE PROSPECT	266
	APPENDIX	277
	BIBLIOGRAPHY	294
	INDEX	305

PART ONE

Commercial Drama

I

The Legacy of Henry Arthur Jones

After Henry Arthur Jones's *Saints and Sinners* opened at the Vaudeville Theatre on September 25, 1884, the author received a letter of praise from Matthew Arnold, who was no admirer of the commercial drama of the time, but the praise was tempered with "I must add that I dislike seduction-dramas. . . ."[1] If Arnold's approbation indicates that *Saints and Sinners* was comparatively a serious play, his reservation is an exact description of the work that Jones had produced. In it, Letty, the daughter of Jacob Fletcher, an incredibly good dissenting minister, falls into the clutches of Captain Eustace Fanshawe, an aristocratic rotter, and is only just saved from going off with her seducer to India and irreparable degradation. Jacob, anticipating *Michael and His Lost Angel*, makes public confession of his daughter's sin and loses his chapel; the two of them almost starve to death, but in the end Letty's first love, honest George Kingsmill, comes back from Australia, rich with money and forgiveness, to get her to marry him. In the printed version of the play, Letty, in the true tradition of the nineteenth-century fallen woman, dies before she can accept George's offer. After the play had opened, Jones was persuaded to convert to a happy ending, which provoked Matthew Arnold to say, "the marriage of the heroine with her farmer does not please me as a *dénouement*."[2]

[1] Quoted, Henry Arthur Jones, "Preface" *Saints and Sinners*, London, Macmillan, 1891, p. xxiv.
[2] Quoted, Clayton Hamilton, "Introduction," Henry Arthur Jones, *Representative Plays*, Boston, Little, Brown, 1925, I, xl.

The play is nineteenth-century in technique—asides, soliloquy-like musings that provide necessary information, stock villains and good folks—as it is in theme. Its appearance probably depended as much on the success of W. G. Wills's *Olivia*, a version of *The Vicar of Wakefield*, at the Court Theatre four years earlier, as it did on Jones's desire to bring something new to the English theater. Yet, in its crude and sentimental way, *Saints and Sinners* reintroduced the possibility of religion as a serious consideration in the English drama. The two canting deacons, Hoggard and Prabble, are set up in opposition to Jacob Fletcher, and, although they are plainly caricatures, they have enough validity and enough vitality to retain some life more than seventy years after their creation. At the time, they caused something of a sensation, largely because they persisted in quoting scripture even while they were trying to get their hands on the widow Bristow's property and when they were spying on Letty in the hopes of getting something on Jacob. "Half the audience thought I was canting, and the other half thought I was blaspheming," Jones wrote in the preface to the published play.[3] It was the half that suspected blasphemy that provoked Jones to write the essay "Religion and the Stage" which appeared in *The Nineteenth Century* in January, 1885.[4]

In this essay, Jones, whose writings on the theater have retained a vitality that is only sporadically in evidence in his plays, made a forceful statement of his position on the use of religion on the stage. He attacked ordinary playgoers with "The idea of human life as being about six-sevenths secular and one-seventh sacred keeps possession of them, and they do not wish to have this convenient fiction disturbed or examined."[5] Jones knew his audience. Although the discussion of religion and religious con-

---

[3] Jones, *Saints and Sinners*, p. xxi.
[4] Reprinted as Appendix to *Saints and Sinners*, pp. 117–142.
[5] Jones, *Saints and Sinners*, p. 125.

troversy was popular in intellectual circles at the time, the theater was little concerned with the preoccupation of intellectuals. It seems odd at this distance that Hoggard and Prabble should have caused a disturbance in the decade in which Samuel Butler was writing his controversial pamphlets and Charles Bradlaugh, the most vociferous advocate of free thought, was fighting his finally successful battle to hold his seat in Parliament. Jones was not seeking to turn the stage into a discussion hall, where the Butlers and the Bradlaughs could be attacked or defended: "In no case could it be profitable for the stage to become the backer or antagonist of any doctrine or creed."[6] He was intent simply on using religion for the dramatic values that it contained; "The drama claims for its province the whole heart and nature and soul and passions of man; and so far as religion has to do with these, so far is the dramatist within his right in noting the scope and influence of religion upon the character he has to portray."[7]

Had Jones felt that the stage was the place to display dogma, he would have lacked for material. He quite obviously had no dogma to display. He had been brought up "in the rigorous creed of English Puritanism".[8] At twelve, he had gone to work for an uncle who kept a shop in Ramsgate, a deacon of a Baptist chapel, who became the model for Hoggard, or so Jones later told his daughter.[9] "Till I was twenty I accepted, almost without question, the creed that I had been taught. . . . Since those years in the 'seventies, when to the best of my power I diligently searched into the truth of these things, I have never been able to accept the dogmas of orthodox Christianity."[10] His plays were marked with his distaste for the Puritanism of his childhood ("The bleak cant, the cold, sour Puritanism of our nation has twisted the meaning

[6] Jones, *Saints and Sinners*, p. 129.   [7] *Ibid.*, p. 127.

[8] Henry Arthur Jones, "My Religion," *My Religion*, New York, Appleton, 1926, p. 85. The book was a collection of reprints from a series in the London *Daily Express*.

[9] Doris Arthur Jones, *The Life and Letters of Henry Arthur Jones*, London, Gollancz, 1930, p. 93.   [10] Jones, *My Religion*, pp. 85, 88.

of the word 'morality' until it signifies only a breach of the seventh commandment."[11]) and by his feeling that the multitude of sects in England was basically ludicrous.[12] Yet if his discontents worked on his portraits of Hoggard and Prabble and of similar figures in the later plays, he was more carefully conventional—almost certainly out of respect to the audience—in his treatment of major religious themes.

Judah (1890), the first Jones play to deal with religion since *Saints and Sinners*, concerns a fiery preacher who finds himself pleading the cause of a phony mystic. In it, Jones hit upon a situation that was to serve him again in his best-known play, *Michael and His Lost Angel* (1896). In both plays, the hero is a man of God whose principles are compromised by his love for a woman. The parson unfortunately in love is as old, dramatically speaking, as Wilkie Collins's *The New Magdalen*, which had appeared in 1873; M. Willson Disher says of the Collins play, "The hero who had the right to preach as well as the right to fall in love was a new inspiration to the drama."[13] With Jones, however, the two rights came into conflict, and the clash, allowing always for the author's penchant for sentimentality and melodrama, grows out of a character whose religious beliefs and moral standards have some claim to dignity.

In *Michael and His Lost Angel*, Jones produced two characters whom even Bernard Shaw could praise, although he did not approve of the way Jones made them behave. The Reverend Michael Feversham is something of a theologian (author of a book called *The Hidden Life*), very High Church (occasioning Shaw's

---

[11] Henry Arthur Jones, "Middleman and Parasites," *New Review*, VIII, 650 (June, 1893).

[12] Henry Arthur Jones, "The Bible on the Stage," *New Review*, VIII, 187 (February, 1893). The point is made more extensively in Henry Arthur Jones, "A Lay Sermon to Preachers," *Vox Clamantium*, ed. Andrew Reid, London, A. D. Innes, 1894, pp. 232–243.

[13] M. Willson Disher, *Melodrama*, New York, Macmillan, 1954, p. 110.

remark that Jones was "harmonizing the old Scarlet-Letter theme in the new Puseyite mode . . ."[14]), and notoriously intransigent in his attitude toward sin. The theological work testifies to Michael's seriousness and his importance to the church. The affinity for Edward Pusey, which is explicit only in Shaw's review, may explain the last act conversion to Roman Catholicism; after all, John Henry Newman was an early colleague of Pusey in his devotion to pre-Reformation teaching. The intransigence sets up a situation against which Michael must place his own sin and judge it, for, as the play opens, he has just forced Rose Gibbard, the daughter of Andrew, his secretary, to testify openly to her sin. "Would you," Michael asks Andrew, "rather that she held up her head in deceit and defiance, or that she held it down in grief and penitence?"

In the first act, too, Michael meets his lost angel, Audrie Lesden, a beautiful and strangely mysterious woman. "Don't let me play with your soul," she warns him. If all five acts were as well constructed as the first, if the characters continued to develop by being played as skillfully one against another, *Michael and His Lost Angel* would be a fine play. It becomes increasingly stagey, however, and the last act dissolves into bathos. In Act II, Audrie seduces Michael. In Act III, he discovers that her husband is still alive and, unable to make an honest woman of her (or, more properly, an honest man of himself), he decides to keep his secret. Andrew, who knows all, is going to be a kind of thorn in Michael's flesh. The third act curtain comes down on the two men, working in Michael's study, having reached Psalms 51. 3 in their translation of the Bible: "For I acknowledge my transgressions, and my sin is ever before me." In Act IV, Michael, over the protests of family and friends, makes a public confession of his sin, resigns his church and leaves, after: "Pray for me, all of you! I have need of your prayers! Pray for me!"

---

[14] Bernard Shaw, *Our Theatre in the Nineties*, London, Constable, 1932, II, 20.

The end of the play finds Michael, now in Roman orders, seeking peace at the Monastery of San Salvatore, but the last act really belongs to the lost angel who has come to Italy to die. Shaw quite rightly points out that "Audrie is dying of nothing but the need for making the audience cry. . . ."[15] She dies at length, hoping for forgiveness and possible eternal reconciliation: "I've been dreadfully wicked. But I've built a church—and—I've loved him —with all my heart—and a little bit over." Since she is Audrie and sophisticated, her dying words paraphrase the last words of Heine, "*Le bon Dieu nous pardonnera: c'est son métier,*"[16] but Jones, who always manages to glance behind, catches a glimpse of Lady Isabel in *East Lynne* and Audrie adds, conventionally, "You won't keep me waiting too long?" The conflict between Michael's beliefs and his desire would, in the hands of Graham Greene, come as no surprise today: it is not the theme, but the sentimentality and the theatrical excesses of the play that so date it.

Although the conflict of love and faith was Jones's most effective vein, he also mined—however surface the mining—many other religious themes. In *The Dancing Girl* (1891), for instance, there is the break with and the return to faith. Drusilla Ives has become a dancer and kept woman in revolt against the too-strict background in which she was raised.

And the things they think sinful! Living is sinful! Loving is sinful! Breathing is sinful! Eating and drinking are sinful! Flowers are sinful! Everything is sinful! Oh, so good! Oh, so stupid! And the time they give to their prayers, and their harmoniums!

Dru finally dies, off-stage, in New Orleans, at peace with God. Since the Duke of Guisebury (her lover) is a fallen man rather than a fallen woman, he is allowed to live. On the edge of suicide

[15] Shaw, *Our Theatre in the Nineties*, II, 17.
[16] Heine is supposed to have said, "Dieu me pardonnera. C'est son métier." *Oxford Dictionary of Quotations*, London, Oxford, 1953, p. 240.

throughout the play, he is at last saved by the love of a good woman, Sybil Crake, a salvation that involves the return to the eternal verities, however vaguely defined: "all the watchwords and passwords—Faith, Duty, Love, Conscience, God. Nobody can help believing them. Turn them out at the door, they only fly in at the window. . . ." A similar regeneration comes to Dr. Lewis Carey in *The Physician* (1897), in which Edana Hinde (named for St. Edana, who used to cure lepers) restores to the doubting doctor his faith in himself and in his work and perhaps in a little something more.

The descendants of Hoggard and Prabble are active in some of the later plays of Jones. Jorgan and Pote, in *The Triumph of the Philistines* (1895), are the canting deacons all over again, this time in a weak comedy which shows, according to the subtitle, "how Mr. Jorgan preserved the morals of Market Pewbury under very trying circumstances." Hypocrisy turns up again, this time with no comic overtones, in the precisely titled *The Hypocrites* (1906). The plot of this conventional play about seduction across classes is simply an excuse to display the honesty of a simple clergyman in contrast to the sham morality of the landed gentry and the time-serving of a fashionable dean.

Jones's most forceful attack on the varieties of hypocrisy is probably *The Galilean's Victory* (1907), which made a brief appearance as *The Evangelist* in New York and none at all in London. There are enough faults in the play to explain its lack of success, but one reason for its failure may have been the bluntness with which Jones attacked his targets. The titular evangelist is Sylvanus Rebbings, who uses living pictures of scriptural scenes to attract crowds. He is invited to Trentistown by Sir James Nuneham, who hopes that a little religion will take the minds of the workers off strikes. Three clerical caricatures—the Reverend Mark Shergold, Vicar of Trentistown; the Reverend Joseph Cushway, D.D., Minister of the Congregational Church; the Reverend Maltman

Toddy, Pastor of the Ebenezer Baptist Chapel—are set up in opposition to Rebbings. The three ministers are carefully drawn to define conventional religion in three different classes; the division is apparent in the tag ends that they speak, in the behavior of their wives, and even in the way they get to Sir John's to meet the imported revivalist—Shergold has a carriage, Cushway hires a fly and Toddy takes the tram. When Rebbings is at last arrested for his use of the living pictures, it is apparent that what his opposition really cannot forgive him for is his taking Christ too literally, particularly in his treatment of a drunk and a fallen woman whom he has befriended. Although Jones is harsh in his satirical portraits, he treats Rebbings as an admirable person and, typically, allows him to save Sir John's daughter-in-law from adultery and to bring her finally to the faith she has been longing for.

Despite the excesses in Henry Arthur Jones, which lead so easily to tongue-in-cheek descriptions of his plays, he was the first of the modern playwrights to treat religion as a serious subject for the stage. The plays described here have treated the struggle between faith and adultery, the uses of expiation, the loss of and need for faith, the confrontation of hypocrisy with genuine belief, and these ideas—however watered with sentimentality they may be in Jones's hands—are the bases of many of the religious plays that have become popular since World War II. Jones also dabbled in diabolism in his one excursion into verse drama, *The Tempter* (1893), and suggested the possibility of divine intervention in *Mrs. Dane's Defense* (1900). In the latter, Sir Daniel's account of why he never ran away with Lionel Carteret's mother ("She was a deeply religious woman, though she loved me, and she had vowed to God that if her child's life was spared she would never see me again.") places Jones temporally, dramatically and theologically between Dion Boucicault's *The Long Strike* (1866), where the miracle of Jane Learoyd's praying the wireless into operation is a simple melodramatic device, and Graham Greene's *The Potting*

Shed (1957), where the Lazarus miracle is acceptable to the author and most of the characters, if not to most of the audience. Jones also played with dramatic symbols like the broken bowl that was Guisebury's broken life in *The Dancing Girl* and the leper's window in *The Physician*, and often with as much subtlety as playwrights could manage fifty years later (e.g., the chess board in Charles Morgan's *The Burning Glass*).

Despite the range of Jones's theatrical ideas, there is a chronic timidity that explains, as much as his debt to nineteenth-century melodrama, why his plays are no longer taken seriously. In a letter to Clayton Hamilton, Jones wrote, "I think, however, that I may claim that I have always done the best work that there was a good chance of offering to the public."[17] In taking care not to offend his public too greatly—in his aesthetics, his morality and his religion—Jones produced plays that are interesting as examples of polite pioneering, but which have little significance beyond the historical. Yet, he did break ground. Some of the playwrights who followed Jones in his concern for religion chose to emphasize his positive side, to concern themselves with conversion and with redemption that was social if not spiritual; ordinarily they were as sentimental and as conventional as Jones. As large a group chose to follow the course implicit in the figures of Hoggard and Prabble, and some of them extended Jones's attack on hypocrisy into an attack on religious belief in general.

In the Wake of Sybil Crake. The success of Henry Arthur Jones with religion on the stage was not lost on Arthur Wing Pinero, whose ability to sense changes in public taste once gave him a reputation for higher seriousness than that of his colleagues who clung too long to old themes or rushed too precipitately toward the new. In early Pinero plays, there are few references, even casual ones, to God or religion. Typical of those which do appear

[17] Jones, *Representative Plays*, IV, xx.

is Aubrey Tanqueray's platitude to his daughter Ellean, after he
has explained that Hugh Ardale is not for her: "You're able to
obtain comfort from your religion, aren't you?" Ellean's convent
upbringing is important in *The Second Mrs. Tanqueray* (1893), but
only so that her purity may serve as a balance to Paula's sinful
past. It was in 1895 that Pinero decided that the time was ripe for
him to indulge in what Shaw later called ". . . those grotesque
flounderings after some sort of respectably pious foothold which
have led Mr Pinero to his rescue of the burning Bible from Mrs
Ebbsmith's stove, and his redemption of Mrs Fraser by the social
patronage of the Bishop's wife. . . ."[18] That was the year of both
The Notorious Mrs. Ebbsmith and *The Benefit of the Doubt*.

The Notorious Mrs. Ebbsmith opens at that point in the relationship of Agnes Ebbsmith and the married Lucas Cleve when she
realizes that she cannot hold him in a platonic alliance, when she
must cease to be the fiery secularist reformer and become a woman.
While her romantically pure affair disintegrates around her, while
she is forced to decide whether or not she can let herself dwindle
to the status of Lucas's mistress, she is continually under pressure
from the Reverend Amos Winterfield and his sister Gertrude to
seek the consolation and shelter of their north-country rectory.
The famous scene in the play comes at the end of Act III when she
snatches up the Bible that Winterfield has left for her and tosses it
into the stove. "You foolish people, not to know [beating her
breast and forehead] that Hell or Heaven is here and here!" The
act does not end in biblical immolation, however, for, moved by a
subconscious knowledge of what makes a good curtain, Agnes
drags the burning book from the stove. In the final and anti-
climactic act, Agnes has an interview with Lucas's much-wronged
wife and goes quietly to the north country, promising: "Lucas,
when I have learnt to pray again, I will remember you every day
of my life."

[18] Shaw, *Our Theatre in the Nineties*, II, 15.

In *The Benefit of the Doubt,* Theophila Fraser's reputation is soiled when the judge in the Allingham separation case, although he clears her of guilt, makes a speech giving her the benefit of the doubt. After several acts of moral maneuvering, Pinero finally turns her over to the Bishop of St. Olpherts, whose wife is Mrs. Fraser's aunt. The Bishop plans to take a house in town for the season, during which, although the play does not make the point, the business of the diocese can apparently take care of itself while the wronged Mrs. Fraser gets reinstated in society. After these two excursions into Jones's territory, Pinero returned to his concern with the double standard and worked it over without the assistance of clerical duennas or spiritual gimmicks.

If Pinero's use of religion was plainly theatrical, Hall Caine's may unfortunately have been sincere. Shaw thought not. In 1895, attacking a number of plays that exploited sentimental religion, including an anonymous adaptation of Caine's novel *The Manxman* (perhaps by Wilson Barrett, who put his name to a version of it the next year), Shaw wrote: "This is not Spurgeon, it is Stiggins; and his lying lips are an abomination. The whole thing is put on to make money out of us."[19] Yet Shaw judged from the play alone, and incompetence can occasionally resemble venality. Hesketh Pearson insists that Caine was sincere:

He believed that he had been sent into the world with some kind of mission, in which moral uplift and purifying thoughts had their part. He took himself very seriously, and when he read one of his plays to a theatrical company the members felt like a church congregation listening to the lesson.[20]

Sincere or not, Caine is responsible for some of the most unlikely plays of the early part of this century. He made his reputation as a novelist, a kind of Manx Marie Corelli, in the eighties

[19] Shaw, *Our Theatre in the Nineties,* I, 266.
[20] Hesketh Pearson, *Beerbohm Tree, His Life and Laughter,* London, Methuen, 1956, p. 139.

and nineties, and worked doggedly at being a successful playwright in the first decade of the nineteen hundreds. As early as
1888, Wilson Barrett helped Caine turn his novel *The Deemster*
into a play, *Ben-My-Chree*, and Barrett dramatized Caine's *The
Manxman* in 1896. By 1897, Caine was apparently ready to go it
alone. That year his own version of his novel *The Christian* was
acted on the Isle of Man; it went on to New York and London.
It is the love story of John Storm, a priest, fighting wickedness in
London, and his childhood sweetheart, Glory Quayle, who has a
London success as a singer and almost, but not quite, succumbs
to her patron. The play is completely devoid of characterization,
motivation, and plot construction. Caine's sentimental attitude
toward the church is implicit in an exchange between John and
Father Lamplugh. When Glory first turns down John's offer of
marriage, he asks, "Father, if a man had just met with an over-
whelming disappointment, and felt that there was nothing left for
him in life, if he wanted to escape from the world, would you
receive him?" The priest answers, "That is what a monastery is
for, my son." Caine's idea of satire is evident in the name he gives
to a fashionable minister, the Archdeacon Wealthy, and his capa-
city for the bathetic is most obvious in the scene in which Glory,
not wanting her love to disturb John's work, secretly kisses his
cloak. The words of *The Times* reviewer, describing a 1907 revision of *The Christian*, sums up not only the play, but all of Caine's
work for the theater: "Mr. Hall Caine's relation to the drama is
that of the pavement artist to painting."[21]

Had Caine's plays appeared when his novels did they might
have seemed less incongruous. His insistence on turning out play
after play in the manner of Jones's *The Silver King* long after Jones
had gone on to *Michael and His Lost Angel*, and had, indeed,
become old-fashioned in the face of Shaw and Granville Barker,
indicates a complete indifference to the course of serious English

[21] *The Times* (London), September 2, 1907, p. 6.

drama. The indifference may have grown out of the sense of mission that Pearson allows him or out of the popular success which was his for a time. In a heavily condescending review of *The Prodigal Son* (1905), *The Times* suggested that Caine was necessary to the tastes of the people: "They are interested in the big banalities of life, and so is he."[22] Although the quality of *The Times* reviews of this period is not consistent enough to justify the lofty tone taken toward the "teeming millions," the definition of Caine and the product that he had to offer is exact.

The tradition of the gently reforming religion was to fade away from the commercial stage within the next few years. The few plays that can be said to follow it certainly owe no debt to Hall Caine. Their roots run directly back to Jones, although their surfaces are often formed by a growing critical and satiric treatment of organized religion and conventional beliefs. Perhaps Rudolf Besier's ambivalent excursion into stage religion might serve as an example. In *Don* (1909), Stephen, the son of Canon Bonington, called "Don" after Quixote by his fiancée, disgraces the family and endangers his engagement by dragging Elizabeth Thompsett away from her husband and bringing her first to a hotel, finally to the rectory. Stephen, a kind of poetic reformer or reforming poet, is simply trying to save her from the violence of her husband, a street preacher, who, according to Stephen, "seems to be typical of Puritanism in its stern sensuality, violent narrowness, and lack of interest in anything but the saving of money and the saving of souls." At first, Stephen's interest in Elizabeth is elaborately misunderstood, but even when his purity is accepted, his father remains shocked: "you have trifled with God's ordinance in separating husband from wife. . . ." In the end, Elizabeth goes back to her husband, who promises to be understanding, Stephen gets his Ann and the comedy ends happily for all. The play is resolutely conventional, particularly in its treatment of the

[22] *The Times* (London), September 8, 1905, p. 5.

marriage vows, but Besier's attitude toward his characters is uncertain enough to suggest that he never really decided how to use them. When the violent Mr. Thompsett at last appears, he recounts his conversion with such lyricism that he becomes quite likeable. The Canon is a pillar of kindly rectitude, refusing to hide Stephen's behavior ("It would be acting a lie"), but in the last act he forgets his pronouncements and does try to cover up what has happened. In having made a connection between Stephen and Don Quixote, Besier has implied a seriousness that the play does not have. Stephen is no Don, nor is he—as he might have been— a Gregers Werle, working havoc with his rightness; he is simply a highly obtuse good young man around whom the characters re-arrange themselves for a smiling curtain.

After Hoggard and Prabble. Henry Arthur Jones's recognition that hypocrisy was a possible adornment of the narrow English Puritanism that he detected and even of the Anglicanism toward which he was more sympathetic led inevitably to further dramatic examinations of religious concepts. One of the favorite devices of the playwrights who followed Jones was to create a character who embodied Christian charity and to examine the consequences. St. John Hankin, in *The Charity That Began at Home* (1906), produced a comedy in which the charitable impulses of Lady Denison resulted in a moral and a practical shambles. John Galsworthy, in *The Pigeon* (1912), was more interested in the reactions of the conven-tionally good people to his hero's indiscriminate kindness. In one speech in the play ("I saw well from the first that you are no Chris-tian. You have so kind a face."), one of the befriended wastrels makes explicit the idea that Christ might not be socially acceptable in the contemporary world, an idea which Galsworthy was to develop more fully in his bizarre *The Little Man* (1915), which is subtitled "A Farcical Morality."

In it, the nameless little man sits with a group of people waiting for a train; the crowd is a mixture of nationalities, including an American given to speeches like, "In this year of grace 1913 the kingdom of Christ is quite a going concern. We are mighty near to universal brotherhood. . . ." When the train arrives, the little man is the only one willing to help a mother struggling with a baby and a number of parcels. He and the baby get aboard, but the mother does not make it. He discovers that the baby is spotted with what may be typhus, and everyone deserts his compartment. At the next stop, the little man is nearly arrested for kidnapping, but the mother arrives, the typhus is discovered to be bits of blanket, and the little man is forgiven and momentarily provided with a halo caused by the light of a machine which has been brought on to dispel the typhus germs.

When W. Somerset Maugham turned to the same theme twenty years later in *Sheppey* (1933), he was nothing if not specific. Sheppey, who has won a prize in the Irish Sweeps, decides to live like Jesus Christ, giving to those who need help. His family is appalled and even the thief and the tart whom he befriends do not understand him. His daughter Florrie says, "Well, who ever heard of anyone wanting to live like Jesus at this time of day? I think it's just blasphemous," and Ernie, her intended, says, "If I have a father-in-law who lives like Jesus of course I shall look a fool." In the end, Sheppey is declared insane to save the family from embarrassment and from losing the Sweeps money, but he is saved from that indignity by death. Although Maugham is primarily interested in the behavior of Sheppey's family, he is also, like Galsworthy before him, gingerly approaching the serious theme of the fool as Christ.

In another group of plays, playwrights like J. O. Francis and St. John Ervine deal seriously with religious belief as a major element in the conflict between two generations. In Francis's *Change* (1911), John Price, an old-time Welsh Calvinist, is in conflict with his sons over both religion and politics. His son Lewis,

Socialist and labor leader, has failed him politically, and his son John Henry, who, trained to be a minister, has lost his faith, has disappointed him on religious grounds. The uncompromising position that Price takes is apparent in his refusal to consider a young, liberal minister for his church: "We've got to preach the living truth to men that have got to die; and if the young people won't give heed, so much the worse for them on Judgment Day and for those who've blinded them. New Theology, indeed!" Only Gwilym, the consumptive son, tries to understand the father, tries to be a bridge between the generations, but he is killed in a riot that Lewis has caused. The play breaks down midway, when Lewis, full of remorse for Gwilym's death, goes off to Australia and John Henry goes off—unlikely idea—to be a chorus boy in London. The emphasis shifts too late to the mother, who loses all her sons one way or another, and *Change* misses the chance to be either her personal tragedy or a dramatic analysis of the consequences of John Price's unrelenting Calvinism.

There is some of the same kind of conflict in St. John Ervine's *Mixed Marriage* (1911), in which John Rainey's opposition to his son's marriage to a Catholic is presented unsympathetically, even angrily. It is in *John Ferguson* (1915), however, that Ervine presents his most complete portrait of a man whose faith can destroy. Like John Rainey, Ferguson is another north Irish Protestant, but, unlike Rainey, he is no bigot. He believes that everything happens by God's design, saying when he is on the point of losing the farm that he is too sick to work, "But it's the will of God!" The accidents that pile upon the Ferguson household when a check from John's brother fails to arrive from America are perhaps a little too much for credibility, but they are certainly good tests of John Ferguson's particular kind of faith. Henry Witherow, who has been interested merely in foreclosing on the farm, suddenly takes it into his head to rape John's daughter and John's son Andrew kills Witherow in revenge. Jimmy Caesar, a suitor of the daughter, is mistakenly supposed to have killed Witherow, and John's refusal to protect him ("He must submit himself to the will of God") sets the stage for Andrew's confession, which he slips away to make, conveniently while John is reading II Samuel, Chapter 18, the story of Absalom. At this point, of course, the late check arrives, occasioning Hannah's "God's late, da!" "Feeling the blow to his faith," as the stage direction says, John tries to convince himself, "There *must* be some meaning in it. There *must* be! God doesn't make mistakes." The news of Andrew's confession finishes him off; when his hand touches the Bible he has been reading, he pushes it away.

The first world war was responsible for some theatrical re-examinations of religion, and, for the most part, Christianity was the loser. Often they were no more more specific than the insufficiency of faith implicit in the casual news that the drunken Stanhope in R. C. Sherriff's *Journey's End* (1928) is the son of a country vicar. Strangely, it was W. Somerset Maugham who made the most detailed examination of loss of faith in *The Unknown* (1920), a play that caused Henry Arthur Jones to remark, "And I was hissed on the first night of *Saints and Sinners* for a few scripture quotations."[23] In the play, Major John Wharton (Military Cross, D.S.O.), a kind of conscientious atheist in a foxhole, comes home on leave and is forced, by his refusal to take communion, to confront his devoutly Anglican parents and fiancée with his loss of faith. The play is little more than a series of debates, involving not only the principals and their principles, but a vicar who argues that the war is in some sense a redemption through suffering and a hysterical mother who, having lost all her sons in the war, cries out: "You say that God will forgive us our sins, but who is going to forgive God? Not I. Never. Never!" In the end, when the fiancée tricks John into taking communion, pleading the peace

---

[23] Jones made the remark to his daughter at the opening of the Maugham play. Quoted, Doris Arthur Jones, *The Life and Letters of Henry Arthur Jones,* p. 93.

of mind of his dying father, there is no grace, no revelation, and the two characters go their separate ways.

At a special performance for ministers and intellectual leaders, arranged by the London *Daily Mirror* and Violet Tree, the Bishop of Birmingham defended the play for its seriousness and read a message from Maugham:[24]

I wrote it with no desire to outrage the religious susceptibilities of any religious person. I hope that you will think it is an honest attempt to place on the stage some of the thoughts and emotions which have occurred to many people during the last few years.

On the surface, Maugham seems an unlikely person to have made the attempt. His earlier plays had shown no concern with religion, unless *Loaves and Fishes*, which he wrote in 1902 and which "was refused by every manager to whom it was sent on the ground that the public would not care to see the cloth held up to ridicule,"[25] can be considered a genuine satire on the wordliness of the clergy. For all the epigraph from *Tartuffe*,[26] however, this play, which was finally produced in 1911, tells the story of Canon Spratte's maneuvers to get a bishopric with such offhand good nature that its political clergyman seems more a familiar Maugham hero, witty, worldly and suavely successful, than he does an object of satire. The playwright's concern in *The Unknown*, then— and in *Sheppey* as well—was plainly not proselytism. He made this clear in the Preface to the third volume of *The Collected Plays*, where, admitting that the play is not very good, he went on to indicate his impetus for writing it: "the drama I saw in my mind's eye lay in the conflict between two persons who loved one another and were divided by the simple piety of the one and the lost faith

[24] Quoted, *The Times* (London), August 18, 1920, p. 8.

[25] W. Somerset Maugham, *The Collected Plays*, London, Heinemann, 1952, I, viii.

[26] There was a quotation from *Tartuffe* on the program for the 1911 production, as mentioned in the review in *The Times* (London), February 25, 1911, p. 8.

of the other."[27] Maugham, who has called himself "an agnostic with sympathies,"[28] is, then, in his few essays at religion in the drama, the legitimate successor of the Jones who insisted that religion in the theater be a device and not a dogma.

The early thirties saw a number of plays that gibed at Christianity, either casually or bitterly, sometimes taking for their target some fringe faith that hovered around the edge of the central tenets of Christian belief. Aldous Huxley, for instance, attacked spiritualism in *The World of Light* (1931). The church was also one of the many targets of W. H. Auden and Christopher Isherwood in their plays. There were incidental snipings in Auden's *The Dance of Death* (1933), where the cry to God becomes one of a number of meaningless cries when the people are in danger, but it is in the pompous and finally vicious Vicar who sides with the native fascists in *The Dog beneath the Skin* (1935) that Auden and Isherwood speak most angrily against the church. There is some relaxation of the attitude in the Curate who cannot decide to take sides: "Christ crucified/Be at my side,/ Confirm my mind/ That it be kind/To those who assert and hurt/On either side!/ I must go away,/I must go pray/To One who is greater." But the final allegiance of the returned Sir Francis Crewe, the necessity to take sides, makes the Curate's hesitation a weakness and a self-condemnation. In *The Ascent of F6* (1936) the satire has given way to a groping and an uncertainty; the one possible religious figure, the Abbot, offers Michael Ransom an unacceptable withdrawal from the combination of his will and the world's desire that is forcing him to his destruction on F6. Auden and Isherwood returned to their familiar view of the Christian in *On the Frontier* (1938), in the character of Martha Thorvald, the spinster, whose religion confuses God with the Hitler-like Leader of Westland

---

[27] Maugham, *The Collected Plays*, III, xvi.
[28] In an interview, quoted, Thomas F. Brady, "The Eighty Years of Mr. Maugham," *New York Times Magazine*, January 24, 1954, p. 12.

and in whom the religious impulse is colored with the implication of sex repression.

By the middle and late thirties the two streams of plays that flowed, however haphazardly, from Henry Arthur Jones's defense of religion on the stage began to dry up. The specifically religious drama, that with a foothold in the churches, had began to flourish by this time and had begun to draw the attention even of commercial audiences; both faith and aesthetics had begun to operate against sympathetic portrayals of the problems of Christian belief when, whether out of an exalted sense of piety or of dramaturgy, the portrayal is too deeply embedded in sentimentality. Not that the genre died, of course; it continued to live in the motion picture and even in the simpler forms of church drama.

The fate of the other stream, in which Jones's tilts at hypocrisy in some cases became slaps at Christianity, is evident in St. John Ervine's successful play, *Robert's Wife* (1937). After his early, rather bitter plays, Ervine wrote a series of light comedies, and when he returned to religion on the stage twenty years later, the product indicated not only that he was older, but that the actual and ideational distance from the days of *John Ferguson* was great. In *Robert's Wife*, the doctor heroine dwindles, after a struggle, to nothing more than the wife of her clergyman husband. The author's admiration for Robert, the husband; his sympathetic treatment of the fanatical High Churchman who opposes Sanchia's clinic; and a speech that he puts into the mouth of the Bishop—"A great wave of materialism is passing over the world, and unless a tremendous effort is made, the whole spiritual life of mankind may founder. . . ."—indicated that Ervine had made some kind of reconciliation with Christianity. Ervine's generation, whose attacks on the varieties of implacable Christianity came often out of personal relationships with the generation before them, were unable to sympathize with the intellectual gamesmanship that made Christian-baiting fashionable in the thirties. The younger group did not long retain coherence. Aldous Huxley and Christopher Isherwood went off to look for the mystic way in the East; W. H. Auden turned back to Anglicanism. Ironically, the mannerisms of their plays have been passed on to some of the less original of today's Christian poet-playwrights—Ronald Duncan, for instance.

The bulk of the plays examined in this chapter can lay no claim to permanent literary value. That they flourished, however, is important to an understanding of the return of genuinely religious dramatists to the commercial stage. This postwar phenomenon may be explained partly by the increased interest, particularly among intellectuals, in things religious, and partly as a result of the new vitality that church drama has shown since the thirties. It must also be explained in part by the fact that the plays described here, beginning with those of the unlikely groundbreaker, Henry Arthur Jones, had already given the consideration of religion a legitimate place in the commercial theater.

II

Barrett, the Bible, and the Big Shows

On January 4, 1896, eleven days before *Michael and His Lost Angel* opened at the Lyceum Theatre, Henry Arthur Jones's old associate Wilson Barrett presented *The Sign of the Cross* at the Lyric. Barrett's melodrama, which he had tried out the year before on his American tour, is an archetype for a strange blending of religion, pageantry, and sex that was tremendously popular on the London stage at the turn of the century. Barrett, who had acted in *East Lynne* in 1867, apparently never got over it. He is supposed to have said to Jones, whose one-act comedy *A Clerical Error* he had done at the Court in 1879, "Look here, boy, the sort of play I want is *East Lynne* turned round."[1] The result was *The Silver King* (1882), of which Jones and Barrett's theater manager, Henry Herman, are listed as co-authors. The play, whose hero Wilfred Denver suffers long, noisily and unnecessarily for a crime he did not commit, made both Barrett and Jones rich. Jones then turned to the more serious plays described in Chapter I, and Barrett looked for new fields to plow. He found them in pseudo-historical drama with Christian overtones. At the Princess Theatre, in 1883, he produced *Claudian*, a play that he had written with W. G. Wills, of which the plot, according to M. Willson Disher, "consisted of 'The Last Days of Pompeii' added to 'The Wandering Jew.'"[2] Then came *The Sign of the Cross*.

[1] Reported by critic Chance Newton, quoted, M. Willson Disher, *Melodrama*, New York, Macmillan, 1954, pp. 106–107.
[2] *Ibid.*, p. 108

The plot is a simple one. Marcus Superbus, Prefect of Rome, tries to seduce Mercia, the Christian beauty, and, failing that, falls in love with her and dies with her in the arena. Bernard Shaw, who treated Barrett's play with good-humoured irony in his review, obviously remembered it when he wrote his own *Androcles and the Lion* fifteen years later. Shaw, with as straight a face as possible, wrote of *The Sign of the Cross*:

With scathing, searching irony, and with resolute courage in the face of the prejudiced British public, he has drawn a terrible contrast between the Romans . . . with their straightforward sensuality, and the strange, perverted voluptousness of the Christians, with their shuddering exaltations of longing for the whip, the rack the stake, and the lions. . . .[3]

Under his pretense of respect for Barrett, Shaw correctly characterized the sensuality of the play. Barrett's sexual conversion of the Roman prefect appealed immediately to a wide audience. *The Athenaeum* in its obituary of Barrett eight years later reported that *The Sign of the Cross* had "impassioned greatly a large and rather ignorant public, and proved highly lucrative."[4] Actually, the play impassioned some men who should have known better. *The Clarion* reported that "Dean Hole, of Rochester . . . sent round the fiery cross among the churches, through the clerical *Guardian* by calling on the clergy to lend their 'presence and commendations' to 'this most pathetic tragedy'. . . ."[5] The Bishop of Truro wrote an introduction to the novel version of the play in which he praised Barrett for having purified the stage with *The Sign of the Cross*.[6] The secularist G. W. Foote dignified Barrett's effort by writing a pamphlet, *The Sign of the Cross, A Candid*

---

[3] Bernard Shaw, *Our Theatre in the Nineties*, London, Constable, 1932, II, 12–13.
[4] *The Athenaeum*, No. 4005, July 30, 1904, p. 156.
[5] Dangle, "Stageland," *Clarion*, January 18, 1896, p. 3.
[6] Philadelphia, Lippincott, 1897.

Criticism of Mr. Wilson Barrett's Play, sprightly in style, but pompous in conception, in which he took unnecessary pains to catch Barrett out on historical grounds.[7] To Henry Arthur Jones, however, belongs the last word on the famous melodrama. In a personal letter to Wilson, in answer to the actor's claim that he had been the author of *The Silver King,* Jones wrote:[8]

But if any critic is so wasteful of his leisure as to compare *The Sign of the Cross* with *The Silver King,* will he not discover in both plays a rich flow of pious bathos, a tendency to holy-mouth diarrhoea which he may safely ascribe, in the one case to your pen, and in the other to your influence?

Barrett next turned to *The Daughters of Babylon* (1897), of which Shaw wrote: "Mr Wilson Barrett has found that he can always bring down the house with a hymn: the first act of The Daughters of Babylon, after driving the audience nearly to melancholy madness by its dulness, is triumphantly saved in that way."[9] In 1900 Barrett adapted *Quo Vadis* for the stage, having got permission from Henryk Sienkiewicz, partly, according to M. Willson Disher, to still rumors that he had plagiarized it for *The Sign of the Cross.*[10] By that time, however, Lena Ashwell had already brought Stanislaus Strange's version of the Sienkiewicz novel to the Adelphi, an event which aggravated *The Times* reviewer to write:[11]

The success of *The Sign of the Cross* revealed the prevalence and strength of the public taste—or perhaps it would be doing less violence to the English language to say the public appetite—for plays compounded of crude sensationalism and quasi-religious sentiment. However the

---

[7] London, Forder, 1896.
[8] Quoted, Doris Arthur Jones, *The Life and Letters of Henry Arthur Jones,* London, Gollancz, 1930, p. 71.
[9] Shaw, *Our Theatre in the Nineties,* III, 45.
[10] Disher, *op. cit.,* p. 124.
[11] *The Times* (London), May 7, 1900, p. 3.

judicious may grieve at the spectacle of "conversions" brought about under the influence of sexual passion, of Christian humility, and even the recital of sacred texts employed as mere ingredients in a theatrical hodgepodge, the fact remains that this spectacle excites not disgust but delight among a large section of the public, and that, human nature being what it is, this section of the public may reckon on getting what it wants from one playhouse caterer or another.

Barrett moved forward in history with *The Christian King* or *Alfred of Engle-Land*,[12] in 1902, but perhaps he had begun to lose his touch. The play lasted only a little more than a month. Barrett died two years later, by which time his particular kind of spectacle had almost run its course.

For a time, however, the section of the public that *The Times* frowned on in the review quoted above did get what it wanted. Herbert Woodgate and Paul M. Berton adapted for the stage in 1897 *The Sorrows of Satan*, a novel by Marie Corelli, who, according to Shaw, had said of Barrett that he had "the unpurchasable gift of genius."[13] A stage version of General Lew Wallace's *Ben Hur*, by William Young, with music by Edgar Stillman Kelly came to the Drury Lane in 1902.[14] In 1907, Alfred C. Calmour's *The Judgment of Pharaoh* opened at the Scala and was greeted by a review in *The Times* which said, "the 'religious element' is exploited to the full."[15] These are examples of the kind of religious melodrama that is best characterized by *Maria, the Martyr* by Mr. Godly-Slime, an invention of Henry Arthur Jones. Jones used this mythical play as a whipping boy in his essay "The Censorship Muddle and a Way Out of It," in which *Maria, the Martyr* was presented as the type of corrupt drama that was acceptable to the Censor and its author was identified as a pious fraud: "it is

[12] Reviewed, *The Times* (London), December 19, 1902, p. 4.
[13] Shaw, *Our Theatre in the Nineties*, III, 42. This was in Shaw's review of *The Daughters of Babylon*. Shaw's review of *The Sorrows of Satan* appears in III, 14–21.
[14] Reviewed, *The Times* (London), April 4, 1902, p. 4.
[15] *The Times* (London), April 22, 1907, p. 6.

quite likely that Mr. Godly-Slime himself supposes he is a great moral elevator, and thrills with the delightful sensations of having morally benefited the public, and of having made a pot of money by the process."[16] Even though the essay was written after Barrett's death, it is obvious that Barrett is the Mr. Godly-Slime that Jones had in mind. It is true that Barrett made a success of *The Sign of the Cross* and its immediate successors. His imitators did less well, and the melodramas of early Christian days shortly gave way to more restrained Biblical plays, which were, in their way, just as much theater pieces.

Allied in spirit to the Barrett melodramas, although not so insistently certain of their own spiritual value, were the romantic plays, set in a pseudo-historical Italy or in a purely mythical country. Clerical figures move through these plays, occasionally making spiritual pronouncements, more often acting as simple plot mechanisms to bring the lovers together or to save the hero from death. Typical is Louis N. Parker's *The Cardinal* (1903), in which the churchman of the title (Giovanni De' Medici) pretends madness to get Andrea Strozzi to confess publicly to a murder of which the Cardinal's brother is accused. The Cardinal's trick allows him to uphold the sanctity of the confessional (Strozzi has confessed to him) and still to save his brother for marriage to Filiberta Chigi, the beautiful cause of Strozzi's crime. Despite much talk of the confessional and of the need for leaving things in God's hands, and despite Filiberta's pervasive faith throughout all her misfortunes, *The Cardinal* is plainly romantic piffle.

Stephen Phillips. With actors like Henry Irving and Beerbohm Tree operating on the stage at the turn of the century, there was a demand for verse plays as well as for romantic ones. Still the verse plays had to have the same ingredients—the fustian and the fancy

---

[16] Henry Arthur Jones, *The Foundations of a National Drama,* London, Chapman and Hall, 1913, p. 310.

dress—that filled the romantic stage, and the theatrical poet needed an eye, like that of his prose-writing competitor, for the use of quasi-religious ideas and characters. Until Stephen Phillips came along with *Herod* (1900), however, there were few successful practitioners. Henry Irving, who had refused Alfred, Lord Tennyson's *Becket* when it was written in 1879, finally put it on the stage in 1893, but the actor had cut heavily (and necessarily), transposing scenes and speeches to achieve greater economy. He had retained Tennyson's concept of Becket, who, for all of his "Into Thy hands, O Lord—into Thy hands!," was a politcal and not a religious figure. In the same year, Beerbohm Tree played the Devil in Henry Arthur Jones's one attempt at verse drama, the unsuccessful *The Tempter.*

Stephen Phillips, whose theatrical poetry now reads almost as heavily as that of Jones, had his brief success in the first decade of this century. Beginning with *Herod,* Phillips dealt with a series of characters, all of whom were likely prospects for religious plays. Phillips, however, was interested in grand passion not in religion, so the plays never did more than touch on that aspect of their subject. *Herod* is the story of that unfortunate king and his love for and distrust of Mariamne. Although the play is spiced with lines like Herod's "I hear a whispering of some new king,/A child that is to sit where I am sitting," the emphasis is almost completely on the personal tragedy of the king. The Chief Priest closes the play:

> Now unto Him who brought His people forth
> Out of the wilderness, by day a cloud,
> By night a pillar of fire; to Him alone,
> Look we at last and to no other look we.

The speech, however, is not important for its content; it is obviously a quiet rounding-off, an easing of the tension that ideally should have been roused by Mariamne's death, Herod's madness and his final catalepsy over her corpse.

Paolo and Francesca (1902), Phillips's greatest success, is concerned with the death of the lovers, not with their damnation. *Sin of David* (1904) transfers the story of David, Bath-sheba and Uriah to England at the time of the Puritan wars. Sir Hubert Lisle sends Colonel Mardyke to certain death at the Castle of Bolingbroke so that he can have Miriam, the colonel's wife; the equivalence is made clear when Sir Hubert closes Act II by reading the pertinent biblical passage, II Samuel 11. 14–15, 17. Phillips's triangle, like its biblical counterpart, is more a love story than a fable of sin and punishment. *Nero* (1906) presents the emperor as a self-defined artist, even in murder and arson. The Christian Acte, who was the emperor's mistress before Poppaea, wanders in and out, voicing predictable sentiments, but she is decidedly on the periphery of the play. In 1908, Phillips, with J. Comyns Carr, adapted *Faust* for Beerbohm Tree, a version that sticks fairly close to Part I of Goethe's play with the addition of Faust's salvation through Margaret. In his last play *Armageddon* (1915), Phillips mixed prose and verse in a play that can best be characterized by its epigraph, a remark of Robert Bridges: "This war is a war of Christ against the Devil."[17] The play, which has a prologue and an epilogue in Hell, showing Satan sending Attila's shade to stir up the Germans, is an episodic affair, making use not only of the familiar stereotypes of the evil German and the quietly brave Englishman, but also of the spirit of Joan of Arc. *The Times*, in its obituary of Phillips later that year, was speaking with restraint when it said, "in *Armageddon* . . . there were unmistakable signs of impaired powers and shaken judgment."[18]

Phillips was the only practising poet of the period to write genuine theater pieces, with or without a religious orientation. Of the other poetic attempts of this period, the most interesting, in

[17] According to Phillips, he got the Bridges' quotation from *The Times*. *Armageddon*, London, John Lane, 1915, p. iv.
[18] "Death of Mr. Stephen Phillips." *The Times* (London), December 10, 1915, p. 11.

conception if not in poetical achievement, is W. G. Hole's *The Master*, which was published in 1913 with an approving introduction by Phillips. The play was never performed, perhaps because of the rule against the depiction of Christ on the stage, for in *The Master* a figure that is supposed to be Christ appears, although he does not speak. The play, set in the seventeenth century, shows Christ's return and his eventual sacrifice by the Church. The Cardinal, who comes to believe that the new wonder worker is indeed Christ, decides that the Master must die to save the work of the first Incarnation and its fruit, the Church: "So this is my commission, this my part:/To be as Caiaphas was, working through death/The effective instrument of life. . . ." *The Master* is somewhat confused in construction, often undramatic and written in undistinguished verse, but it retains a certain fascination by virtue of the workings of the cardinal's mind.

The Biblical Play. The appearance of the biblical play on the English stage in this century was delayed by the practice of the Lord Chamberlain, who refused to issue licenses for plays on scriptural subjects until one was granted to Beerbohm Tree for a production of Louis N. Parker's *Joseph and His Brethren* in 1913. *The Times* greeted what it considered the beginning of a new policy with, "Hitherto, the only form of religion that has been denied a voice in the theatre has been the Christian religion."[19] Granville Barker, one of the most articulate opponents of the censorship, welcomed the license to Tree and Parker less enthusiastically, "Is it not a little unfortunate that this rule should be broken, or this exception made, in favour of two of the Censorship's most ardent supporters?"[20]

The liberalization of the censorship was not a sudden or surprising reversal of policy. Agitation had long been going on

[19] "Religious Drama," *The Times* (London), June 17, 1913, p. 9.
[20] Letter, *The Times* (London), June 17, 1913, p. 5.

against the Lord Chamberlain, who had banned, among other plays, *Oedipus Rex* and *The Cenci*. The furor over the failure to license Shaw's *The Shewing-up of Blanco Posnet* led in 1909 to the appointment of a Parliamentary Committee, headed by Sir Herbert Samuel, to investigate the censorship. No change in the law came from the hearings, although the committee had recommended that plays be allowed to perform without license, but the publicity occasioned by the investigation weakened the position of the censorship enough to set the stage for the changes that were to come. The first evidence of the censorship's new liberality, its treatment of Parker's biblical play, was, however, partly the result of several incidents that were in no way connected with the Parliamentary investigation. One was the presentation of *The Miracle* at the Olympia in December, 1911. Karl Vollmoeller's pantomine story of the wayward nun whose place is temporarily taken by a statue of the Virgin Mary come to life, the dramatization of an old legend that Maurice Maeterlinck had used in *Sister Beatrice* in 1904, was widely welcomed, largely because it introduced the rococo splendor of Max Reinhardt to London. In content, *The Miracle* is very little different from the pseudo-religious extravaganzas that Barrett had produced in his heydey. Yet the Reinhardt production and the American movie *From the Manger to the Cross*, which opened at the Albert Hall on December 24, 1912, "were welcomed by many of the clergy of all denominations, and helped to prove that irreverence and blasphemy are not essential features of a theatrical display."[21] The film version of the life of Christ, which was not subject to the censorship, was probably the strongest argument for the acceptance of plays on scriptural subjects.

The hole in the censorship's dike, *Joseph and His Brethren*, is not a particularly religious play. Parker calls it a pageant play, by which, oddly enough, he means a presentation of the entire life of the leading character. Its narrative follows the biblical story very

[21] "Religious Drama," *The Times* (London), June 17, 1913, p. 9.

carefully; Parker lists at the head of each act the chapters of Genesis on which it is based and, particularly in the section about the interpretation of the dreams, he lifts his speeches almost completely from the King James Version. He does enlarge the part that Potiphar's wife plays in the story, and he contrives a sentimental romance around Joseph's marriage to Asenath. *The Times* correctly characterized the play with the remark that "the susceptibilities that may be offended will not be religious; they will be literary."[22]

Although the biblical play never became as popular on the commercial stage as the wide welcome of the license for *Joseph and His Brethren* implied that it might, a number of practicing playwrights did make attempts at the genre. Arnold Bennett, largely at the instigation of Lillah McCarthy, for whom the play was written, turned to the Apocrypha for his *Judith* (1919). The play, stilted and semibiblical in style, focused its attention on the means that Judith uses to approach and murder Holofernes. If it can be said to have a theme, the play is concerned with political morality rather than religion; there is a running contrast between the selflessness of Judith's action and the desire of Ozias, the governor of Bethulia, for personal prestige.

Clemence Dane's *Naboth's Vineyard* (1925), like Bennett's *Judith*, is more political than religious. Miss Dane's story of Jezebel centers upon the machinations of Jehu and the corrupt priests who want to rule in Samaria. The queen is presented sympathetically, even to the suggestion of a romance with Jehu, and in the end she becomes a symbol for toleration against the narrow ecclesiastical nationalism of Jehu and Zedekiah. The play actually contains little biblical material, although it holds to the bare outlines of the story as it is told in the two versions in I and II Kings, and it does retain the fine line, "Bury her, for she is a king's daughter."[23]

[22] *The Times* (London), September 3, 1913, p. 6.   [23] II Kings 9. 34.

Writers as different as D. H. Lawrence and James M. Barrie turned to the story of the youthful David for plays. In both cases, the biblical story was marked with the recognizable personalities of the writers. In Lawrence's *David* (1926), the real hero, the dying hero, is Saul. David represents a new concept of God ("For when the seed of David have put the Lord inside a house, the glory will be gone and men will walk with no transfiguration!"), the making of God in man's image, that has come to replace the indwelling flame, the faceless God that Saul has known. Saul is a visionary; David, a practical man. Saul, to borrow Lawrence's terminology from his essay "The Novel," is quick; David is dead. "We have to choose between the quick and the dead. The quick is God-flame in everything. . . . And the sum and source of all quickness, we will call God. And the sum and total of all deadness we may call human."[24] Yet in the play, Saul's defeat is inevitable. Samuel, whose God is Saul's God, acts as a bridge to the change, but his regret in his function is apparent in a speech that best defines the two ideas of God:

Thou seest thy God in thine own likeness, afar off, or as a brother beyond thee, who fulfils thy desire. Saul yearneth for the flame; thou for thy to-morrow's glory. The God of Saul hath no face. But thou wilt bargain with thy God. So be it! I am old, and would have done.

David's victory, however, is not to be complete. He and his God will pass too. In a moment of vision Saul speaks:

Yea, David, the pits are digged even under the feet of thy God, and thy God shall fall in. . . . Oh, men can dig a pit for the most high God, and He falls in. . . . And the world shall be Godless, there shall be no God walk on the mountains, no whirlwind shall stir like a heart in the deeps of the blue firmament. And God shall be gone from the world. . . . And Men shall inherit the earth!

[24] D. H. Lawrence, "The Novel," in *The Later D. H. Lawrence,* ed. William York Tindall, New York, Knopf, 1952, pp. 193–194.

If Saul in his visionary ramblings is not specific about what happens beyond David, Samuel is: "But after many days, men shall come again to the faceless flame of my Strength, and of Saul's." Jonathan gets the curtain speech. He has met David at their secret meeting place and has learned that there can be no reconciliation between David and Saul. He chooses to go with his father:

For my twilight is more to me than the days to come. In the flames of death where Strength is, I will wait and watch till the days of David at last shall be finished, and wisdom no more be fox-faced, and the blood gets back its flame. Yea, the flame dies not. . . .

Lawrence's *David* is a kind of twilight of the Gods, to use Jonathan's word, but one in which there is a hint of rebirth, of the undying flame of deity. It is a genuinely religious play, rare among the biblical plays, although the religion is personal to Lawrence.

In James M. Barrie's *The Boy David* (1936), there is, according to Granville Barker, "the contrast between the respondings of the two—of the man once chosen now rejected, and of youth newly elected—to the ways of the Lord with them."[25] Saul fights the fact that God no longer reaches him directly, that Samuel and his agent Nathan must mediate between Saul and his Lord. David is little more than a vessel—at least as the play begins—one which can be filled with the power of God. "David becomes all but a child so that he may strangle the lion and the bear and overcome the Philistine by no possible strength of his own . . . but because the Spirit of the Lord is upon him."[26] Before the play ends, David has learned something of the "Other One" about whom Samuel talks, the God that is defined by Barker as "the god of every man of genius who builds better than he knows how to build. . . ."[27] Although the play does not carry David to Saul's throne, it does presage what is to happen, directly with a series of visions in the

[25] Harley Granville Barker, "Preface" to J. M. Barrie, *The Boy David*, New York, Scribner, 1938, p. xxvi.
[26] *Ibid.*, p. xxiii.　　[27] *Ibid.*, p. xxvii.

third act and indirectly with David's final triumphant attempt to lift Goliath's heavy spear without God's help—"I want to do something all by myself!" Although Barker manages to find theological significance in David's boyishness, Barrie's conception of the character too much resembles his depiction of Mary Rose and Peter Pan and the rest of his eternal children. That Elizabeth Bergner could play the title role during the play's initial, unsuccessful run is indicative of the kind of David that Barrie created.

The New Testament, too, attracted the playwrights, although they were understandably hobbled by the impossiblity of using Christ as a character. E. Temple Thurston in *Judas Iscariot* (1923) portrays a Judas who betrays Christ, hoping to force Him to reveal himself as the Messiah. At the end of the play, he waits for news that Christ has come down from the Cross and only when word comes that Christ is dead does he go and hang himself. In Act One, the First Chaldean (Wise Man) has a line which Simon repeats in the play: "All that a man doeth in the eyes of a man and of himself, he doeth of his will, but knows not the result."

The same Judas appears briefly in *Caesar's Friend* (1933), by Campbell Dixon and Dermot Morrah. At least Judas, who at the opening of the play has been striking a hard bargain for his thirty pieces of silver, explains the betrayal to Mary Magdalene in terms that suit the Thurston play; he says that he wants to force Jesus to declare himself the political Messiah that Judas wants him to be. The play shifts quickly to Pilate, however, for he is the central figure. He is presented as a man who wants to do justice, one who would like to act on the pleas of Mary Magdalene and of his wife Claudia, one who envies the certainty of others. He is, however, caught by the political priests, Caiaphas and Annas, who are presented as nonbelievers, politicians who hold their power through the established church. Caiaphas's "If you let this man go, you are not Caesar's friend!" defines the political pressure, the danger of Christ as a revolutionary, that forces Pilate to accept his death. The play is full of references that show Pilate touched with the idea of the incarnation of some god, any god, but with an inability to see that Christ might be that god. For instance, in an exchange with his general, Pilate asks, "Tell me, Balbus, if a new god *did* appear—to-night—what would you do?" Balbus answers, "I'd double the guard." The intended irony of Pilate's position is brought out, too, in his curtain line: "What is Truth? Oh God—if there be a God—show your face before our eyes—rid us of doubts that torture minds, and hate that eats away the hearts of men."

The kind of melodrama that made Wilson Barrett famous disappeared from the stage early in the century, largely for practical reasons. The American *From the Manger to the Cross* (1911) and the Italian *Quo Vadis?* (1913) proved that that kind of story could best be told on the screen, where the sweep of armies, the movement of chariots and the crackle of sacrificial fire has space and a verisimilitude that the stage cannot achieve. The long career of Cecil B. DeMille, crowned with his lengthy excursion into Genesis, *The Ten Commandments* (1956), indicates that the public taste for the mixture of sex and religion did not die with Barrett; it simply changed media. The romantic play, with its swash and its buckle, also proved to be more comfortable on film.

For the most part, the verse play and the biblical play passed out of the commercial theater into the hands of men like Laurence Housman and John Masefield, who sometimes joined the two in their work for small groups which were concerned with the welfare either of religion or poetry. With T. S. Eliot and Christopher Fry, of course, the religious verse play returned to the commercial stage after World War II. The biblical play, has remained alive mainly in church drama, and even there the genre runs mostly to Nativities and Passion plays.

III

Sentimental Supernaturalism

One of the uses of religion on the commercial stage that has proved most popular has been the manipulation of supernatural characters or concepts for sentimental or comic effects. In such plays, a heavenly or a diabolic figure, often specifically Christ or the Devil, appears to interfere directly in human lives. The archetype of that kind of play for this century is Jerome K. Jerome's *The Passing of the Third Floor Back* (1908). Jerome, who had made a name for himself as a humorist, a short-story writer and an editor, had tried the stage before 1908, but never with the kind of success that came with *The Passing of the Third Floor Back*. His *The Rise of Dick Halward* (1895), a play about a swindler who is forgiven, caused Bernard Shaw to call him a "maudlin pessimist."[1] But if *Dick Halward* plumped for forgiveness on the ground that all men are scoundrels, as Shaw pretended that it did, *The Passing of the Third Floor Back* worked its magic on the theory that all men are really good.

The play, adapted from a story of Jerome's, brings a stranger to a boarding house in Bloomsbury. The landlady is a thief, the serving girl is a sluttish slavey, and all the guests are either fools or villains. When the stranger arrives, he effects immediate changes in the lot by pretending that they have virtues which they have not seen in themselves. Even his look has great power toward softening them into sweetness. Although the stranger is never specifically identified as Christ, it is apparent from his first entrance that he is supernatural: "A beam of sunlight has

[1] Bernard Shaw, *Our Theatre in the Nineties* London, Constable, 1932, I, 225.

softly stolen through the dingy fanlight. It lies across the room,
growing in brightness." In some of his speeches, the stranger
appears to be directing the audience to make an equivalence
between him and Jesus. Comforting the slavey about her menial
position, he says that he knew her father (read, Father) and adds,
"A King, once, was born in a stable. . . . So, you see, Stasia, the
place doesn't matter." If the stranger is indeed Christ returned
He has unfortunately lost His New Testament power of speaking
simply and dramatically, for the stranger is too often given to
sentences like, "It is the Helpless and the Fallen that hold in their
hands the patents of nobility." Jerome's characters are no more
than stage stereotypes (including, unfortunately, a stage Jew complete with lisp), but the neatness of the reversal was enough to
keep the play popular for years. It was revived as late as 1949.

In 1925, Jerome adapted another of his early stories for the
stage, the much less successful *The Soul of Nicholas Snyders*. This is
the story of a miser who learns from a pedlar (the Devil) how to
exchange souls with another person. He traps young, open-
hearted Jan into an exchange, and Nicholas becomes as good as he
once was evil and Jan becomes as grasping as Nicholas has been.
Christine, who works for Nicholas and loves Jan, is horrified at
the change in her lover and is ready to marry the aged Nicholas,
but the reformed miser learns that she still loves the young man,
despite all, and he makes the last sacrifice of his new goodness,
another shift in souls. Jerome's short story recounts the double
exchange and no more, with Nicholas Snyders forced to die a
villain, but the playwright, probably hoping for another *The
Passing of the Third Floor Back*, introduces a little child who trusts
and loves old Nicholas and who, before the final curtain, frightens
the Pedlar-Devil away.

The success of Charles Rann Kennedy's *The Servant in the House*
(1907), which made its commercial appearance at the Adelphi in
1909, is another example of the popular taste for the mysterious

and ordering stranger. Kennedy's stranger comes to the home of
the Reverend William Smythe in the guise of a new butler, just
in from India; his name is Manson, which, as Joseph Wayne
Barley pointed out, is an anagram for the Son (of) Man.[2] In the
course of the play, Manson reconciles Rev. Smythe to his work-
man brother Robert, whom the Smythes have shunned since
Robert took to drink after his wife's death. Manson also ticks off
James Ponsonby Makeshyfte, D.D., the Bishop of Lancashire,
Rev. Smythe's brother-in-law, who represents the church at its
most corrupt and worldly. Throughout the play, there is talk of
some smelly drains that make William's church impossible to
worship in. At the end, Robert has traced the source of the corruption to beneath the church itself, a graveyard (of Ibsenite old
ideas, presumably) that is rife with poison and rats. William
strips off his polite churchman's clothes and gets ready to join
Robert in an attempt to clean up the corruption. The two
brothers, William's wife and Robert's daughter join hands, forming a cross on stage. At this point, Manson reveals that he is
Joshua, the unknown brother who has been expected throughout
the play. "In God's name, who are you?" asks William. Manson
answers, "In God's Name—your brother."

Although *The Passing of the Third Floor Back* and *The Servant in
the House* were popular, they did not, perhaps because of the censorship, initiate a series of dramas with lightly disguised Christ-
figures. It was the Devil who proved to be more stageworthy.
Diabolical characters began to turn up in comedies where occasionally, as in Richard Hughes's *A Comedy of Good and Evil*
(1924), they took unexpected forms. In it the Reverend John
Williams's guardian devil is an innocent-looking little girl, whom
Mr. Williams and his wife Minnie take into their home. Minnie,
who has been very lonely, thinks at first that Gladys, as they call

[2] Joseph Wayne Barley, *The Morality Motive in Contemporary English Drama*,
Mexico, Mo., 1912, pp. 60–61.

the child, must be an angel, but when she burns her hand on the Bible, they know her origins. For the most part, Gladys behaves like a little girl, although now and then she stops to make rousing, pro-evil speeches, "Oh, we know the odds we're up against, don't you think we don't! It's *that* that makes the fight so glorious, a few poor weak defenceless fiends fighting against all the battalions of Heaven—." She replaces Minnie's wooden leg, but the new leg wears a silk stocking and a Paris shoe, kicks up its heel without Minnie's assistance and positively refuses to pump at the harmonium whenever Minnie wants to play a hymn. Just as the town folks are ready to declare Minnie's leg a miracle, Owain Flatfish, the fishmonger, who is revealed in the last act as "The plain-clothes angel for the district—guardian, you call it," turns up with bell, book and candle and exorcises Gladys. In the last act, Mr. Williams is dead and Gladys and Owain contest for his soul. There is no contest really, for Owain is a highly legalistic angel, quite ready to give up Mr. Williams to Gladys; the clergyman has after all harbored a devil. Gladys finds herself defending the man she set out to damn: "There never was a better saint in Wales, I swear it, and I ought to know: It was pure charity got him damned." In the end, Gladys gets him into Heaven on a technicality. Minnie's attempts to console Gladys for having done good, almost win the little devil over, but in the end, crying, "If I'm not bad—I'm nothing!" she rushes away from Minnie. Hughes's charming play is an illustration of an early speech of Mr. Williams's: "It is a grand, terrible thing to be a humble soldier, fighting the shadowy battles of the Lord; fighting for the forces of Good against the forces of Evil. Yes. But there are times when it is not easy to tell which is which."

The devil also fails to work his evil in Benn W. Levy's *The Devil* (1930), which was called *The Devil Passes* in the United States. In the play, the Reverend Nicholas Lucy, an obvious combination of Old Nick and Lucifer, listens to a group playing a

game of Truths in which each tells what he most wants. Lucy
gives each a chance to achieve his desire, but in every case the
fulfillment involves either a dishonest act or the inflicting of pain
on another person, and the supposedly self-centered seekers
decide to settle for what they have. Early in the play, when Rev.
Lucy is still a socially amiable young minister, he says: "I believe
in God. . . . The Devil, after all, is only God's advertising agent:
the Devil's complete failure being proof of God's success." The
play is an extension of this remark, and it is told in terms that can
best be characterized by underlining the phrase "God's advertising agent."

If Levy's trafficking with the devil is pious and moralistic after
the manner of Jerome K. Jerome and that of Hughes fantastic and
funny with a moral bite at the edge of it, G. K. Chesterton's use
of diabolic forces in *Magic* (1913) is, for all the near slapstick,
seriously theological. The play insists on the existence of spirits,
good and evil, that have more than a stage validity. When the
Duke in the play brings in a Conjurer to cure his Irish niece's
belief in fairies, the Conjurer is met by the girl's American brother,
a young man who is a believer in science and a proud debunker of
charlatans. In anger, the Conjurer calls up real magic, for he has
contact with evil spirits, and turns the red light over the doctor's
door blue; when no rational explanation for the trick can be
found, Morris, the young man, runs mad. The Conjurer decides
to invent a practical reason for the light's having changed color,
and he goes into the garden (the biblical garden?) to seek help in
finding something that will bring Morris back to his senses: "I
am going to ask God whose enemies I have served if I am still
worthy to save a child." While the Conjurer is out in the garden,
the presence of the devils is felt inside by the doubters—the Duke,
Dr. Grimthorpe, and the Reverend Cyril Smith. Although the
Conjurer invents his lie to save Morris, he will not pass it on to the
three men:

Because God and the demons and that Immortal Mystery that you deny has been in this room to-night. Because you know the spirits as well as I do and fear them as much as I do. . . . But if I tell you a natural way of doing it. . . . Half an hour after I have left this house you will be all saying how it was done.

The Conjurer also gets the young lady, of course, suggesting that love (of man as well as of God) can help overcome diabolical forces. Chesterton's seriousness in the play is most evident in the scene in which the Conjurer denounces the young clergyman:

But what the devil are you for, if you don't believe in a miracle? What does your coat mean, if it doesn't mean that there is such a thing as the supernatural? What does your cursed collar mean if it doesn't mean that there is such a thing as a spirit? Why the devil do you dress up like that if you don't believe in it?

Magic is the only one of Chesterton's plays that ever became a stage piece. His *The Surprise* (1932) did not even see publication until twenty years after it was written. According to Dorothy L. Sayers, it criticizes "the attitude of mind which takes security, happiness, or life itself to be no more than what our own merit entitles us to."[3] The play is several plays. An author stops a wonder-working friar and shows him a puppet play in which the Princess gets the Poet and the King gets the girl he loves, the happy ending resulting from each character's doing his duty as he sees it. The puppets are then given real life, which the author has wanted for them, and the play begins again; this time, moved by human pettiness, the happy ending goes awry. At the end, the Poet and the King are fighting, the girl has been struck mad, and the author runs on the stage to try to save his creations. The theme that Miss Sayers has found in the play is there in the discussion that runs throughout about the value of surprise over certainty,

[3] Dorothy L. Sayers, "Preface" to G. K. Chesterton, *The Surprise*, New York, Sheed and Ward, 1953, p. 8.

but there is also a theological point being made. The author has said, "I am like a little god in my own mimic world," and the friar, in explaining miracles ("God's miracles always free man from captivity and give them back their bodies."), indicates that the author may be like a god, but not like God. The author, Chesterton seems to be saying, may be able and willing to manipulate his characters to get a happy ending, but God lets man go his own way to an unhappy ending, which logically, given Chesterton's beliefs, implies the possibility of damnation. *The Surprise* is perhaps too slight to carry such a weight of theologizing, but these ideas, which are implicit in the puppeteer and his twice-told tale, might have become clearer and more specific had the play ever received the revisions that Chesterton apparently intended when he put it aside after he wrote it.

Death of sorts. Another favorite supernatural subject for the theater is death, envisioned often as a figure or a condition; almost always it is gentle. James M. Barrie managed a rather cozy concept of death in *A Well-Remembered Voice* (1918), in which a recently dead soldier returns to earth to comfort his father. The dead, Barrie's soldier tells us, are cheered by the brightness of the living and saddened, even punished by their despair. Dick describes crossing over:

When you have been killed it suddenly becomes very quiet; quieter even than you have ever known it at home. . . . When I came to, the veil was so thin that I couldn't see it at all; . . . By that time the veil was there, and getting thicker, and we lined up on our right sides. . . . Ockley came after us. He used to be alive, you know—the Ockley who was keeper of the fives in my first half. . . . As soon as I saw it was Ockley I knew we would be all right.

Barrie's public-school concept of death turns up again in *The Boy David* in the visionary scene in Act III which shows Saul after death. Samuel, who was apparently keeper of the fives in Saul's first half, comes out to meet the dead king: "Then, to guide you, I was sent hither, as one who in a past time had, in some way now forgotten by me, been tied up with you in the bundle of life." Greater restraint, perhaps, but essentially the same view of death.

It was Sutton Vane, however, and not James M. Barrie who provided the *The Passing of the Third Floor Back* of the life-after-death dramas. Vane, who early in his career as playwright joined Arthur Shirley in *The Better Life* (1900),[4] a dramatization of the Reverend Charles Sheldon's *In His Steps*, made his one indelible mark on the modern theater with *Outward Bound* (1923). In the play, an assortment of passengers—a business man, a clergyman, a drunk, a society matron, a char, a young couple—find themselves on a strange ocean liner, not quite aware how they got there and with no idea of their destination. In the course of the play, they discover that they are dead, they attempt to organize some system that they can use in facing the examiner (a kindly but stern clergyman) and they are judged and placed, each according to his merits, into a fitting position in an afterlife that is presumably Heaven. Although the businessman and the society woman are scheduled to suffer for a while, there is no final Hell in Sutton Vane's cosmography. Damnation, like characterization, is only skin deep. Vane had such success with death in *Outward Bound* that he tried to render the same sentimental service to birth in *Overture* (1925), a play in which another disparate group—a judge, another society matron, a spinster, a pair of lovers, an actor, a Cockney panhandler—are waiting, in the form that they will finally take in life, to be born. They are born and they do achieve what they want, but in each case—except for the Cockney—things turn out badly. The message of the play, and its quality, is apparent in a speech of Youth, a young lady who at first refuses to be born and then at the end decides to go on with it, "'K-I-N-D' yes, that's what I'm going to try to be downstairs—'K-I-N-D,' kind and leave the

[4] Reviewed, *The Times* (London), February 6, 1900, p. 10.

rest to 'G-O-D.'" *Overture* is such an awkward and confused play, so without the slickness of *Outward Bound*, that it is unlikely to make anyone think of G-O-D. It is much more likely to conjure up the U-N-K-I-N-D thought that someone other than Vane must have got his hands on *Outward Bound* between its initial performance at the Everyman Theatre on September 18, 1923, and the opening of the revised version at the Garrick on October 16.

J. B. Priestley. The manipulation of the supernatural, or at least of the unnatural, is not limited in the theater to the ghostly appearances of heavenly or diabolic figures or to journeys into the unmapped country of a comfortable beyond. Playwrights have used the material of fantasy or the framework of magic to make a convenient moral point or to exhibit a sociological or psychological observation. James M. Barrie provides a mysterious wood in *Dear Brutus* (1917) that allows a group of stock characters, each of whom blames his condition on an accidental wrong turning, to live their lives again. The new lives differ from the old only on the surface. Since the play is a three-act illustration of Shakespeare's "The fault, dear Brutus, is not in our stars/But in ourselves, that we are underlings," the characters remain essentially the same. Although Matey the butler calls Lob, the fey old gentleman whose wood works the transformation, "the most lovable old devil," the play makes no pretense at religion; it is simply a bit of Midsummer's Eve magic. John Galsworthy in *The Little Dream* (1911) lets his Seelchen follow first the Wine Horn, the call of the city; then the Cow Horn, the call of nature; finally the Great Horn, the call of the mountain which says, "Where light and dark, and change and peace,/Are One—Come, little soul, to MYSTERY!" Seelchen is ecstatically calling, "Great One, I come!" when she awakes and mutters, "My little dream!" The soul apparently is always in search of a mystery that it cannot fathom, one that may, in fact, not exist. Stephen Phillips in *Aylmer's Secret*, published in the posthumous *Collected Plays,* allows his scientist to bring to life a mock man that he has created. Although there is a suspicion of religious concern in Aylmer's horror when his creation kneels and worships him—"This is a sin—idolatry! I am no God,/But man, as thou art."—the play is primarily pseudo-philosophic. Only Aylmer's daughter Miranda (that would be the name) is able to pity and love the creature and when Aylmer forbids the two to see each other, the creation dies. The obvious message: man is not man without love.

This sampling of plays indicates the ways in which a variety of playwrights have used the marvelous. J. B. Priestley, however, is the English playwright who has most consistently made theatrical capital out of the supernatural. There are, for instance, his time plays, of which he says, "We can offer you Split Time, Serial Time, and Circular Time."[5] Split Time is used in *Dangerous Corner* (1932), his first play. The play is built around the idea that there are dangerous corners in life, at which, if the truth is told, disaster follows. Such a moment comes to an amiable group gathered at Robert Caplan's for dinner. A chance remark leads to another and another and another until we learn that the Caplan parlor houses, among others, a thief, a slut, a homosexual, and a smattering of adulterers. Robert, who finds the revelations too much, shoots himself and, on the sound of the shot, the scene fades back to the original remark, which leads this time in another direction—to dance music and a happy ending to a good dinner.

Priestley borrowed the concept of Serial Time from the theories expounded by J. W. Dunne in *Experiment with Time* and *The Serial Universe.* As Priestley explains the concept:[6]

We are each of us a series of observers in a corresponding series of times, and it is only as Observer One in Time One that we can be said

[5] J. B. Priestley, "Author's Note for This Edition," *Three Time-Plays,* London, Pan Books, 1947, p. x.
[6] *Ibid.,* p. viii.

to die, the subsequent observers being immortal . . . when we are no longer functioning as Observer One it is our Observer Two who catches a glimpse . . . of events that await our Observer One moving in Time One.

This idea is used in *Time and the Conways* (1937). In Act I, Kay Conway is celebrating her twenty-first birthday in a house full of noisy and happy Conways, made happier and noisier by the party and by the fact that it is 1919 and the two boys have just been demobilized. Kay is left alone for a moment at the end of the act and, operating as Observer Two, she fades into Act II, into 1937, where all the Conways, except for the quietly unsuccessful Alan, have made messes of their lives. In Act III, we are back at the party, but Kay is troubled by the 1937 that she has sensed. She asks Alan for comfort and he says that he cannot give it yet, but that he will some day. He will, Act II has shown, in 1937.

For Circular Time, there is *I Have Been Here Before* (1937). The theory of time used here, borrowed, Priestley says, from P. D. Ouspensky's *A New Model of the Universe*, is embodied in a casual remark of Sam, the landlord of the inn where the action takes place: "if I had my time over again." Each of us, according to Dr. Görtler, the scientist of the play, does have his time over again. He explains that we live in a system of spirals, always the same life with slight variations. He has come to the inn to make an experiment, to try to control the cycle by using his knowledge of what is to happen in the lives of the other guests at the inn. In an earlier life Janet Ormund left her husband Walter for the young schoolmaster Oliver Farrant. Walter's suicide and the ensuing scandal wrecked the lives and the love of the two young people, and Dr. Görtler, who remembers having known the unhappy Farrants in an earlier life, hopes to keep the pattern from repeating. Janet and Oliver do fall in love again, Walter does again go for his gun, but in the end Dr. Görtler prevails. He persuades Walter to let the lovers go off together and not to resort to suicide:

In the end the whole universe must repond to every real effort we make. We each live a fairy tale created by ourselves. . . . We do not go round a circle. That is an illusion. . . . We move along a spiral track. It is not quite the same journey from the cradle to the grave each time. . . . When a soul can make a fateful decision. I see this as such a moment for you Ormund. You can return to the old dark circle of existence, dying endless deaths, or you can break, the spell and swing out into a new life.

Ormund makes the break. Priestley uses the theory simply for melodramatic purposes.

Although *Desert Highway* (1945) was not included with the plays above when Pan Books collected *Three Time-Plays*, it belongs with them. In the play, which makes no specific use of time theories, a collection of army clichés—the Jewish sergeant, the intellectual, the Cockney comic, the young boy—are stranded on the Syrian desert, waiting death from thirst or the enemy. They are strafed, and the young man dies. In an Interlude that moves the same characters in different guises to 703 B.C., where they are part of an Egyptian caravan crossing the same spot, the young man again dies, a sacrifice to Moloch to gain free passage for the caravan. It is Joseph, the Jewish guide in the Interlude, who comforts the young man with quotations out of Amos and Micah. It is Sgt. Joseph, when the scene switches back to the present, who states why they are fighting, why the destruction of the Jews by the Nazis is part of a greater destruction:

Because they want to destroy, once and for all, that idea which the two tribes of Judaea have never quite lost—the idea of the great invisible Lord of Hosts, the one God of righteousness, to whom every man belongs, and to whom every man is precious, and who should reign on earth through man's free choice, as He reigns in Heaven.

Although Joseph speaks in specifically religious terms, it is clear that Priestley sees the war as a defense of every man's dignity as a human being. Of all the time plays, *Desert Highway* is the only one that can be said to attempt any statement that is not simply theatrical, unless the action of Ormund in *I Have Been Here Before* is to be taken as an assertion of the power and dignity of the human individual.

For the most part, the time plays—even when they try to go deeper than stage surfaces—are little more than tricks. Priestley is not even particularly interested in the theories of time that he uses. Of his borrowings from Ouspensky, he says, "it does not follow because I make use of them that I necessarily accept them."[7] Of the plays in general, he says," . . . I make no grand metaphysical pretensions, for I am a dramatist and not a philosopher, and if I were a philosopher I would not choose the Theatre as the place in which to expound my ideas."[8] As a dramatist, he also makes use of the life-after-death convention in the expressionistic *Johnson Over Jordan* (1939) and in *They Came to a City* (1943) and of the mysterious visitor in *An Inspector Calls* (1946), but in all three plays he is more interested in his moral, that each man is every man's responsibility, than he is in the validity of his supernatural devices.

The variety of plays described in this chapter indicates the persistent popularity of supernaturalism on the commercial stage. It produced not only sentimental essays like *The Passing of the Third Floor Back* and *Outward Bound,* but comedies as good as *A Comedy of Good and Evil* or as interesting as *Magic.* It also provided, as Priestley's plays show, a framework for plays in which the concern was not primarily religious. The genre retained its vitality in the English theater after World War II, when, in playwrights like T. S. Eliot, it was infused with a new religious seriousness.

[7] J. B. Priestley, *The Plays of J. B. Priestley,* London, Heinemann, [1950], I, 202.
[8] Priestley, *Three Time-Plays,* p. vii.

IV
A Doctrine of Substitution

In the early years of the century, playwrights such as Bernard Shaw and John Galsworthy looked toward the stage as, in some sense, a substitute for the church. They did not intend that the stage should take over the church's concern with display, that part of religion that is already theatrical. They hoped that the drama might embody the spiritual, the inspirational, the pedagogical content that traditionally belongs to religion; that, in short, drama should regain its ancient religious function, although the religion that the new drama espoused was not specifically Christian. It was more likely to be ethical and social in Galsworthy and Granville Barker, biological and political in Shaw. Shaw, who was comfortable with conventional religious terminology, although he seldom used it in a conventional way, expressed the idea of the religious theater in these words:

The theatre is really the week-day church; and a good play is essentially identical with a church service as a combination of artistic ritual, profession of faith, and sermon. Wherever the theatre is alive, there the church is alive also. . . . The fundamental unity of Church and Theatre —a necessary corollary of the orthodox doctrine of omnipresence—is actually celebrated on the stage in such dramas as Brand, and in the Parsifal performance at Bayreuth, which is nothing less than the Communion presented in theatrical instead of ecclesiastical form.[1]

Even Henry Arthur Jones expressed such a view of the stage. In his essay "The Science of Drama," he described a lady who told him, "I place the Stage next to the Church," and his answer,

[1] Bernard Shaw, *Our Theatre in the Nineties*, London, Constable, 1932, I, 264.

"Why put it second?"[2] Elsewhere, he wrote, "The more the Church becomes an archeological museum of fossil dogmas, the less hold and command will it have upon the religion and the morality of the nation. If the Pulpit loses its power, will the Drama take its place?"[3]

In some ways, John Galsworthy is typical of the new dramatists. Scattered through the earlier chapters, have been references to Galsworthy plays in which religion is presented in one or more of its conventional theatrical usages—for instance, the attack on lip Christianity in *The Pigeon* and *The Little Man* and the attempt at supernaturalism in *The Little Dream*. What these plays share with his more serious and more successful work—*Strife* (1909), *Justice* (1910), and *Loyalties* (1922)—is an ethical view of man's duty to his fellow man, which he has described in terms of faith:

For our drama is renascent, and nothing will stop its bursting the old bottles. It is not renascent because this or that man is writing, but because of a new spirit. . . . It is part of an unobvious, inevitable religious movement; part of a slow but tenacious groping towards a new form of vital faith—the faith of "All for One, and One for All." A faith so far removed from, and so transcending mere party politics, that it will ever increasingly inspire and influence the life of all sects, from Tories to Anarchists, from Roman Catholics to Quakers. A faith, like a great visiting wind, sweeping into the house of our lives through a hundred doors, of which the drama is one, and not the narrowest.[4]

Sometimes, as in *A Bit O' Love* (1915), with its flute-playing, poetry-writing curate who is saved by a little child, the playwright displays a strain of softness and sentimentality, an attempt to grasp an essentially amorphous idea of love and religion, one

    [2] Henry Arthur Jones, *The Renascence of English Drama*, London, Macmillan, 1895, p. 101.
    [3] Jones, "The Future of English Drama," *The Renascence of English Drama*, pp. 130–131.
    [4] John Galsworthy, "Some Platitudes Concerning Drama," *Fortnightly Review*, N.S., LXXXVI, 1009 (December, 1909).

which, although it sounds Christian at times, appears to reject Christianity. He is on safer ground in plays like *Strife* and *Justice*, in which his faith is more ethical than mystical, and in which man's potential is shown negatively.

Granville Barker does not speak of the stage as though it were a church, but there are indications in his plays that he was searching for a way to express the religious impulse, which, for him, was divorced from conventional Christianity. In *Waste* (1906), Henry Trebell has changed his party allegiance in an attempt to control the use of the church money that will be freed by Disestablishment. The money is to go to education, without dogma, and Trebell speaks of it always in religious terms: "I shan't explain to them that education is religion, and that those who deal in it are priests without any laying on of hands," or again, "A man's demand to know the exact structure of a fly's wing, and his assertion that it degrades any child in the street not to know such a thing, is a religious revival . . . a token of spiritual hunger." After Trebell is rejected and commits suicide, it becomes clear that Barker, who always built his plays thematically, is concerned with a great many kinds of waste; one of them certainly is the waste of the religious nature that is unable to find its workable form. In a letter to Gilbert Murray, Barker describes Trebell as "The man of no religious ideas who when he gets one at a great crisis in his life is so superstitiously possessed by it that it drives him monomanical [*sic*] and kills him. . . ."[5] In *The Voysey Inheritance* (1905), there is also a suggestion of a religious vocation transferred to a situation which is not ordinarily religious. Edward Voysey's decision to take over his father's business, including the rotten structure of swindling on which it is built, is important in economic, social, and psychological terms; but Alice Maitland's "You have a religious nature. . . . Therefore you're not fond of creeds

[5] Quoted, C. B. Purdom, *Harley Granville Barker,* Cambridge, Mass., Harvard University Press, 1956, p. 95.

and ceremonies" is an apt description of Edward, for there may
be a kind of religious transference in the young man's dedication.

In *Waste*, Henry Trebell says: "The supernatural's a bit blown
upon . . till we re-discover what it means. But it's not essential.
Nor is the Christian doctrine . . . . the tradition of self-sacrifice and
fellowship in service for its own sake . . that's the spirit we've to
capture and keep." Although Barker, according to C. B. Purdom,
had "no ascertainable religion in his life or work,"[6] he seemed at
times to be attempting to find a secular and moral equivalent for
religion. Galsworthy's attempt was much the same. Bernard
Shaw, who was not only the best English playwright of the century, but also the best religious playwright, went beyond Barker
and Galsworthy. He could have adopted Trebell's statement as his
own, but with two important reservations. He would have insisted on defining "the tradition of self-sacrifice and fellowship"
in political terms and he would have staked out a claim for his
own re-discovery of the supernatural.

Bernard Shaw. Whenever Bernard Shaw makes metaphorical use
of biblical or Christian terminology, his statements take on an air
of fantasy; they engender a suspicion that he is playing with the
familiar phrases to shock the faithful. Yet some kind of serious
truth lurks at the bottom of even his most unlikely pronouncements. He turns so often to Christian terminology and so often
in the same words that it becomes clear that he felt the need to
describe his religion in a verbal frame that would be familiar to a
nominally Christian West.

Although there have been a variety of attempts to explain
Shaw's religious ideas, he has always been his own best inter-
preter. In his will, he wrote:[7]

⁶ Quoted, C. B. Purdom, *Harley Granville Barker*, Cambridge, Mass., Harvard
University Press, 1956, p. 282.
⁷ Bernard Shaw, *Last Will and Testament*, Flint, Mich., Apple Tree Press, 1954, p. 1.

As my religious convictions and scientific views cannot at present be more specifically defined than as those of a believer in Creative Evolution I desire that no public monument or work of art or inscription or sermon or ritual service commemorating me shall suggest that I accepted the tenets peculiar to any established Church or denomination nor take the form of a cross or any other instrument of torture or symbol of blood sacrifice.

More than fifty years earlier, in *An Essay on Going to Church* (1896), he had said:[8]

My own faith is clear: I am a resolute Protestant; I believe in the Holy Catholic Church; in the Holy Trinity of Father, Son (or Mother, Daughter) and Spirit; in the Communion of Saints, the Life to Come, the Immaculate Conception, and the everyday reality of Godhead and the Kingdom of Heaven. Also, I believe that salvation depends on redemption from belief in miracles. . . .

There is no contradiction between the two statements. Shaw, who never accepted the basic tenets of orthodox Christianity—the incarnation, the atonement and the resurrection of Christ—was willing to use the Christian phrases—once he had redefined them —to declare his own beliefs.

Shaw was baptized a member of the Protestant Episcopal Church of Ireland and raised in a family that was nominally, if not actively, Christian. After discarding Christianity, he first embraced atheism. In the Preface to *Back to Methuselah*, he describes how in the late seventies he shocked a roomful of skeptics by defying God to strike him dead. "Now in those days," he wrote later to G. K. Chesterton, "they were throwing Bradlaugh out of the House of Commons with bodily violence; and all one could do was to call oneself an atheist all over the place, which I accordingly did."[9]

[8] Bernard Shaw, *An Essay on Going to Church*, Boston, John W. Luce, 1905, p. 55.
[9] Quoted, Maisie Ward, *Gilbert Keith Chesterton*, New York, Sheed and Ward, 1943, p. 227. The letter is dated March 1, 1909.

By the 1880's Shaw had discarded atheism and also rationalism, which he has called "a stronger position, being a positive one."[10] In one of his letters to the Abbess of Stanbrook (written in 1924), Shaw said, "I exhausted rationalism when I got to the end of my second novel at the age of twenty-four, and should have come to a dead stop if I had not proceeded to purely mystical assumptions."[11] Certainly in *The Quintessence of Ibsenism* (1891), Shaw wrote:[12]

the reasonable thing for the rationalists to do is to refuse to live. But as none of them will commit suicide in obedience to this demonstration of "the necessity" for it, there is an end of the notion that we live for reasons instead of in fulfilment of our will to live.

Shaw had become the mystic that he spent the rest of his life insisting that he was.

His statement of faith in *An Essay on Going to Church* is, then, essentially true. Shaw was a Protestant, officially in his childhood, actually in his adulthood, accepting always that "The true Protestant is a mystic"[13] and that Saint Joan was, as Shaw's play insisted, the first Protestant. He did believe in the Holy Catholic Church, although he demanded that it become catholic enough to accept him, a freethinker. The trinity was no more than the obvious father and son in the same person with the addition of spirit, Holy Spirit, which he found in all men, although he sometimes called it the Life Force. The Communion of Saints included anyone who operated by inspiration, as Shaw said he did; the Life to Come was a continuation of Life, the life that was everlasting

[10] Bernard Shaw, "What is My Religious Faith?" *Sixteen Self Sketches,* London, Constable, 1949, p. 74.

[11] Bernard Shaw, "The Nun and the Dramatist," *Atlantic,* CXCVIII, 30 (July, 1956).

[12] Bernard Shaw, *Major Critical Essays,* London, Constable, 1932, p. 21.

[13] Bernard Shaw, "Our Great Dean," *Pen Portraits and Reviews,* London, Constable, 1932, p. 152.

only in that it was passed from person to person; the Immaculate Conception was possible because it was "an instalment of the sacred truth that all conceptions are immaculate."[14] The reality of Godhead and the Kingdom of Heaven is in evidence in all men. Shaw's special use of all the Christian doctrines can best be seen in the sentence: "To me no man believes in the Resurrection until he can say: '*I* am the Resurrection and the Life,' and rejoice in and act on that very simple and obvious fact."[15]

Shaw returned again and again to the idea of God in man. In his most detailed examination of Jesus, the "Preface on the Prospects of Christianity" (1915) to *Androcles and the Lion,* he picked what he considered the four central doctrines of Jesus. The first of them is:[16]

The kingdom of heaven is within you. You are the son of God; and God is the son of man. God is a spirit, to be worshipped in spirit and in truth, and not an elderly gentleman to be bribed and begged from. We are members one of another; so that you cannot injure or help your neighbor without injuring or helping yourself. God is your father: you are here to do God's work; and you and your father are one.

Almost twenty years later, in the Preface to *On the Rocks* (1933), Shaw wrote a short Passion Play, one in which Jesus is a talking, not a mute protagonist. "I am the embodiment of a thought of God: I am the Word made flesh: that is what holds me together standing before you in the image of God." Pilate, who is something of a debater, compliments Jesus and tries to best him. "That is well argued; but what is sauce for the goose is sauce for the gander; and it seems to me that if you are the Word made flesh

[14] Shaw, *Sixteen Self Sketches,* p. 74.
[15] Bernard Shaw, "The Chesterbelloc: A Lampoon," *Pen Portraits and Reviews,* p. 76.
[16] Bernard Shaw, *Selected Plays and Prefaces,* New York, Dodd, Mead, [1948–1949], I, 796–797.

so also am I." Jesus answers, "Have I not said so again and again? . . . The Word is God. And God is within you."[17]

Shaw is willing to find practical, political, and social theories in the Gospels. For him, the other three important contributions of Jesus are His suggestions by His life and words that man should get rid of property, of judges, punishment and revenge and of family entanglements. The idea that Shaw found most offensive about the worship of Christ was that it should center around the cross ("which I loathe as I loathe all gibbets"[18]) and that it should be based on the doctrine of atonement, of blood sacrifice, of a man's sins being forgiven or paid for through the efforts of another. This emphasis on suffering and pain was Shaw's chief target in the Preface to *Androcles* and at length in *The Black Girl in Search of God*, in which the conjuror (Jesus) says, "People idolize me as the Dying Malefactor because they are interested in nothing but the police news."[19]

All of Shaw's comments on religion give evidence that he accepted whatever of Christianity he found congenial and rejected all that he found distasteful. The cataloguing of acceptances and rejections is fascinating in a way, but it does not help to define positively what Shaw's faith actually was. There is little point in conjecturing whether or not Shaw was really Christian, unless, like the Abbess of Stanbrook, one is interested in saving the playwright's soul. There are other terms that better serve to describe the beliefs of Shaw. In his ninety-third year, he wrote: "For nomenclatory purposes I may be called a Fabian Communist and Creative Evolutionist if I must have a label of some sort."[20]

[17] Bernard Shaw, *Too True to Be Good, Village Wooing & On the Rocks, Three Plays,* London, Constable, 1934, p. 180.

[18] Shaw, *Selected Plays,* I, 322.

[19] Bernard Shaw, *The Black Girl in Search of God and Some Lesser Tales,* London, Constable, 1934, p. 56.

[20] Bernard Shaw, *Buoyant Billions, Farfetched Fables, & Shakes Versus Shav,* New York, Dodd, Mead, [1951], p. 84. From the Preface to *Farfetched Fables.*

Although Shaw once said "we must make a religion of Social-ism,"[21] his political beliefs have less religious weight than his evolutionary beliefs. For him, political action and economic reform are methods; their results are no more than improvements, steps in the direction of an end that cannot be imagined, one that is farther, even, than thought can reach. His socialism, engendered by Henry George, matured by Karl Marx, corrected by Stanley Jevons, was one of distribution as well as of production. Its aim, as the Preface to *Major Barbara* indicates, was the abolition of poverty, but that, as the play itself says, was to be only the be-ginning. Shaw's concern with the man of action, from Captain Bluntschli in *Arms and the Man* (1894) to King Charles in "*In Good King Charles's Golden Days*" (1939) (although in the last case the only possible action is talk) shows his healthy respect for the man who gets things done. He was preoccupied to the end of his life, as the *Farfetched Fables* indicate, with a way of discovering the Bluntschlis and the Charleses in the hope that they might really be allowed to rule. But his political vision of a society in which all men worked and all men shared, ruled over by the most capable men available, was a hope, not a faith. The plays of the thirties, particularly *Too True to Be Good* (1932), emphasized his growing doubt about the possibility of achieving his goal. While two world wars effectively crippled his political optimism, his faith in Creative Evolution remained strong. At ninety-three, he wrote, "Providence, which I call The Life Force, when not de-feated by the imperfection of its mortal instruments, always takes care that the necessary functionaries are born specialized for their job."[22] He may have become more and more aware of the imper-fections of the mortal instruments, although he had certainly never been sanguine on that point, but the Life Force was still

[21] Quoted, Eric Bentley, *Bernard Shaw*, Norfolk, Conn., New Directions, 1947, p. 46. From an unpublished manuscript.

[22] Shaw, *Buoyant Billions*, p. 63. From the Preface to *Farfetched Fables*.

operative for Shaw and through him: "I present myself there as an instrument of the Life Force writing by what is called inspiration. . . . "23

The fullest statement of Shaw's faith in Creative Evolution comes in the Preface to *Back to Methuselah* (1921). There he reveals himself as an opponent of the idea of Natural Selection (a negative idea of evolution) and a supporter of Jean Lamarck, whose theory of evolution embodies the will to evolve. This will is Shaw's Life Force, Bergson's *élan vital*, and, in the Shavian theology, an evolving God. In a letter to Tolstoy in 1910 Shaw wrote:24

Whoever admits that anything living is evil must either believe that God is malignantly capable of creating evil, or else believe that God has made many mistakes in his attempts to make a perfect being. But if you believe, as I do, and as Blanco Posnet finally guesses, that the croup bacillus was an early attempt to create a higher being than anything achieved before that time, and that the only way to remedy the mistake was to create a still higher being, part of whose work must be the destruction of that bacillus, the existence of evil ceases to present any problem; and we come to understand that we are here to help God, to do his work, to remedy his old errors, to strive towards Godhead ourselves.

In *The Black Girl in Search of God*, Shaw's heroine finds and rejects Abraham's God of vengeance, Job's argumentative God, the doubt of Ecclesiastes, the simple God of Micah, the scientific God of Pavlov, the Roman faith in empire, the particular churches and sects, the suffering Christ, the Mohammedan heaven and hell, and nineteenth-century rationalism. She ends finally in Voltaire's garden, where she meets an Irishman, a humble and familiarly unfamiliar Shaw, who says, "Sure, God can search for me if he

23 Shaw, *Buoyant Billions*, p. 64. From the Preface to *Farfetched Fables*.
24 Quoted, Archibald Henderson, *George Bernard Shaw: Man of the Century*, New York, Appleton-Century-Crofts, [1956], p. 590.

wants me. My own belief is that he's not all that he sets up to be. He's not properly made and finished yet."[25] In the end, the black girl helps God one step farther along by stopping her search and raising a family. 'I myself have never lost an opportunity of warning Man that he is not God's last word, and that if he will not do God's work God will make some more serviceable agent to supplant him," Shaw had written in 1922.[26] It is plain, however, that Man is God's last word to date, for Shaw, and that it is man's duty, as man and as God and as an embodiment of the Life Force, to do his best to achieve the perfection toward which God is evolving, even though his mortal condition and God's unfinished condition make the nature of that perfection at best highly conjectural. Shaw's politics and economics are his attempts to show man how he can best do the job for which he was put on earth. His religion is the faith that a purposive will created man and operates through him: "I, as a Creative Evolutionist, postulate a creative Life Force or Evolutionary Appetite seeking power over circumstances and mental development by the method of Trial and Error, making mistake after mistake, but still winning its finally irresistible way."[27]

When Lady Britomart in *Major Barbara* complains to Barbara that she talks too much and too fondly of religion, Andrew Undershaft says, "I do not find it an unpleasant subject, my dear. It is the only one that capable people really care for." Certainly it was the subject that Shaw returned to again and again in his plays, whether he was measuring Christian doctrine and morality by a personal yardstick or whether he was illustrating his own faith, providing, as he put it, "my beginning of a Bible for Creative Evolution."[28]

[25] Shaw, *The Black Girl in Search of God,* p. 69.
[26] Bernard Shaw, "Again the Dean Speaks Out," *Pen Portraits and Reviews,* p. 159.
[27] Shaw, *Buoyant Billions,* p. 72. From the Preface to *Farfetched Fables.*
[28] Shaw, *Selected Plays,* II, lxxxix. From the Preface to *Back to Methuselah.*

The first of Shaw's plays that faces specific religious problems is *The Devil's Disciple* (1897). In this mock-romantic play, set in the American Revolutionary War, Dick Dudgeon, a declared worshiper of the Devil, habitually displays a gentleness and kindness that becomes, in the scene in which he lets himself be arrested in the place of the Reverend Anthony Anderson, what might be called Christian sacrifice. He is contrasted first with the mockpious family, particularly his cold and bitterly Puritan mother; then, more importantly, with the Presbyterian minister, "an altogether secular authority," who discovers in the excitement of the Revolution that he is a man of war and not a preacher of peace. Dick is willing to die in the place of Anderson, but the clergyman, preferring the lives of both men to the life of one, organizes an uprising that frees Dick. Anderson summarizes:

I thought myself a decent minister of the gospel of peace; but when the hour of trial came to me, I found that it was my destiny to be a man of action, and that my place was amid the thunder of the captains and the shouting. So I am starting life at fifty as Captain Anthony Anderson of the Springtown militia; and the Devil's Disciple here will start presently as the Reverend Richard Dudgeon, and wag his pow in my old pulpit, and give good advice to this silly sentimental little wife of mine.

Declare your colors, says the play; do not mask your behavior by dressing it in the doctrine of God or the Devil.

Caesar and Cleopatra (1898) is primarily the presentation of the strong and wise governor instructing the infant ruler in the use and misuse of power. "If one man in all the world can be found, now or forever, to know that you did wrong," Caesar says to Cleopatra after she has had Pothinus killed, "that man will have either to conquer the world as I have, or be crucified by it." Caesar's choice of conquest over sacrifice, the choice of Anderson over Dudgeon, is a Shavian advocacy of salvation through action and not through outside expiation. In the Notes to the play, Shaw writes: "It may have been the failure of Christianity to emancipate itself from expiatory theories of moral responsibility, guilt, innocence, reward, punishment, and the rest of it, that baffled its intension of changing the world."[29] In *Caesar and Cleopatra*, too, there is the first indication in the plays of the idea of Creative Evolution, in Caesar's speech: "And so, to the end of history, murder shall breed murder, always in the name of right and honor and peace, until the gods are tired of blood and create a race that can understand." Until that race is achieved, however, Shaw's Caesar will do what is in his power to make over the world.

". . . in 1901," Shaw wrote in the Preface to *Back to Methuselah*, "I took the legend of Don Juan in its Mozartian form and made it a dramatic parable of Creative Evolution."[30] The play, of course, was *Man and Superman* the first of the Shaw plays that specifically presented his religion. If Act III, the section that has become known as "Don Juan in Hell," is removed, as it usually is in production, the play can be performed simply as the story of Jack Tanner, Shaw's Don Juan, an intellectual adventurer, and his eventual capture by Ann Whitefield. It is Ann and Violet Robinson, who know exactly what they want—husbands and families—and how to get them, that embody the Life Force, and not Jack with his "The Revolutionist's Handbook and Companion." At best, Jack is a man concerned with the needs of society; at worst, he is a talker and no more. Ann's famous last line, "Never mind her, dear. Go on talking," is the Life Force's unconscious insistence that it will go on with its work outside and beyond the immediate and necessary activity of any individual. Jack, in warning Octavius away from Ann, states that the purpose of woman "is neither her happiness nor yours, but Nature's. Vitality in a woman is a blind fury of creation. She sacrifices herself to it: do you

[29] Shaw, *Selected Plays*, III, 480–481.
[30] *Ibid.*, II, lxxxviii.

think she will hesitate to sacrifice you?" Yet Ann's vitality needs Jack's intellect to make its forward step.

The point about Creative Evolution that is played with in the battle between Jack and Ann for Jack's independence is stated explicitly in the not really dispensable third act. Tanner dreams a philosophical discussion involving Don Juan (himself), the Devil (Mendoza, the brigand who has captured him), Ana (Ann) and the Statue of Ana's father (Roebuck Ramsden, the outdated radical of the play). Hell is presented as a gratification of all the familiar pleasures and to Don Juan, a philosopher by nature, a killer and a seducer by default, it is a bore, just as heaven, a place of contemplation, is tiresome to the statue. Here Shaw plays a variation on the reversal of roles in *The Devil's Disciple*. Juan goes off to Heaven, because it is there that he will be able to take part in man's struggle to outreach himself:

Are we agreed that Life is a force which has made innumerable experiments in organizing itself; that the mammoth and the man, the mouse and the megatherium, the flies and the fleas and the Fathers of the Church, are all more or less successful attempts to build up that raw force into higher and higher individuals, the ideal individual being omnipotent, omniscient, infallible, and withal completely, unilludedly self-conscious: in short, a god?

Ana, who, like the Ann that she is, represents woman at her most conventional, at first heads for Heaven on the assumption that it is the destination of all the good people—meaning the pious ones. When she learns what Heaven is really like, she still chooses it over the pleasant Hell because in Heaven she hopes to find the superior man whom she needs: "Then my work is not yet done. I believe in the Life to Come. A father! A father for the Superman!" Jack Tanner's dream is Shaw's first dramatic presentation of his concept of God in the act of becoming and his idea of the Life to Come as the simple process of birth.

If the Heaven and Hell between which Don Juan swings in *Man and Superman* may be taken as two conditions of man, and they quite obviously should be taken that way, Jack Tanner's dream goes on in Father Keegan's vision in Shaw's next play, *John Bull's Other Island* (1904). Keegan is a defrocked priest, considered mad because he thinks the Earth in general and Ireland in particular is hell. Keegan's message is that "For me there are but two countries: heaven and hell; but two conditions of men: salvation and damnation." He describes his heaven:

it is a country where the State is the Church and the Church the people: three in one and one in three. It is a commonwealth in which work is play and play is life: three in one and one in three. It is a temple in which the priest is the worshipper and the worshipper the worshipped: three in one and one in three. It is a godhead in which all life is human and all humanity divine: three in one and one in three. It is, in short, the dream of a madman.

In the end, the repatriate Irishman Larry Doyle and his caricatured English partner go on with their plan to turn Rosscullen into a tourist's paradise instead of into Father Keegan's paradise. *John Bull's Other Island* speaks through Father Keegan the language of familiar religious metaphor. Yet Father Keegan's hell is a country (or a world) exploited for selfish gain; his heaven, for all its invocation of the trinity, is a kind of socialistic vision.

Shaw's next play, *Major Barbara* (1905), is probably his most perfect study of a religious personality as well as his most beautiful play. Barbara Undershaft's desire to save souls is never for a moment bogus or canting. She faces real spiritual suffering in the defeat of her faith at the hands of her father and genuine spiritual triumph in her acceptance of his faith and her knowledge that she will transcend it, as he means that she should. When Andrew Undershaft visits his family for the first time in years, it is plain within a few moments that Shaw has sent him to challenge Barbara's method of saving souls. He agrees to visit her Salvation

Army shelter ("In West Ham. At the sign of the cross. Ask anybody in Canning Town.") if in return she will visit his munitions factory ("In Perivale St Andrews. At the sign of the sword. Ask anybody in Europe.") In the shelter, Barbara is following the usual Salvation Army procedure, passing out food and reaching out for souls, and she has her share of politic converts. The action in the shelter is double. First, Bill Walker, who has hit Jenny Hill, is put under spiritual attack by Barbara. She infects him with guilt and refuses to let him buy forgiveness either with money or with a beating which he gets at the hands of a wrestler turned Salvationist. Only Bill's soul will do, and she almost has it, when the other action intervenes. Her father matches a donation from Bodger, the brewer, and, as far as Barbara is concerned, buys the Army, for to her Bodger and Undershaft are the forces she is fighting. The act ends with the defeat of Barbara, her withdrawal from the Army and the heartbreaking taunt of Bill, "Wot prawce selvytion nah?"

In Act II, also, Undershaft, who calls himself a "confirmed mystic," tells Barbara, ". . . I am a Millionaire. That is my religion." Later he explains to Adolphus Cusins, the Greek professor who has turned Salvationist to be near Barbara, that there are just two things necessary to salvation: "Yes, money and gunpowder; freedom and power; command of life and command of death." This is the gospel to which he must convert Barbara:

Leave it to the poor to pretend that poverty is a blessing: leave it to the coward to make a religion of his cowardice by preaching humility: we know better than that. We three must stand together above the common people: how else can we help their children to climb up beside us? Barbara must belong to us, not to the Salvation Army.

In the last act, Barbara bears the scars of her defeat:

BARBARA. . . . Yesterday I had a man's soul in my hand. I set him in the way of life with his face to salvation. But when we took your money he turned back to drunkenness and derision. [*With intense conviction*] I will never forgive you that. If I had a child, and you destroyed its body with your explosives—if you murdered Dolly with your horrible guns—I could forgive you if my forgiveness would open the gates of heaven to you. But to take a human soul from me, and turn it into the soul of a wolf! that is worse than any murder.

UNDERSHAFT. Does my daughter despair so easily? Can you strike a man to the heart and leave no mark on him?

BARBARA [*her face lighting up*]. Oh, you are right: he can never be lost now: where was my faith?

CUSINS. Oh, clever, clever devil!

BARBARA. You may be a devil; but God speaks through you sometimes. [*She takes her father's hands and kisses them.*] You have given me back my happiness: I feel it deep down now, though my spirit is troubled. .

UNDERSHAFT. You have learnt something. That always feels at first as if you had lost something.

The final capitulation of Barbara is tied to the choice that Cusins must make as to whether or not he will become Undershaft's heir. It is Barbara, however, and not Cusins that needs convincing. When Cusins asks, "You do not drive this place: it drives you. And what drives the place?" Undershaft answers, in good Shavian metaphysics, "A will of which I am a part." Barbara cries out, "Father! Do you know what you are saying; or are you laying a snare for my soul?" A few speeches later, he challenges her directly:

It is cheap work converting starving men with a Bible in one hand and a slice of bread in the other. I will undertake to convert West Ham to Mahometanism on the same terms. Try your hand on my men: their souls are hungry because their bodies are full.

Cusins accepts the inheritance and Barbara accepts Cusins, making it clear that she would never have taken him had he not become the next Undershaft. The play ends on a note of spiritual triumph:

BARBARA. . . . My father shall never throw it in my teeth again that my converts were bribed with bread. [*She is transfigured*]. I have got rid of the bribe of bread. I have got rid of the bribe of heaven. Let God's work be done for its own sake: the work he had to create us to do because it cannot be done except by living men and women. When I die, let him by in my debt, not I in his; and let me forgive him as becomes a woman of my rank.

CUSINS. Then the way of life lies through the factory of death?

BARBARA. Yes, through the raising of hell to heaven and of man to God, through the unveiling of an eternal light in the Valley of The Shadow. [*Seizing him with both hands*] Oh, did you think my courage would never come back? did you believe that I was a deserter? that I, who have stood in the streets, and taken my people to my heart and talked of the holiest and greatest things with them, could ever turn back and chatter foolishly to fashionable people about nothing in a drawing room? Never, never, never, never: Major Barbara will die with the colors. Oh! and I have my dear little Dolly boy still; and he has found me my place and my work. Glory Hallelujah!

Major Barbara has suffered a great many interpretations, and it is rich enough to sustain them all. A few things about it, though, appear obvious. First of all, its major insistence is that no soul can be saved in a hungry body. The play, as well as the Preface, is an attack on poverty, a fact that is apparent in Shaw's remark, ". . . Salvationists divine that they must actually fight the devil instead of merely praying at him? At present, it is true, they have not quite ascertained his correct address."[31] The emphasis on Undershaft's religion, his money and gunpowder, his freedom and power, implies that wishing will not make anything so; action— revolutionary action—is metaphorically supported in the play as

---

[31] Shaw, *Selected Plays*, I, 317. From the Preface.

it is specifically supported in the Preface. Most important, however, Shaw chose to make his points about poverty and the battle against it in the terms of a spiritual journey. At the end of the play, Barbara is talking about salvation in good Shavian terms—the God that needs man to do his work, the work that is done without the bribe of heaven—but her religious mission is as genuine—perhaps more genuine because she has suffered—at the end as it is at the beginning. *Major Barbara* remains Shaw's most important religious play and its heroine is a religious figure in many ways more impressive even that Shaw's Saint Joan.

The next specifically religious play of Shaw's is the one-act *The Shewing-up of Blanco Posnet* (1909), which Shaw calls "A Sermon in Crude Melodrama." It is the story of Blanco Posnet, a rough, obscene, villainous cowboy who, touched by a woman and a dying child, gives up the horse he has stolen so that the woman can try to reach a doctor. Blanco is caught and about to be hanged for his crime. The spirit that caught him off guard and made him give up the horse, moves Feemy, the whore, to swear that she never saw him riding the stolen horse. The play ends with a sermon in which Blanco preaches the God of Creative Evolution:

It was early days when He made the croup, I guess. It was the best He could think of then; but when it turned out wrong on His hands He made you and me to fight the croup for Him. You bet He didn't make us for nothing; and He wouldn't have made us at all if He could have done His work without us.

The God is Shavian, but the man who revolts and runs away from God only to be snapped back against his will is as old as Jonah. Blanco's description of God is in words that fit Shaw's cowboy-novel concept of the American West, but its tone is familiar in the literature of Christianity. "He's a sly one," Blanco says. "He's a mean one. He lies low for you. He plays cat and mouse with you. He lets you run loose until you think you're shut of Him; and then, when you least expect it, He's got you." The hound of heaven apparently has a Creative Evolution kennel.

Androcles and the Lion (1912), with its reminders of Wilson Barrett's lush melodramas, forces a variety of Christians to face death in the arena and saves them through Ferrovius's sudden reversion to violence and Androcles's old friendship with the lion. It is a fable not so much of Christianity facing Roman tyranny as of any infant religion (or political creed) facing its oppressor. Lavinia makes this point clear:

> But when men who believe neither in my god nor in their own—men who do not know the meaning of the word religion—when these men drag me to the foot of an iron statue that has become the symbol of the terror and darkness through which they walk, of their cruelty and greed, of their hatred of God and their oppression of man—when they ask me to pledge my soul before the people that this hideous idol is God, and that all this wickedness and falsehood is divine truth, I cannot do it, not if they could put a thousand cruel deaths on me.

Androcles with his love of animals and men, his gentleness, his patience, and his willingness to suffer is touching and admirable in the play, but it is Ferrovius and Lavinia who are more nearly Shavian religious figures. Ferrovius is Anthony Anderson all over again. Just before he is to enter the arena, Lavinia comforts him. "You will find your real faith in the hour of trial." "That is what I fear," he answers. "I know that I am a fighter. How can I feel sure that I am a Christian?" When his doubts prove true, he accepts himself: "The Christian God is not yet. He will come when Mars and I are dust; but meanwhile I must serve the gods that are, not the God that will be." In the Notes at the end of the play, Shaw suggests that the clergymen who took so enthusiastically to the war (World War I) would have been more honest had they emulated Ferrovius and refused to proclaim themselves fighters and Christians at the same time. Lavinia, whom Shaw calls a freethinker, believes in the doctrine of Creative Evolution. She tells the Captain: "I think I'm going to die for God. Nothing else is real enough to die for." When the Captain asks, "What is God?" she answers, "When we know that, Captain, we shall be gods ourselves." At the end, she says, "I'll strive for the coming of the God who is not yet." In the context of Shavian thought, this is obviously an avowal of the God-in-the-making that Don Juan and Blanco Posnet have glimpsed in earlier plays.

Back to Methuselah (1921) is Shaw's most determined effort to present Creative Evolution in dramatic terms. This five-part play tries to look into the future, to find the evolutionary changes that man can will, but in its need to be specific it violates the Shavian idea that the end cannot be determined. In many ways the first part, "In the Beginning," is the most effective. Here, Adam and Eve discover death and the secret of birth; here, too, Eve learns to put her trust not in the diggers (Adam) nor the killers (Cain), but in the poets, the creators, the thinkers. Adam defines the Life Force when, in answer to the Serpent's "The voice in the garden is your own voice," he says, "It is; and it is not. It is something greater than me: I am only a part of it." The Serpent, in refusing to take a vow as Adam has, to live precisely one thousand years, reaffirms the indeterminate end, the unending end, "If I bind the future I bind my will. If I bind my will I strangle creation." Part II, "The Gospel of the Brothers Barnabas," reaffirms, in the words of Franklyn Barnabas, Shaw's contention that ". . . God proceeds by the method of Trial and Error. . . ." It also sets up the ideal of long life—three hundred years as a beginning—as the first step, the first act of faith in the newly conscious Creative Evolution. Part III, "The Thing Happens," takes the world to 2170, when some long-lifers are already in operation, but for the most part it is concerned with the pompous inefficiency of British politicians, the kind of joke that is more typical of Shaw's plays of the thirties. Part IV, "Tragedy of an Elderly Gentleman," finds the long-lifers in Ireland, occasionally consulted as oracles by the short-lifers.

In Part V, "As Far as Thought can Reach," mankind has evolved into a race of thinkers, Don Juan's Heaven realized. Man is now hatched from an egg, full-grown, articulate, replete with sexual appetite. He spends a four-year childhood, concerned with love, sex, art, all the things that presently occupy man for a lifetime, and then turns to contemplation. Life lasts until it is erased by a fatal accident. The ancients are striving to get away from the body (the cause of the accidents), to become vortices of thought. Shaw is successful with his gentle, grown-up children, but his ancients are something else again. In depicting their life of contemplation, their aim toward bodilessness, Shaw faces the problem that confronts every writer who tries to conceive of Heaven. The picture must be unrelentingly desirable and it must at the same time be described in the limiting language that has to do with the real world. A man is just as likely to get impatient with Shaw's slightly smug ancients as he is to get bored with Dante's vision of the rose. Shaw saw this, of course. In *Farfetched Fables* (1948), one of the vortices, for the body has learned to become vortex in that play, reincarnates itself, a feathered being; the end of thought seems to have become a pointless curiosity. *Back to Methuselah* is not to be taken literally, of course. Shaw, who so often fulminated against the Fundamentalists who held exactly to the word of the Bible, would never expect the Bible of Creative Evolution to be accepted as more than a myth. That the method should be willed longevity, that the end—even a temporary one—should be contemplation is simply the accident of Shaw's personality. The point is made in the last, lovely speech of Lilith, which ends, "And for what may be beyond, the eyesight of Lilith is too short. It is enough that there is a beyond."

Then came *Saint Joan* (1923). In it, Shaw was able to use a

Christian story in a way that he had never done before. His Joan is
the Catholic saint and martyr, but she is more than that. She is also
a Shavian saint and martyr. Like Shaw's Caesar, she is a natural
genius; she is a variation on Major Barbara. She is—in the history
lesson scene between the Earl of Warwick and the Bishop of
Beauvais—the first nationalist and the first Protestant. She can
produce practical reasons for all her actions, for instance, to
appease the unbelieving Dunois, and her practicality does not
desert her even when she talks of her visions. She answers Robert
de Baudricourt, who tells her that her voices come from her own
imagination, with " Of course. That is how the messages of God
come to us." One half of Joan is, then, a Shavian man of action,
an embodiment of the Life Force, although the label is never used
in the play. The other half is the French peasant girl who sincerely
believes in her voices, the mystic acting by instinct or through
revelation—in short, the saint. In scene after scene, she is given
moments of spiritual exaltation or anguish—when the wind
changes at Orleans, when she is warned after the coronation at
Rheims, when she recants. Having allowed Joan so much of herself, Shaw faced a problem with the play's intention. The heart of
Saint Joan is the Epilogue, where all those who loved her, all those
who persecuted her and all those who sainted her are still unable
to accept her, save as a dead saint. The pain of her famous line,
" O God that madest this beautiful earth, when will it be ready to
receive Thy saints? How long, O Lord, how long?" depends for
its irony on the Shavian assumption that Joan's death is an unnecessary horror. Yet for Joan the Catholic, her death is not a
misfortune, but a triumph. Shaw has written his saint's play so
well, has entered so effectively into the personality of Joan that
the play carries an ambivalence within it. *Saint Joan*, in Shaw's
terms, is a tragedy, but the play has always had those advocates
who, sharing Joan's final triumph, consider the Epilogue an
accretion, those whose admiration for the play caused Israel

Zangwill to wonder if Shaw might "die in the odour of Sybil Thorndike's sanctity."[32]

For Shaw, of course, the tragedy is that the saints should have died at all, that their usefulness to the world should be destroyed by the world. The death of Joan becomes more ironic and more terrible in Shaw's play because he insists that the men who desert her and the men who kill her are not villains. At worst, they are fools. "To understand a saint, you must hear the devil's advocate. . . ."[33] Shaw wrote years earlier in *The Sanity of Art*. He leans over backward to make all of Joan's opponents understandable, most of them honorable within their own sphere of action. Even De Stogumber, the English chaplain who begins as a caricature and ends as a suffering human being, is more ignorant than evil. The well-meaning, narrow-visioned, selfish men of the world, like those who opposed Joan, became the protagonists of the Shaw plays that followed *Saint Joan*—after a six-year lag. The playwright became increasingly preoccupied with the world that was not yet ready to receive its saints. The change had begun in *Heartbreak House* (1916) with its curious atmosphere of sorrow and disenchantment. Even *Back to Methuselah*, although it was Shaw's most nearly complete statement of his faith in Creative Evolution, was not a completely positive play. The goal was disembodiment, an asceticism that might conceivably be a withdrawal, a solving of the world's problems by transcending them, and the satirical depiction of the British politicians was, for all its farcical fun, a statement of ineffectuality.

Prior to the first world war, Shaw had mixed his faith in Creative Evolution with a belief in the efficacy of practical politics, but the prevailing tone of the plays after *Back to Methuselah* is very nearly defeatist. The optimism of *Man and Superman* and *Major Barbara* is gone. Shaw's fear for the future, which allowed

[32] Israel Zangwill, "My Religion," *My Religion*, New York, Appleton, 1926, p. 69.
[33] Shaw, *Major Critical Essays*, p. 284.

him to look momentarily longingly at Hitler and Mussolini, which allowed him to see the virtues and be blind to the vices of Soviet Russia with a naiveté that marks some of his plays, like *Geneva* (1938), as clearly as the same quality of mind marks and informs all the later work of Sean O'Casey. There is still fun in his plays; they still end in positive statements. Shaw does not discard his faith in Creative Evolution, nor does he drop his belief in practical measures and the socialism toward which they are to be aimed. But the Shavian strong men begin to grow weak. There are no more Caesars and Undershafts; no more Barbaras and Lavinias. Joan is his last vital character, and she is a martyr, rejected by the world; there is no Ferrovius and no Androcles to save her from burning. Joan dwindles to King Magnus in *The Apple Cart* (1929), to Private Meek in *Too True to Be Good* (1932), to Sir Arthur Chavender in *On the Rocks* (1933), and to King Charles in *"In Good King Charles's Golden Days"* (1939). They no longer imagine, like Undershaft, that they can lift the world; they are intent on hanging on to a semblance of order and sanity.[34]

The muted despair of these last plays, which are largely political, is stated in religious terms in *Too True to Be Good*. Since this is an "Extravaganza," it is impossible to reduce the plot to a few coherent sentences. After a mock robbery, a mock kidnapping, an attack by desert troops, a handful of sudden and unlikely appearances, most of the cast is assembled in a kind of grotto. Aubrey, a not very professional burglar, the ordained son of an atheist father, climbs up on a rock and begins a sermon:

I must have affirmations to preach. Without them the young will not listen to me; for even the young grow tired of denials. The negative-monger falls before the soldiers, the men of action, the fighters. . . .

[34] A valuable discussion of Shaw's last plays can be found in Katherine Haynes Gatch, "The Last Plays of Bernard Shaw: Dialectic and Despair," in *English Stage Comedy*, ed. W. K. Wimsatt, Jr., New York, Columbia University Press, 1955, pp. 126–147.

Their way is straight and sure; but it is the way of death; and the preacher must preach the way of life. Oh, if I could only find it! I am ignorant: I have lost my nerve and am intimidated: all I know is that I must find the way of life, for myself and all of us, or we shall surely perish. And meanwhile my gift has possession of me: I must preach and preach and preach no matter how late the hour and how short the day, no matter whether I have nothing to say or whether in some pentecostal flame of revelation the Spirit will descend on me and inspire me with a message the sound whereof shall go out unto all lands and realize for us at last the Kingdom and the Power and the Glory for ever and ever. Amen.

As Aubrey speaks, the characters go out singly or in pairs. A mist comes up and covers him. He goes on talking. In a note at the end, Shaw contradicts everything that the play has been saying about the drifting, rootless uncertainty that is too true to be good:

The author, though himself a professional talk maker, does not believe that the world can be saved by talk alone. He has given the rascal the last word; but his own favorite is the woman of action, who begins by knocking the wind out of the rascal, and ends with a cheerful conviction that the lost dogs always find their way home. So they will, perhaps, if the women go out and look for them.

These last words are as much an invocation of faith as Ann White-field's advice to John Tanner to go on talking, but the faith is here being sorely tried. Shaw is twenty-five years past Major Barbara's vision.

Shaw's Day of Judgment comes at last in *The Simpleton of the Unexpected Isles* (1934). In the play, two superior Eastern types, Pra and Prola, convince a number of Englishmen to join an experiment in communal living which produces four beautiful children, who speak all the catchwords of art, patriotism, and romance, but are sterile. An English clergyman called Iddy (short for Idiot) is taken into the community in the hope that, since he has been raised on a special nitrogen diet by his scientist father, he will be able to bring life to the young. He is impotent, however, a Shavian comment on both the church and science. An angel comes to announce the Shavian judgment which calls for the disappearance of all useless people. The Angel says, "The Day of Judgment is not the end of the world, but the end of its childhood and the beginning of its responsible maturity." The beautiful young people disappear first, then Iddy, finally the rest of the Englishmen. The play ends with Pra and Prola welcoming the future, but the extermination rate has been high. The mature world involves not the raising as in *Major Barbara*, but the erasing of the weak.

"*In Good King Charles's Golden Days*" is Shaw's last major play. In it, sadness prevails. There are always men able to run a country, King Charles says in Act II, but they can never be chosen (by inheritance or by vote) to do the job. In Act I, however, Shaw has reaffirmed his basic religious tenet. The long discussion involving Charles II, Isaac Newton, George Fox, and the artist Godfrey Kneller, enlivened with the romping of Nell Gwynn and the Duchesses of Cleveland and Portsmouth, seems designed to show that the inspiration that touches Fox, Newton, Kneller, and Charles is all the same inspiration. "Divine grace takes many strange forms," according to George Fox, and Charles says, "Do you think God so stupid that he could invent only one sort of conscience?" To Fox falls the specific avowal of the Life Force: "I am not one of those priest-ridden churchmen who believe that God went out of business six thousand years ago when he had called the world into existence and written his book about it." In the Preface to *Farfetched Fables* nine years later, Shaw, at ninety-three, made his final restatement of faith in Creative Evolution, his acceptance—even after a second world war—of George Fox's still-growing God.

The attempt to sort out the religion in Shaw's plays, the attempt to isolate it and say that Shaw said this and this about God and the Life Force involves a number of complications. First, Shaw was never willing to separate religion from the rest of life—as nominally religious people sometimes do. His statements of faith move in all his plays, informing their ideas and their action. "It is not that I have too little religion in me for the Church," says his King Charles. "I have too much. . . ." For Shaw, every action became a religious action and every idea a religious idea. "But the more you let life come to you," says Pra, "the more you will find yourself bothering about religion." Second, Shaw was an artist and a playwright. He never doubted that the theater was a place in which to preach and teach, but he complicated the simplicity of thesis drama by consistently writing plays in which the characters have human validity and vitality, which means that they cannot be expected to act simply as mouthpieces for ideas. Every one of Shaw's plays is about ideas, but—except for the fantastic and caricatured plays of the thirties—the ideas always take form in relation to human beings. Lastly, Shaw's work divides into two main groups. Prior to *Heartbreak House* his plays are suffused with optimism, restrained always by a realistic power of observation; after that, the optimism remains but becomes tempered, occasionally almost defeatist. Two world wars and a depression marked Shaw's work as obviously as it marked the world. On practical matters, Shaw's opinions changed—for instance, his ideas about socialism, revolution, and parliamentary government altered with the circumstances—but his faith in Creative Evolution remained basically unchanged. Although his personal doctrine of free will still flourished at the end of his life, it was quite obviously touched with the sadness that marks his last plays, even at their most farcical and most foolish. This much can be said about Shaw as a religious playwright. He produced in *Major Barbara* and *Saint Joan* two of the most moving religious plays in the English language. He made a sincere if not completely successful effort in *Back to*

Methuselah to construct a mythology for his own religion, and in *Man and Superman* he came closer to such a mythology without the ponderousness that sometimes marked the later play. He was adept at religious-moral parables, like *The Devil's Disciple* and *Androcles and the Lion.* And more than any other playwright of the century, Shaw was aware of the theater as the home for religious drama and was most active in seeing that the genre got home.

James Bridie. James Bridie, who wrote out of Glasgow and, as often as not, for the Scottish theater, is the playwright who comes closest to Shaw in his use of religious figures and religious idiom in specifically personal terms. Bridie, whose real name was Osborne H. Mavor, wrote mainly comedies, but comedies in which such harsh realities as death, disease, and drunkenness are accepted and transcended. His penchant for puns and obvious verbal jokes was even more insistent than Shaw's, and he had a sense of fantasy that often shattered conventional play structure and placed his work close in form to the late Shavian extravaganzas. The chief criticism that was aimed at him all through his career was that his plays fell apart before the end or that his ideas were never fully developed. Actually, Bridie preferred to approach an idea skippingly, to run around it rather than to build it slowly and carefully; most of his plays, although they often leap from character to character, from place to place, from reality to fantasy, have a unity that is recognizable as Bridie's approach to life, as his point of view about the meaning and importance of the human being.

Although his career was dogged with comparisons to Shaw, Bridie never had political or religious views that were carefully articulated, as Shaw's were. According to Winifred Bannister, "Bridie's political views were rather like his religion: so liberal minded, so humanitarian that they were unfixed."[35] Certainly

[35] Winifred Bannister, *James Bridie and His Theatre*, London, Rockliff, 1955, p. 36.

Bridie's religion, at least on the evidence of the plays, is amorphous; only in two of his last plays—*The Queen's Comedy* and *The
Baikie Charivari*—did he appear to be working toward some
specific statement about religion. For the most part, his plays
express a faith in and a fondness for the individual, a distrust of
institutions—government and the church—a distaste for social
compulsion, a suspicion of the overdedicated man, and a feeling
for a God who is distant and impersonal, unconcerned with and
uninvolved in the activities of men. This concept of God is best
seen in *A Sleeping Clergyman* (1933), a play in which three generations are manipulated to show that the strain of genius in them
overcomes their strain of violence, the operation of a Life Force,
more accidental, less purposive than that of Shaw. The title of the
play refers to a white-bearded clergyman who dozes in a chair in
the Chorus openings to each act, clubroom scenes in which one
man tells another the story. Bridie specifically identifies the clergyman and explains why he should sleep through the whole story:
"God, who had set it all going, took his ease in an armchair
throughout the play."[36]

Bridie's supernatural plays are more likely to call on the devil
than on God. Beelzebub, for instance, appears in *The Sunlight
Sonata* (1928), where he infects seven characters, each with one of
the deadly sins. The comic point of the play is that when some
chattering heavenly messengers manage to remove the sins, the
characters lose their liveliness. This early play is really little more
than an extended joke. Later, in *Mr. Bolfry* (1943), the playwright
was to write a more serious diabolic comedy. In it, three young
people, two English soldiers and the minister's niece, outargued
by the Reverend Mr. McCrimmon, a Puritanical Scottish Presbyterian, conjure the devil—Mr. Bolfry, neatly dressed, with umbrella—and find to their distress that he and Mr. McCrimmon
agree. As Mr. Bolfry says, " we cannot begin our battle for the

[36] James Bridie, *One Way of Living*,n, Londo Constable, [1939], p. 278.

souls of these persons until they realise that they have souls to battle for." McCrimmon consents that Bolfry should preach, and the visiting devil begins a sermon about Good and Evil being in league against Death. He goes on to call on Life, to ask for the breaking away from Christian restrictions, echoing Shaw's Saint Joan in the process: "How long, O Lucifer, Son of the Morning, how long? How long will these fools listen to the quaverings of impotent old priests, haters of the Life they never know?" Realizing that he is being bested in argument, McCrimmon snatches up a knife and chases Bolfry into the night.

McCrimmon's victory is no victory of Scottish Puritanism over a more liberal view of life, however, for his is the triumph of violence not of persuasion. Besides, as Bolfry preaches, McCrimmon cries out, "you are my own heart speaking in a dream." McCrimmon's involuntary support of Bolfry seems to indicate that his is not the way of life, but the play is more than a simple reversal, as in *The Sunlight Sonata*. Bolfry is, after all, the force of evil and his defeat is necessary. He makes this clear in a conversation with Jean. She says, "I believe that the Kingdom of Heaven is within me," and Bolfry accepts the idea with reservations: "So far as it goes, you are quite right. But you are also the receptacle of the Kingdom of Hell and of a number of other irrelevancies left over in the process of Evolution." Mr. Bolfry is one of Bridie's attempts to personify the spirit of evil that opposes man. In the Scottish setting of this play, his defeat must come at the hands of McCrimmon, but the preacher is plainly identified as in some ways in league with the devil. Still, the three young people who appear to believe nothing are not let off either; they are helpless in the face of both McCrimmon and Bolfry. Jean explains to Bolfry why he was conjured, why they need someone to argue against her uncle, "He's got the advantage of believing everything he says." Bridie is suggesting, as he often is, that some kind of belief is necessary.

Bridie's biblical plays are probably his best known and most widely performed works. The first of them was *Tobias and the Angel* (1930), which has much of the charm of the original story in the Apocrypha. In it, the charity of Tobit is rewarded—after he has suffered poverty and blindness—when his son Tobias goes off, accompanied by Raphael in disguise, and comes back with wealth, a bride, and a cure for Tobit's eyes. In Bridie's play, as in the Apocrypha, Raphael beats Asmoday, the daemon, and so saves Tobias's life and his marriage to Sara. Raphael, in an explanation of his purpose and, incidentally, that of Asmoday, sounds a little like the Mr. Bolfry who was yet to come:

A daemon, spelt with an "a" is a creature by whose agency you write immortal verse, go great journeys, leap into bottomless chasms, fight dragons, starve in a garret. . . .
When it is necessary to Jahveh's purpose they make contact, often with extremely disturbing results; for daemons are not all equally expert and conscientious, and their material is not invariably well chosen.

The daemon, then, is the power for inspiration to acts beyond the ordinary, the power for creativity, for courage and for destruction. To Tobit belongs the best line in the play and the one that subsumes Raphael's explanation. After he has got his eyesight back, the old man says, "Jahveh has made me a very happy man. Jahveh is full of unexpected moments."

As Bridie was drawn to the story of Tobit and his just reward, so he was attracted to Jonah and the lesson that God taught him outside Nineveh. *Jonah and the Whale* appeared in its first form in 1932. In a program note Bridie described the play and its relation to the world in which it appeared: "*Jonah and the Whale* is placed in an era when prophets grew sourly on every bush as they do to-day, and this is the story of a prophet who was proved by a series of grotesque circumstances, not to know what he was talking about."[37] His Jonah is a pompous, consequential little man, strutting in importance as the prophet of Gittah-Hepher. Angered by a fast-talking travelling salesman, Jonah rashly promises to go to Nineveh to preach repentance. After the interlude of the Whale, who warns him, "Forgive me, little man, you are an instrument of God in your fantastic way, but you are not at all in His secrets," Jonah gets to Nineveh, where he appears before the Semiramis Club, a parody of all ladies' clubs, and prophesies the destruction of the city. In the moment of prophecy, Jonah is more than the self-important little man who figures in most of the action; he transcends his own character, is genuinely inspired. To Eudoias's "Aren't you a little bit sorry for them, Jonah?" he answers, "Of course I am sorry for them. I am a man and not God." By the time he gets to the hill outside of town, however, he is concerned solely with his reputation. God teaches him the lesson of the withered gourd and the unhurt city and Jonah says, "I have learned a bitter truth. I am not in God's confidence."

Bridie rewrote *Jonah* as a radio play in 1942, as *The Sign of the Prophet Jonah*, in which most of the side characters—the salesman, for instance—are dropped and in which the satire on contemporary foibles largely disappears. The main story, the chastening of Jonah, is kept and a charming scene of Jonah as a child, stumbling accidentally on his power as a prophet, is added to initiate the idea of his self-importance. In the same year, Bridie rewrote the long play, as *Jonah 3*, for F. Sladen-Smith at Manchester, who wanted to do a wartime version with fewer characters. By way of introduction, this version has the ghost of Jonah seeking out the Whale, who cannot quite remember him, and the prophecy no longer takes place before the ladies' club, but at the end of a scene involving the wise-cracking King of Nineveh. In all of the *Jonahs* Bridie insists on one point: that the prophet had best not confuse his inspired message with his quite ordinary self.

[37] Quoted, Bannister, *op. cit.*, p. 87.

In *Susannah and the Elders* (1937), Bridie manages to do two things—to save Susannah from false accusation and, at the same time, to endow the lecherous old men with a pathetic dignity. In Bridie's enlargement of the Aprocryphal story, the two Assyrian judges are self-indulgent old gentlemen, fond of good food, good company, good conversation; their attitude toward the law and the religion that they administer is clear in Kabbittu's speech, "I may not be a very religious man, but I think that religion should be taken seriously." They are concerned with form not substance. Having maneuvered Susannah, pure to the point of foolishness, into their garden, they stoop to violence, to lies, to murder (of the young man who comes in answer to her cries for help and whom the judges accuse as her lover). In the court scene, they are easily defeated by Daniel, but in the face of the penalty against them, they manage a dignity that they have not been able to achieve as judges and certainly not as would-be seducers. Daniel is drawn as a bright and angry young Jewish lawyer, defeating the oppressing Assyrians in the name of the oppressed Jews—as he is pictured in a number of the Apocryphal stories. In saving Susannah, Daniel has done what he knows had to be done; yet when one of his admirers suggests that God has spoken through his mouth, Daniel says, "I hope He did, Meschach. I do not know," as though he suspects that in some sense the Lord also spoke through the desires and the unhappiness of the defeated old men.

Two plays that Bridie wrote in 1942 for the Pilgrim Players, the wartime company that operated across the English and Scottish countryside under the direction of E. Martin Browne, are related to his biblical plays. *The Dragon and the Dove*, based on a story from Helen Waddell's *The Desert Fathers*, tells the story of a holy monk who becomes a roaring soldier, a kind of *miles gloriosus*, to save his niece whom a less holy monk has seduced by reading Song of Songs to her. *A Change for the Worse*, the companion piece, is a short rhymed-verse play in which Satan inadvertently does good and the smug St. Eloi takes the credit. As Christian comedies, these plays—like the biblical ones—are eminently acceptable to Christian church groups; they are also dramatic parables of Bridie's humanitarian religion.

In two of his later plays—*Holy Isle* (1942) and *John Knox* (1947)—Christianity, in so far as it is institutional and restrictive, comes under attack, but in both plays comparable secular attitudes are just as harried. In *Holy Isle,* Torquil, a kind of sailor-philosopher-reformer, leads an expedition—which includes Grettir, a businessman; Father Innocence, a missionary; and Queen Margause, in disguise—to the island Ru-rhush. Having once visited the island and been impressed by the simplicity of life there, Torquil feels compelled to bring his version of civilization to the benighted natives. On the island, there is only a casual government with the Ponderers (as far as Shaw's thought can reach) in advisory control; the chief of the Ponderers is a woman, identified simply as She. Each of the newcomers introduces his particular brand of virtue to the island. Grettir teaches greed; Margause, display and the idea of social classes; Father Innocence, prudery and repressive religion. At the beginning of his mission, Innocence tells the story of the Fall from Eden, and She compliments him, "It is a most interesting story and very well told; and it confirms us in our wish not to have gods on our Island." She then tells of an islander who once managed to retain the corner of a magic book that had been banned from the island, a corner that read, "Blessed are the meek, for they shall inherit the Earth"; she goes on to explain how "from that fragment came efforts to be meek, rules of meekness, quarrels about meekness and finally a repressive hierarchy of meekness." Grettir, Margause and Father Innocence finally succumb to the island; only Torquil refuses to give in; his desire to control and discipline the island grows stronger. Margause finally saves the island from its would-be benefactors, but not before Bridie has drawn a forceful picture of the reformer turned represser. Father Innocence has the last important word:

Our Lord taught us the alphabet very simply, and when His disciples had learned that, He went on to teach them the mysteries. But we haven't learned the alphabet, have we, sir? We don't know how to live at peace with our neighbors. How can we understand the mysteries?

John Knox is Bridie's historical lesson in overdedication. In the play, Knox is shown fighting for the establishment of a society in which the Kirk is to share power with the government—a society, incidentally, which looks forward to such highly acceptable reforms as universal education. His advocacy of Protestantism leads him into opposition to the Catholic Mary Stuart. The action of the play involves the attempts of Lord James Stuart to balance the conflicting ideas of Knox and Mary. The play ends in bloodshed. Hector, the divinity student who acts as narrator, says of Knox's goal, "Long years afterwards his dream came true and it proved to be no great matter." Knox, who is presented sympathetically as a person, but not as a purveyor of ideology, is pictured as a compulsive preacher; in the scene at the end in which he and Mary evaluate their actions in retrospect, he involuntarily breaks into a sermon. Still, he summarizes his own defect, like Jonah in Bridie's other play about a misdirected prophet, "I thought there was a man sent from Heaven whose name was John, but I took the ordinary road for getting here. It was ill luck that I got a voice that could talk Kings off their thrones and I thought too much of it."

In *The Queen's Comedy* (1950) and *The Baikie Charivari* (1951), the latter performed at the Edinburgh Festival the year after the author's death, Bridie's religious ideas found their most effective dramatic form. *The Queen's Comedy* is a decidedly free working of Books XIV and XV of the *Iliad*, the section in which Juno seduces Jupiter (Bridie uses the Roman names) and gives the Greeks a chance to triumph momentarily over the Trojans. As in Homer, the action swings between earth and heaven. Bridie's gods are even more frivolous than those in Homer. The action on earth, except for some Colonel-Blimpish portraits of the Greek officers, is confined to discussions between a medical orderly and a plain foot soldier, conceived unfortunately in the clichés of contemporary colloquialism, and between the nurse Hecamede and the young doctor Machaon. When the four chief human characters are killed after the Greek advance is turned back, they are given a chance to confront the gods. It is the orderly who does the attacking, "Call yourself gods! I've seen savages up in Scythia make better gods in an old clay puddle. . . ." His indictment becomes a plea for the cessation of heavenly intervention, for the sleeping-clergyman concept of God:

I worked hard and I done the dirty to no person. Why not? Because I didn't want to, see. It wasna nothing them that bossed me around told me, the Priests or the Sergeant or that. . . . You great, stupid, lazy, good-looking sticks of barley sugar! They say you send us the rain and the sunshine and the wheat in the fields. Well, get on with it and leave us alone!

Jupiter appears and makes a speech, telling how, as a child, he accidentally constructed the Universe and how he has been working on it ever since, not certain where it is to go. In substance, his speech hints at the Shavian will; in tone, it sets him off from both man and the gods, makes him as distant as an impersonal force:

But long ago I put a little swelling at the end of the primitive spinal cord of a sort of fish. I am happy to observe that in some of the higher apes, the lump has taken on extensive and peculiar functions. One of these functions appears to consist of explaining me and my little Universe. I have no doubt at all that these explanations are very interesting

and stimulating. Perhaps, in time, these little objects will attain to the
properties and activities of the Immortal Gods themselves. Who knows?
I have not nearly completed my Universe. There is plenty of time.
Plenty of time. You must have patience.

If *The Queen's Comedy* is Bridie's last clear statement about God,
The Baikie Charivari, or The Seven Prophets is his last dealing with
the devil. In this play, Bridie's most elaborately conceived and
most carefully worked out, man triumphs over the devil and his
agents. This "Miracle Play," as Bridie calls it, is told on two levels
—the realistic and the fantastic—and it runs freely from one to
another. The characters in it are real residents of the Scottish
village of Baikie; they are also characters out of Punch and Judy
and, beyond that, diabolic agents. In the fantasy scenes the play
breaks into verse, sometimes rhymed, that achieves an intensity
that is not so much the result of verbal ingenuity, as it is of the
emotional and intellectual investment of the hero in his search for
knowledge in and of the new world in which he finds himself. The
action is inaugurated by the De'il who announces his intention to
use the seven figures to try the hero. At the end of a career in
India, a retired civil servant, named Pounce-Pellott, a combination
of Punch and Pontius Pilate that suggests "Pounce Pilat" from
"The Cutler's Play" in The York cycle, comes to Baikie with his
wife (Judy) and his daughter (Baby). He meets an assortment of
people and asks them all to dinner. Each of them offers a standard
solution for the world's ills. The Reverend Dr. Marcus Beadle
(Beadle) offers Christianity; Robert Copper (Policeman), the civil
servant's social science; Councillor John Ketch (Hangman), Communism; Joe Mascara (Clown), in the name of art, the self as sole
order; Dr. Jean Pothercary (Doctor), psychiatry in particular,
science in general; Lady Maggie Revenant (Ghost), shades of
the past; Mrs. Jemima Lee Crowe (Jim Crow), the lure of
money.

When Rev. Beadle and Ketch insist on their brands of order, Pounce-Pellot makes his important speech:

> I know order and I know disorder.
> Order I have forever loved and ensured.
> . . .
> This is the order of two dead stones—
> Two dead, flat stones, pieces of machinery.
> I will not lie down and be crushed by those horrible stones.
> I will be a King and a Priest again.
> I was a stupid priest and a dull king;
> But an honourable king and an honest priest.
> . . .
> I never imagined Destruction, much less
> Made Destruction my goal and my god.
> . . .
> I have washed my hands of my God and killed Him.
> I have sold Him for Order.
> Therefore I must be punished.
>
> But by the God I sold, I will not go quietly.
> Where is my stick?

Like Punch, he lays about him with his stick. There is wryness in his curtain speech:

> If you don't know, who knows? Nobody knows. Nobody
> knows.
> I've killed all those fools who pretended to know.
> And so . . . and so . . .
> With the soothsayers littered about the stage
> That I slew in my rage,
> Who did not know . . . and no more do I . .
> I must jest again and await my reply . . .
>
> Good-bye.

This end, however, is not defeatist. Pounce-Pellott has accepted his guilt in mankind's guilt and he has rejected easy solutions, the crutches that might protect him without helping him. In wielding his stick, he has also saved his daughter, for, as in Punch and Judy, the Seven Prophets have been after Baby. She decides to marry Toby Messan, the apprentice plumber, the man who does not work with theories. Bridie with a depth and a sadness that does not appear in many of his plays is reminding man that he still must beware the devil who takes so many and such provocative human forms.

With the death of Bridie in 1951, following so closely on that of Bernard Shaw the year before, modern English religious drama has been left almost completely in the hands of the more orthodox Christian practitioners. Unfortunately, few of them approach Shaw and Bridie as playwrights; few, too, are so exuberant in their confession of faith.

PART TWO

Church Drama

V

Up from Everyman

By 1933, the revival of religious drama (church drama in contrast to commercial drama) in England was well under way. The plays of T. S. Eliot, Christopher Fry, and Charles Williams lay in the future, but a body of serious religious drama, of which John Masefield's *The Coming of Christ* is the best-known example, was already forming. The Religious Drama Society and the Canterbury Festival were already four years old and "the first Director of Religious Drama in an English diocese since the Reformation,"[1] E. Martin Browne, appointed by George K. A. Bell, the Bishop of Chichester, had been operating for three years. In that year, the actor Harding Steerman wrote a letter to *The Times*[2] to remind the world that Miss A. M. Buckton's *Eager Heart* (1904) had been the first modern mystery play and that William Poel's production of *Everyman* at the Charterhouse on July 13, 1901, had been the first modern presentation of an ancient mystery. Steerman, who had played Adonai in the Poel *Everyman* and had appeared as Joseph in some of the productions of *Eager Heart,* was essentially—if not technically—correct in his declaration. Laurence Housman's Nativity play *Bethlehem* and a number of less well-remembered works had preceded *Eager Heart,* but the popularity of Miss Buckton's play and the flurry of medieval productions that followed Poel's *Everyman* gave the first real force to the revival that was to continue through the teens and the twenties

[1] E. Martin Browne, "Introduction," Viscount Duncannon, *Like Stars Appearing,* London, Heinemann, [1953], p. vii.
[2] *The Times* (London), January 12, 1933, p. 8.

and was to bring forth plays of literary significance in the thirties.

It is impossible, of course, to put a finger on a particular play or a particular production and to say that with it the movement began. There are almost always forerunners. Joseph Wayne Barley cites, for instance, the Bethlehem Tableaux given at Kensington in 1898.[3] In the same year, Bernard Shaw's duties as drama critic for *The Saturday Review* took him to the Great Hall of the Church House, Westminster, to see *The Conversion of England*, an ecclesiastical drama by the Reverend Henry Cresswell, an event which moved him to random thoughts on the commercial theater, but to no understandable account of the play itself.[4] The few quotations that he did give seem to indicate that his failure to deal with the play at length was the result of kindness rather than critical laxity. The Kensington tableaux and the Westminster play are examples of a kind of tentative gesture toward religious drama before the turn of the century, but the Poel revival of *Everyman* is the first clearly generative production.

The Medieval Revival. Poel seems an unlikely source for a religious drama revival. The director emerges from Robert Speaight's biography, *William Poel and the Elizabethan Revival*, as a Victorian radical, one who grew up in the strongest days of rationalism. He was generally anticlerical and particularly anti-Catholic. Of Poel's own play *The First Franciscans* (1905), also called *The Temptation of Agnes*, an account of a follower of Francis in opposition to the Order, Joseph Wayne Barley wrote, "The theme of this play is the bigotry and arrogance of the Catholic church."[5] Poel's attitude toward organized religion is also made

[3] Joseph Wayne Barley, *The Morality Motive in Contemporary English Drama*, Mexico, Missouri, 1912, p. 9.
[4] Shaw's review is in *Our Theatre in the Nineties*, London, Constable, 1932, III, 292–297.
[5] Barley, *op. cit.* p. 39.

clear by a note that he wrote to Allan Gomme in 1909, shortly after Granville Barker produced the Gilbert Murray *Bacchae* at the Court Theatre:[6]

To make Euripides alive today what is wanted is to show the modern rationalist that Euripides is the great model for all those who today want to show the immorality and irreligion of the Christian religion as it is used by the Church for her own interests. . . .

There was a positive side to Poel's faith, too—a strong ethical quality and an admiration for the simplicity of Christ, which, for him contrasted to the artificiality of the church as a dogmatizing institution.

Poel came to *Everyman* under unusual circumstances. At A. W. Ward's suggestion, he read the play for the first time shortly after his mother's death. Perhaps his mourning made the play particularly attractive to him, but, for whatever reason, he decided that he wanted to direct it. He had already made his reputation with his Shakespearean revivals, and he had done two plays which might be considered religious—Christopher Marlowe's *Dr. Faustus* (at St. George's Hall, 1896) and John Milton's *Samson Agonistes* (at the Lecture Theatre of the Victoria and Albert Museum, 1900) —although Speaight's account of the two productions indicates that Poel did not treat them primarily as religious plays. He hoped to present *Everyman* in the cloister of Westminster Abbey, but the Dean and the Chapter refused their permission. He did get an acceptance from Dean Farrar at Canterbury, but the chapter there overruled the Dean. Poel ended by producing it in the Master's Court of the Charterhouse, under the auspices of the Elizabethan Stage Society, for whom he had done much of his work. *The Sacrifice of Isaac* made up the bill. *The Times* greeted the production respectfully,[7] but with no sense of occasion, no indication that

[6] Quoted, Robert Speaight, *William Poel and the Elizabethan Revival*, Cambridge, Mass., Harvard University Press, 1954, pp. 174-175.

[7] *The Times* (London), July 15, 1901, p. 8.

there was anything out of the ordinary in a production of *Every-man* in London. The revival of religious drama had begun quietly enough.

Poel dipped again into the medieval repertory when he produced *Jacob and Esau* at the Little Theatre in London in 1911, and he restaged *Everyman* (on a program with his own *The First Franciscans*) in 1926; but by that time the 1901 production had done its seminal work. The immediate popularity of *Everyman* allowed Ben Greet to put it on at the Imperial Theatre for a month and, in association with Charles Frohman, to take it on tour in the United States. The most important successor to Poel, however, was Nugent Monck, who had acted in the 1901 *Everyman*. In 1905, he founded the English Drama Society, which performed *The Interlude of Youth* that year, and in 1906 he put on the Nativity group from the Chester cycle in Chelsea and later at the Old Music Hall in Chester. The police intervened when he attempted to revive the *Ludus Coventriae* in 1909, charging violation of the Blasphemy Law, and the English Drama Society came to an end. Monck went to Norwich in 1910 to stage one production and stayed to become director of the Norwich Players and finally of the Maddermarket Theatre, a post which he held until 1953. Over the years the Norwich Players branched out into all kinds of drama, but they returned frequently to the medieval plays. George Bell, then Dean of Canterbury, invited Monck to stage *Everyman* at the first Canterbury Festival of Music and Drama in 1929. In 1938, Monck finally produced the Passion cycle of the *Ludus Coventriae* that had caused such a furore in 1909, but even then he did it before an invited audience at the Maddermarket; it was not until 1952 that he received the Lord Chamberlain's permission for a public performance, which the Bishop of Norwich called "one of the most moving experiences of my life."[8] If Poel was, in a

[8] Quoted, June Ottaway, "Nugent Monck of Norwich," *Christian Drama*, II, 22 (Spring, 1953).

sense, the originator of the religious drama revival, Monck was one of the most important influences that pervaded the movement.

Monck and Greet were not the only producers to follow in the wake of Poel's *Everyman*. Although the Pilgrim Players in Birmingham, formed in 1907, were not primarily a religious group, they performed *The Interlude of Youth*, *Everyman*, and *Eager Heart*. F. R. Benson's Shakespeare company did four of the Chester miracle plays at Stratford-on-Avon in 1909. As Monck's career testifies, the production of the medieval plays has been continuous since the beginning in 1901. Rutland Boughton's choral drama *Bethlehem*, first performed at the Glastonbury Festival School on December 28, 1915, introduced a variation on the usual medieval revival by using an adapted version of the Coventry Nativity Play as libretto for Boughton's music. Around 1930, E. Martin Browne adapted a number of medieval plays—*The York Nativity Play*, *The Sacrifice of Isaac* from the Brome MS, and *The Play of the Maid Mary* and *The Play of Mary the Mother* from the *Ludus Coventriae*—by rearranging them into scenes and modernizing the verse. The thirties were particularly busy years for medieval productions among church groups, in universities and schools, and at festivals. Browne's Chichester Diocesan Players contributed many performances of his adaptations. The movement which began with Poel culminated a half-century later in the York Festival, instituted in 1951, at which Browne directed a shortened version of *The York Cycle of Mystery Plays*, twenty-nine of the original forty-eight plays, in a slightly modernized version prepared by J. S. Purvis.

Eager Heart. The purpose of this study is not to examine the staging of the ancient mysteries in modern times. The work of Poel and Monck and their successors is important here only in that it helped create an atmosphere in which modern religious drama could develop. Laurence Housman's Nativity *Bethlehem* is the first important landmark on the path of that development. He wrote it, he says, "solely for my own satisfaction," but having made an unexpected financial success of *An Englishwoman's Love-Letters,* decided to produce it because "I wish to show that it is possible for the drama to come near, without irreverence, to the central truths of Christianity. . . ."[9] He had been unable to obtain a license from G. A. Redford, the Censor, and so was forced to form the "Bethlehem Society" to give his production the appearance of private performance. The play was given in the Great Hall of the University of London in December, 1902, under the direction of Gordon Craig.

It was not the Housman play, however, but A. M. Buckton's *Eager Heart* that first attracted wide audiences. This play, which was first performed in 1904, was given a license because, according to Housman, the Censor never noticed that the Holy Family was in the cast.[10] It is the story of the maiden Eager Heart who waits on Christmas Eve to see the King, who traditionally is supposed to put in an appearance on earth on the night of His birth. Her sisters Eager Fame and Eager Sense try to lure her to the palaces of power and luxury to find the King, but she stays at home, guarding the meager fare that she has to offer Him when He arrives. A poor family—a man, his wife, and a child—present themselves at her door, and she is unable to resist the impulse to give them the food and shelter that she has prepared for the King. She then runs out and meets the shepherds—all but one of whom are grousing and unbelieving—and the wise men—only one of whom, the one wearing "the spiked circlet of Inspiration"— understands the nature of the King they seek. The shepherds and the wise men return to Eager Heart's home, where the family to

[9] Laurence Housman, "In Spite of the Censor," *Critic,* XLII, 141 (February, 1903).

[10] Laurence Housman, *The Unexpected Years,* Indianapolis, Bobbs-Merrill, [1936], p. 212.

whom she has given shelter are revealed, dressed in white and bathed in light, in the traditional grouping of the adoration. Eager Sense and Eager Fame return too late for the vision and are cautioned, by a wise man and a shepherd to prepare themselves for the reception of the King. To hammer home the point, the old man who has spoken the Prologue returns and speaks directly to the audience: "Is *your* hearth ready?"

The play is written in blank verse and the speeches are interspersed with the singing of traditional Christmas hymns. The mixture of speech and song became standard for the Nativities that were to come later, whether they were straight biblical narratives or attempts, like *Eager Heart* to use the Nativity material imaginatively. Miss Buckton's verse contains a plethora of *thou's* and *wilt's* and other archaisms, but that kind of vocabulary could be expected of most stage verse at the turn of the century. Despite the verse, the play retains an appealing simplicity, probably because of the schoolgirl enthusiasm of the heroine. *Eager Heart* was greated warmly. *The Times* found it "an artistic pleasure, and a tender and reverent appeal to associations of which few are destitute."[11] Max Beerbohm wrote that "Such plays as 'Eager Heart' are written, necessarily, with an archaistic impulse. They are attempts to revive a form that is past,"[12] but, for all his reservations, his review was very favorable.

Eager Heart became "almost an institution,"[13] as Percy Dearmer called it in 1922. An Incorporated Company of Eager Heart was formed shortly after the play was introduced, and the play was revived year after year. By 1925, *The Times* reported that 119 performances had been given,[14] which, considering that it was only performed around Christmas, is a respectable, if not consecutive,

[11] *The Times* (London), December 8, 1904, p. 7.
[12] Max Beerbohm, "Eager Heart," *Saturday Review*, XCVIII, 729 (December 10, 1904).
[13] Percy Dearmer, "Religion and Drama," *The Times* (London), May 23, 1922, p. 16.
[14] *The Times* (London), December 18, 1925, p. 12.

run. In time, *Eager Heart* came to be accepted as inevitable and
was greeted less cheerfully on its annual appearances. *The Times*, in
1922, found it "burdened with rhetoric and too vague in its
thought,"[15] an opinion that mirrors the change in taste between
1904 and 1922 as much as it presents an objective view of *Eager
Heart*. Miss Buckton's play was performed into the thirties. Ben
Greet gave a benefit production of it at Sadler's Wells in 1933,
and as late as 1938 it was presented in the Abbot's Hall at Westminster Abbey.

The Morality Play Society. Briefly, in the years immediately before
the first world war, the Morality Play Society presented religious
plays in London. Mabel Dearmer was the initiator and the chief
force of the Society, which was formed to produce her *The Soul of
the World* (1911). Mrs. Dearmer, wife of the Reverend Percy
Dearmer, had a slight reputation as a novelist (*The Difficult Way*),
a contributor to *The Yellow Book*, and an artist and a writer of
verse about children. She was also the author of a play, *Nan
Pilgrim*, about the marital problems of a minister and his artist's-
model wife, which was performed at the Royal Court in 1909, and
of a dramatized version of *Don Quixote*. As Stephen Gwynn described her in his Introduction to her *Three Plays* and his "Memoir"
in her *Letters from a Field Hospital*, she sounds like a gifted amateur,
the kind of nonprofessional literary figure who has always
flourished in England. Writing of the potential public for her
work, Gwynn said, "That public will be found, perhaps among
the simpler lovers of literature, who concern themselves more
with the thing said than with the manner of saying it: who value
poetry for other qualities than the technical quality of verse as
verse." He added, "No one understood better than she the value
of craftsmanship; but it was not there that her gift lay."[16]

---

[15] *The Times* (London), December 21, 1922, p. 8.
[16] Stephen Gwynn, "Preface," Mabel Dearmer, *Three Plays*, London, Erskine
Macdonald, 1916, pp. 5, 6.

Her religious plays—*The Soul of the World* and *The Dreamer*
(1912)—apparently grew out of performances that she produced
(one of Housman's *Bethlehem*) for the St. Mary's Choir Fund at
Primrose Hill, where her husband had the living. *The Soul of the
World* (for which Martin Shaw did the music) is the story of the
coming of Christ told in the framework of a discussion between
Time and Eternity over which really rules the world. Eternity
ends the Prologue with the news that an event is about to take
place that will be the end of Time and the beginning of Eternity
on earth—"For in a man, mankind has found his God." The play
is in three acts, in the first of which the coming of the Messiah is
predicted and Mary is introduced. In the second, the Nativity is
celebrated; and in the third, the events of Calvary are described.
The Epilogue finds Time giving way to Eternity, who directly
exhorts the audience: "Ah, ye, who here have watched us, hold
the light,/And in the dust and warfare of the world/ Follow the
Kings and Shepherds to the Cross." The wise men and the shepherds are indeed present at Miss Dearmer's Calvary, afraid that
the cross cancels out the birth, but Mary explains the significance
of what Christ has done. *The Dreamer* tells the story of Joseph,
altering the biblical narrative only to make comparisons between
Joseph and Christ. "In this play Joseph is represented throughout,
first historically, and then symbolically as a type of the Christ to
come," Mrs. Dearmer said in a prefatory note.

Although Mrs. Dearmer's verse, as Gwynn admitted, is fairly
commonplace, her manipulation of symbol can be dramatically
sound. In the first act of *The Soul of the World*, Mary meets Mary
Magdalene at the well in Nazareth. There is no attempt to explain
practically why the Magdalene is there; she is simply present to
point to Jesus's life to come. Also at the well is a child whom she
chases away and whom the Virgin calls back and sends again to
her. The little scene is apparently supposed to represent Mary
Magdalene's early rejection and later acceptance of Christ. This

kind of effect is overdone in *The Dreamer*, where Mrs. Dearmer
strains to equate Joseph with Christ. When his family turns him
out of the feast in the first act, Joseph says, "If it be Thy will/Let
these ills pass from me—and yet, and yet,/Not my will, Lord, but
Thine." The second scene of Act One, the selling of Joseph to
the Midianite trader, is flooded with New Testament analogues.
Joseph is bound to two pieces of wood in the shape of a cross.
Zebulon suggests that the brothers cast lots for his cloak of many
colors. The price that they get for him is thirty pieces of silver.
These Gospel echoes, plus lines like Joseph's "They know not
what they do," and Simeon's "Ah, thou who dreamest, save thy-
self, come down!" more than make the point about the crucifixion. The heavy weight of references in Act One is particularly
noticeable because the analogy to Christ is lost later in the play.
Joseph's problem with Potiphar's wife, his reading of the dreams
in prison, his assumption of political power and his reconciliation
with his family do not fit so easily into an imitation of Christ. At
the end, Mrs. Dearmer is forced to let Joseph directly prophesy
the coming of Christ while the shadow of a cross appears behind
him.

The quality that is most interesting about Mrs. Dearmer's work
is probably what Stephen Gwynn calls "the radiant optimism of
her cult of sorrows."[17] In both plays, there is a heavy emphasis on
the pain of Calvary, which for Mrs. Dearmer informs not only the
life of Christ, but all of life. It is, however, a sorrow that can be
seen as a joy. When Mary first enters in *The Soul of the World*, Mary
Magdalene cries out, "What sorrow has come near us?" but
Elizabeth says, "Nay, 'tis joy." When the three wise men come to
worship the infant, having forsaken worldly wisdom, worldly
power and wordly love to make the journey, Balthazar presents
his gift: "I bring Thee tears, O Child; here is Thy myrrh,/The

[17] Stephen Gwynn, "Preface," Mabel Dearmer, *Three Plays*, London, Erskine
Macdonald, 1916, p. 8.

gift of sorrow; for God loving Thee/Will not withhold earth's anguish from His Son." The idea of myrrh as sorrow, and the sorrow of man, is not a new one, of course, but it is not always customary to invoke Calvary at the Nativity. Calvary is implicit in the Nativity, but simpler plays, such as *Eager Heart,* prefer to focus only on the joy of Christmas. Later religious playwrights, such as Charles Williams, are more likely to see the Nativity whole, to accept the crucifixion that stands beside the incarnation and to celebrate the mingling of sorrow and joy. Although earlier playwrights, like Housman in *Bethlehem* and Robert Hugh Benson in *A Mystery Play in Honour of the Nativity of Our Lord* (1907), did suggest the relationship between the stable and the cross, Mrs. Dearmer was one of the first of the modern religious playwrights to invoke fully the duality of sorrow and joy that is represented by the life and death of Christ and, by implication, of all men.

The Morality Play Society was not simply the Dearmer Play Society and no more. Since there were as yet few plays of this kind, of any quality, in England, William Butler Yeats's *The Hour Glass* and Lady Gregory's *The Travelling Man* were imported from Ireland for the second program. Other English playwrights —Clifford Bax and Edith Lyttleton—were performed. When Percy Dearmer went to Serbia and Greece as an army chaplain, Mrs. Dearmer followed as a hospital orderly. She died of a fever on July 11, 1915, and any possibility that the Morality Play Society might be revived after the war died with her.

St. Silas and St. Martin. The years immediately before and during the war saw the formation of two groups whose activities extended beyond the decade. The St. Silas Players, as they came to be called, were amateurs who began to perform at St. Silas-the-Martyr, Kentish-town, in 1913, with a production of B.C. Boulter's *The Mystery of the Epiphany.* The group, which was apparently devoted to the works of Boulter, is more interesting as

a reflection of changing attitudes toward church drama than it is
for any widespread influence that it had; the Bishop of London, in
whose jurisdiction St. Silas lay, refused permission for its initial
production to be given in the church proper,[18] but a decade later,
The Mystery of the Passion (1923) was presented in the church. The
only unusual thing about Boulter as a playwright—his plays are
conventionally mock-biblical—is that Christ appears and speaks
in his Nativity, and, as E. Martin Browne said as late as 1932, "it
is at present axiomatic in England that the person of Christ shall
not be shown in the church."[19]

The dramatic activity of St. Martin-in-the-Fields lasted longer
and tended to be more professional than that at St. Silas. The
Reverend H. R. L. Sheppard, who is best known for his pacifist
activity in the thirties, was the instigator of drama at St. Martin's.
In a news story about the formation of the British Drama League
in 1919, *The Times* reported: "The Rev. H. R. L. Sheppard urged
that religion and the drama must go hand in hand. It was a mons-
trous thing that the Christian Church did not possess its own
theatre in London, where it could amplify the message that it
gave from the pulpit."[20] Sheppard was already working toward
such a theater at St. Martin's. His first dramatic venture was a series
of missionary and historical tableaux in the churchyard in the
summer of 1916. In 1917, he initiated the annual Christmas mystery play in the church, a presentation that extended beyond
World War II. The St. Martin's Players, which in the early
twenties included professional actors, gave plays in the crypt of
the church and generally made itself available "anywhere that it
was wanted, to give pleasure or earn money for a good cause."[21]
In 1921, Sheppard not only convinced a reluctant Laurence Hous-

[18] *The Times* (London), January 30, 1913, p. 13.
[19] E. Martin Browne, *The Production of Religious Plays*, London, Philip Allan, [1932],
p. 25.
[20] *The Times* (London), June 4, 1919, p. 9.
[21] R. Ellis Roberts, *H. R. L. Sheppard*, London, John Murray, [1942], p. 102.

man to write the *St. Martin's Pageant*, but he also acted the Beggar in it. The pageant, given to raise money for alterations and improvements in the church, was so well received that it was revived in 1922 at the Lyceum Theatre and again at the Strand in 1923. When Sheppard left St. Martin's in 1926, the Reverend Pat McCormick, who followed him as vicar, continued his dramatic work.

The Twenties. The twenties provided an increasing amount of religious drama activity. Laurence Housman's first series of St. Francis plays was produced at the Glastonbury Festival in 1922, and then after they became an annual event of the Dramatic Society at University College, University of London, he added extra plays. John Masefield was experimenting with religious themes—for instance, in his *The Trial of Jesus* (1925)—in private productions at his home, Boar's Hill. Masefield and Housman were exceptions; the bulk of the writing, like most of the production, was amateur. Elsie Fogerty, who was later to coach the Chorus for the Canterbury debut of *Murder in the Cathedral*, did extensive work in choral speaking and wrote a few plays, of which *The Harrying of the Dove* (1920), a well-intentioned peace play in verse, is an example. The work of Margaret Cropper, a staple of amateur groups, began to appear. Charles A. Claye's *The Joyous Pageant of the Holy Nativity* which began in 1922, became a tradition, one which by 1948 had begun to make nervous the more sophisticated adherents of religious drama; Terence Vale, writing in *Christian Drama*, wondered, "Is it not time for the Joyous Pageant to retire to the pages of history . . . ?"[22]

Miss M. Creagh-Henry may be taken as representative of the religious drama movement of the twenties, even though the group that she operated with Miss D. Marten—the Mystical

[22] Terence Vale, "Lest One Good Custom," *Christian Drama*, I, 12 (February 1948).

Players—did not begin to present plays until the summer of 1929. Her plays, for the most part sentimental and undemanding, began to appear before the advent of the Mystical Players. *The Outcasts*, published in 1924, a Christmas play in which three unhappy people learn that "The Christ Child came to the poor and the outcast, poor and outcast too," may be taken as typical. It was groups like the Mystical Players that helped bridge the distance from the amateurism of the twenties to the professionalism of the thirties. Fred Eastman, in an article in *The Christian Century* in 1929, was primarily concerned with the new Canterbury Festival and the formation of the Religious Drama Council (later Society), but he took time to cite the work of Miss Creagh-Henry as typical of the "Mystical plays dealing with spiritual truth in symbolic fashion."[23] that were popular in England at the time. George Seaver, the biographer of Sir Francis Younghusband, one of the founders of the Religious Drama Society, mentions that in the early days of the Society the Mystical Players gave many performances either under the Society's auspices or with its encouragement.[24] Plays like those of Miss Creagh-Henry, of which the intention is more evangelical than aesthetic, continued and will continue to appear of course, because the religious drama movement is necessarily primarily an amateur one, for all that more and more professionals have been drawn to it.

As the amateurs of the twenties went about their work, three important events—the initiation of the Canterbury Festival, the formation of the Religious Drama Society, and the appointment of the first diocesan director of Drama—waited in the wings. These events, in all of which George Bell had a hand, were to attract more men of literary stature to the writing of religious dramas.

[23] Fred Eastman, "Religious Drama in England," *Christian Century*, XLVI, 1213 (October 2, 1929).
[24] George Seaver, *Francis Younghusband*, London, John Murray, [1952], p. 352.

VI

Canterbury, Chichester, and the Religious Drama Society

"The man who has, quietly, taken all the crucial steps toward making a worthy Christian Drama is the present Bishop of Chichester,"[1] wrote E. Martin Browne in his post-World War II pamphlet *Religious Drama*. As Bishop of Chichester, George K. A. Bell appointed the first diocesan drama director of the English religious drama revival, just as, earlier, as Dean of Canterbury, he initiated the movement's most important symbol, the Canterbury Festival. He also gave his name, as President, to the Religious Drama Society from its inception. Dr. Bell's ecclesiastical duties, particularly as Bishop of Chichester, made extensive practical activity in the drama impossible; for instance, although President of the Religious Drama Society from 1929, he first attended one of the Society's annual general meetings in 1954. Nor did he formulate any important statements on religious drama. He wrote occasional letters to *The Times* and made infrequent speeches on particular needs of the church drama movement, but his importance to the religious drama revival in England lay not in the formulating of principles or the presenting of productions, but in the providing of occasions.

As Dean of Canterbury, George Bell invited John Masefield to write a play to be given at the Cathedral. The poet's *The Coming of Christ*, with music by Gustav Holst, was acted on the nave steps

[1] E. Martin Browne, *Religious Drama*, [Glasgow, Iona Youth Trust], n.d., p. 6.

at Whitsuntide, May 28, 1928. The formation of the Canterbury
Festival of Music and Drama followed on the success of the Masefield play. The Friends of Canterbury Cathedral, under the impetus of the Dean, began to organize the first festival for the
summer of 1929. The work that began under Dr. Bell ("I remember in 1929, just before I became Bishop, going to Nugent
Monck and asking him whether he would be willing to come and
present *Everyman* outside Canterbury Cathedral . . .")[2]) was
finished in other hands because he was made Bishop of Chichester
before the Festival was given. Nugent Monck did bring his
Norwich Players to Canterbury, where they gave *Everyman* at the
west door of the Cathedral and *Dr. Faustus* in the Chapter House.
With these productions, the Canterbury Festival was formally
inaugurated.

With the presentation of Tennyson's *Becket* in 1932, the Canterbury Festival began the practice of presenting plays that in some
way dealt with the history of the Cathedral. The version of
Tennyson's play was that prepared by Eileen Thorndike, who also
directed. Her adaptation, largely an extensive abridgement, was
repeated in 1933 with her brother Russell in the title role. The
Canterbury play for 1934 was Laurence Binyon's *The Young King*,
which he had written originally in 1924 and had seen acted in its
earlier form in John Masefield's private theater at Boar's Hill;
once again Eileen Thorndike was the adapter, i.e., abridger. The
play, which has no particular religious significance, deals with the
relationship between Henry II and his rebellious son; its connection with Canterbury is the bare suggestion that the defection of
the son is God's punishment on Henry for having had Becket
killed. T. S. Eliot's *Murder in the Cathedral*, the 1935 festival play,
continued the historical allegiance to the festival city, but the
invitation to Eliot—harking back to Bell's original request to

---

[2] Bishop of Chichester, speech at the annual general meeting of the Religious
Drama Society, November, 1954, *Christian Drama*, II, 15 (Spring, 1955).

Masefield—initiated the practice of asking poets to provide new plays for the Canterbury Festivals.

Eliot was probably the most likely person to begin the new series of Canterbury plays. His international reputation as a poet and his national reputation as an articulate Anglican layman would have been reason enough to call on him, but his newly active interest in the theater, of which his pageant play *The Rock* was evidence, probably made Canterbury as attractive to him as he must have been to it. *The Rock* had been commissioned for presentation as part of the Forty-five Churches Fund drive of the Diocese of London; it was given at Sadler's Wells Theatre from May 28 to June 9, 1934. His *Murder in the Cathedral* opened at Canterbury a year later, on June 15, 1935, with E. Martin Browne directing and Robert Speaight as Becket. In 1936, Charles Williams provided the Canterbury play—*Thomas Cranmer of Canterbury*. In 1937, Dorothy L. Sayers's *The Zeal of Thy House*, the story of William of Sens, the architect of the twelfth-century rebuilding of the cathedral, was the festival production. With Christopher Hassall's *Christ's Comet*, the story of the fourth wise man, in 1938, the Canterbury plays ceased to use a local subject; the history of Canterbury was apparently not that full of dramatic possibilities. When Dorothy L. Sayers returned as the festival playwright in 1939, she presented *The Devil to Pay*, a retelling of the Faust legend. The Canterbury Festival was discontinued during World War II; it was revived in 1947 with the presentation of Laurie Lee's *Peasant's Priest*.[3]

In its first ten years, the Canterbury Festival managed to put a kind of official seal on the religious drama revival. It not only made use of figures already familiar in the religious drama movement—John Masefield and Nugent Monck—it focused attention on T. S. Eliot, Charles Williams, and Dorothy L. Sayers, all of whom were to make sizable contributions to the body of English

[3] Reviewed, *The Times* (London), June 23, 1947, p. 6.

religious plays, contributions which, at least in the cases of Eliot
and Williams, are of literary merit. The festival also attracted professional theater men, actors and directors like E. Martin Browne,
Robert Speaight (who was Cranmer in *Thomas Cranmer of Canterbury* and Artaban in *Christ's Comet*, as well as Becket in *Murder in
the Cathedral*), Harcourt Williams (who directed, and acted in, the
two Sayers plays), and Frank Napier (also in the Sayers plays). It
was the professionalism of men like these, as well as the quality
of the plays, that made it possible for several of the Canterbury
plays—*Murder in the Cathedral*, *The Zeal of Thy House*, *The Devil to
Pay*—to move on to London theaters, transfers that were har-
bingers of the commercial interest in serious religious drama
that was to come after World War II.

Religious Drama Society. In the year in which the Canterbury
Festival of Music and Drama began, the Religious Drama Society
also came into existence. It was functioning as the Religious
Drama Council when on September 1, 1929, it called a meeting on
"Religion and Drama." The "moving spirit"[4] in the formation
of the Society was Mrs. Olive Stevenson, secretary of the Congregational Women's Guild, who obtained the support of Sir
Francis Younghusband, well-known both as an explorer and as a
student of comparative religion, who became cofounder with her.
He served as Chairman of the Council of the Society until his
death in 1942. The Society received its support from a mixed
group of churchmen, professional theater people and practitioners
of church drama. The Bishop of Chichester was made president;
the first group of vice-presidents included Dr. S. M. Berry,
Moderator of the Federal Council of Free Churches, Dr. F. W.
Dwelly, Dean of Liverpool, Laurence Housman, Sir Barry Jackson, and Sybil Thorndike. Other early supporters were Sir Frank

[4] Fred Eastman, "Religious Drama in England," *Christian Century*, XLVI, 1212
(October 2, 1929).

Benson, Charles Williams, Percy Dearmer, and Martin Shaw. As the names—Housman, Dearmer, Shaw—indicate, the lines leading to the Religious Drama Society run back to the early experiments, like the Morality Play Society and the Glastonbury Festival. The Religious Drama Society became, as it hoped to, a focal point for the scattered activity in church drama.

The object of the Religious Drama Society, according to a statement that appears on the title page of each issue of *Christian Drama* the Society's journal, is "To foster the art of drama as a means of religious expression and to assist the production of plays which explore and interpret the Christian view of life." A statement made by Sir Francis Younghusband in 1929 expressed much the same general attitude, but it also indicated some of the practical ways in which the object of the Society could be realized:[5]

Our aim is to encourage the production of plays with a definitely religious motive, which embody religious truth and stimulate religious sentiments. Some will be produced in parish halls, others in school houses, and still others in churches. The council will not produce plays itself but will act as a center of reference for the different church bodies and will assist in suggesting suitable plays and the best methods of producing them.

In time, of course, the Society came to be a producer of plays. It sponsored, for instance, Eileen Thorndike's production of Margaret Cropper's *Christ Crucified* at Southwark Cathedral in 1933 and E. Martin Browne's presentation of Gordon Bottomley's *The Acts of Saint Peter* at St. Margaret's, Westminster, in 1934.

Most of the work of the Religious Drama Society was to be advisory and educational. In 1930, for instance, the British Drama League helped the infant Religious Drama Society sponsor its

[5] Quoted, Eastman, *op. cit.*, p. 1212.

first School of Religious Drama, a week of lectures, performances, and conferences at Bournemouth, under the patronage of
the Bishop of Winchester. Laurence Housman, E. Martin Browne,
and Nugent Monck were among the participants. Following
Bournemouth, the Religious Drama Society continued to sponsor
occasional schools and conferences on religious drama; after
World War II a summer school became an annual event.

In 1938, the Society was reorganized, and E. Martin Browne
became honorary director. The Society offers membership to
individuals and to groups, most of the latter being religious drama
organizations attached to particular churches. The central
organization provides facilities for the improvement of religious
drama at the parish level through its traveling advisor, its library
which acts as a lending library to member groups, and its
selected lists of recommended plays. Under these circumstances,
of course, the emphasis within the Religious Drama Society is on
amateur theatrical work. The aim has been to draw amateur
groups to more difficult and better plays. Even so, *A Catalogue of
Selected Plays*, which Jessie Powell and Kathleen Bainbridge-Bell
prepared for the Society in 1951, contains a large proportion of
plays of no literary interest. Even though its primary concern is
amateur, the Society since World War II has shown a lively
interest in the professional theater's concern with religion, both
through its journal, *Christian Drama*, founded in 1946, and through
its attempts to keep a professional group of its own—the New
Pilgrim Players—alive and operating despite financial difficulties.

Chichester. In 1930, the Bishop of Chichester appointed E.
Martin Brown as Director of Religious Drama in his diocese, the
first such appointment in modern times. Browne is a professional
theatre man who made his acting debut at the Regent Theatre in
1927. His career, more than that of any other person connected
with English religious drama, is a mirror of the history of the

movement since 1930. He has managed to have a hand in most of the important events since then and most of the religious play-wrights, from Eliot and Fry down, have thanked him in print for the help that he has given them. Browne has moved back and forth between the commercial theater, where he has always directed Eliot's plays, to the amateur theater, which he has served as a teacher, a director, and an officer of the Religious Drama Society. He has worked directly with church theater, as at the festivals of Canterbury and Tewkesbury, and has, by virtue of his own Christian allegiance, brought religion to theatrical ventures that need not have had that character at all—his wartime Pilgrim Players, for instance, and the seasons of poetic plays that he and Robert Speaight presented at the Mercury Theatre shortly after World War II.

Browne's work really began in Chichester. The duties of this first diocesan director of drama were twofold. He was expected to give advice and comfort to parishes throughout the diocese which hoped to put on plays of their own. Beyond that, and more important, he was director of a semiprofessional group, the Chichester Diocesan Players, which presented both within the diocese and outside it plays too difficult for ordinary amateur production. In the early days, Browne depended on translations from the French (Ghéon, Claudel) and on his own adaptations of the medieval mysteries for his repertory.

Other dioceses followed the example of Chichester. In 1933, the Bishop of Bristol set up a Diocesan Religious Drama Committee and appointed Mrs. Vera Peareth as Director of Religious Drama. Another diocese that showed an early official interest in religious drama was Chelmsford, where Phyllis M. Potter was Director. None of the dioceses, however, were quite as active or as pro-fessional as Chichester under the direction of E. Martin Browne. Still, the others were capable of unusual productions. If Miss Potter's *From the Nursery of Heaven*, the Chelmsford 1935 Nativity

Play, is typical of the ordinary work that she produced, she has also to her credit Charles Williams's *Seed of Adam*, which she requested and first presented. Her Nativity is a children's play, laboriously constructed of quotes from the Gospel of St. Luke, from some of the medieval Nativities, from Caxton's *The Golden Legend*, and even from Shakespeare, Crashaw, and Giles Fletcher. In it, the little angels carry the news of the birth of Christ to earth, and the children of the world join the wise men and the shepherds in the adoration. *Seed of Adam*, on the other hand, is one of the most subtle and difficult of the modern religious plays.

Exeter and Tewkesbury. The bulk of the religious plays of the thirties, as of the twenties, were amateurish. A few playwrights and a few events, however, stand—with the work at Canterbury —above the average. Gordon Bottomley's *The Acts of Saint Peter* which was written for the Octocentenary Celebrations of the Cathedral Church of St. Peter at Exeter, June 27, 1933, is an example of the kind of religious play that was to become increasingly popular after World War II. The idea of a church's requesting a play for an occasion was not a new one, of course; on such an invitation, Housman had written the *St. Martin's Pageant* more than ten years before. After Canterbury, however, a play or a pageant was a likely prospect for a special religious observance, and, if possible, a playwright with a reputation was given the commission. Not that Bottomley's play is very impressive. It tells the story of Peter from his answering the call of Jesus to his crucifixion in Rome, with the emphasis on his denial of Christ and his attempt to make up for it. The verse is no more than adequate. Although it is fortunately free of the kind of archaisms that one would have expected ten years earlier, it only occasionally takes on any character of its own.

The Tewkesbury Festival, which lasted for a few years before World War II, also grew out of a special occasion. In the summer of 1935, Nevill Coghill directed performances of *Samson Agonistes*, *Everyman*, and *Noah's Flood* at the Tewkesbury Abbey. The motive was to raise money for the restoration of the Norman tower. From this beginning, the Tewkesbury Festival came into being, depending for its plays, as Canterbury had in its early days, on the already existing repertory. In 1938, for instance, James Bridie's *Tobias and the Angel* was performed. In 1939, however, not only was an old play—J. M. Barrie's *The Boy David*—given, but also Christopher Fry's *The Tower*. Fry's play, which according to Derek Stanford[6] showed the influence of Eliot's *The Rock*, was never published. Although *The Tower* was the first of Fry's works to attract much attention, he had already written *The Boy with a Cart* (1937), which was to become his first published play, and *Open Door*,[7] a play celebrating the founder of Dr. Barnardo's homes. If Tewkesbury cannot claim to have initiated Fry into the drama, just as Canterbury cannot claim to have introduced Eliot, at least the cathedral town and the abbey town can be said to have had an important hand in the launching of the two playwrights.

Mostly Amateur. In reviewing a revival of Bottomley's *The Acts of Saint Peter*, *The Times* compared it favorably to the average religious drama performance which ran to "a timid and therefore undramatic pietism, or an embarrassed, defiant heartiness."[8] The characterization is an apt one. Most of the amateur work of the thirties was a predictable extension of the kind of thing that had been done in the twenties. Margaret Cropper continued to write plays for religious groups, but the folksy sentimentality of her plays of the twenties gave way to a more conscious artiness. Her Passion play, *Christ Crucified* (1932), is her best-known work of this period. The ordinary biblical narrative scenes—at Simon's house in Bethany, at the court of Caiaphas, in the lodging of Mary

[6] Derek Stanford, *Christopher Fry Album*, London, Peter Nevill, 1952, p. 15.
[7] Described, *ibid.*, pp. 14–15.
[8] *The Times* (London), March 21, 1934, p. 12.

the Mother—are in no way unusual. They follow the familiar pattern in which—since the protagonist cannot appear—a narrator tells what has happened off stage. Miss Cropper's addition to the story is an Angelic Sphere in which the agony at Gethsemane and the crucifixion are told through four angels, who are also visible in the rest of the scenes, miming horror at the behavior of the human figures. "The Three, who stand together on the one hand, speak in the words of the Old Testament Prophets as they reached forward to the Mystery hid in Christ," the author explains. "The Fourth Angel, who stands alone, speaks the Mind of Christ, as we dimly know it, through the words of the Gospel." Miss Cropper's angels were not always happy additions to her plays; in *The Nativity with Angels* (1934), for instance, they so obscure the event that they are supposedly celebrating that the result is not a play at all, but a series of speeches suggested by the Nativity. In still another Nativity, *A Great and Mighty Wonder* (1938), Miss Cropper has hit upon an interesting symbolic idea—the meeting of the Great Angel of Purpose and the Angel of the Need of Man at the crib of Christ.

The Gardener and *The Last Man In*, both of which appeared in *Poet Lore* in 1930, may stand as examples of the work of Vera I. Arlett. In the first, Phocas, a Christian (A.D. 303), welcomes and entertains the Roman soldiers who come to kill him; he even digs his own grave. His dignity in the face of death apparently converts one of the soldiers. The situation is basically fantastic, but since Miss Arlett's single intention is to convey the idea of Phocas's strength, the play is not ineffective. *The Last Man In* is simply a collection of clichés in which the hero allows assorted relatives to enter heaven before him and refuses to permit his sweetheart to come out and descend the steps with him, thus proving his heavenly eligibility; it is doubtful that it could be interesting even to amateurs. *This Is the Gate* (1939) does not differ greatly from the rest of Miss Arlett's plays in quality, but it is unusual in that it speaks out strongly on a moral question that is also political. In it, a group of Jewish refugees are huddled for shelter on the steps of a church in a totalitarian country, obviously but not specifically Germany; inside, the priest's voice is heard reading a directive: "All persons not of pure Aryan birth shall withdraw themselves from the congregation of this Church. . . ." The statues of St. Anne, the Virgin, St. John, St. Paul, and the crucified Christ come down and depart. Miss Arlett's sermon on a guilt that is in part a Christian guilt is made ineffective by the fact that the parade of rejected statues is described, not seen.

Freda Collins and Lesbia Scott are among the amateur religious playwrights of the thirties whose work continued into the post-war years. Miss Collins's plays include *The Fortieth Man* (1937), "*The Foolishness of God . . .*" (1939), and *The Centurion* (1940). *The Fortieth Man* tells the story of forty Christian martyrs, members of the Roman Legion, who have been deposited on a frozen river where they must freeze to death or deny the Christian God. When one of the sufferers weakens, lured from the ice by the girl who loves him, Lucius, secretly a Christian, runs out to join the dead and dying, taking up the cry that echoes through the play, "Here die forty men for Christ!" In "*The Foolishness of God . . .*" an unlikely group of women at a Church of England mission in China —a believing mission leader, an atheist doctor, a new missionary, a Roman Catholic nun, a Noncomformist missionary—refuse to leave in the face of an impending bandit attack. When a young man protests—"It's crass, bloody foolishness. It's the foolishness of . . . of . . . "—Mrs. Reynolds, remembering I Corinthians 1.25 and recognizing a straight line when she hears one, finishes, "It's the foolishness of God." *The Centurion* is about the centurion of Matthew 27.54, where Miss Collins found the original of her key line, "Truly this man was the Son of God." Lesbia Scott's *That Fell Arrest*, which won a prize as the best unpublished play by a new author in the British Drama League Community Theatre

Festival, 1937, tells of the death of a sophisticated young thing who finds that the life she chose on earth predetermines her life after death; she is condemned—after a glimpse of God—to an eternity of fashionable pleasures. Miss Scott makes her point, but that is about the only positive thing that can safely be said of *That Fell Arrest.*

The War Years. World War II interrupted the steady growth of religious drama activity that had marked the twenties and the thirties. Whether at an amateur, parish level or a professional, festival level, the production of religious plays—particularly new ones—almost ceased during the war years. In two ways, however —through the presentation of religious radio plays and through the operation of The Pilgrim Players—the religious revival kept alive. Since this is primarily a study of the drama of the theater (even if that theater be a church), little attention has been or can be give to radio. It is enough, perhaps, to mention that Dorothy L. Sayers, who had made her radio debut before the war with *He That Should Come* (1938), produced her play-cycle on the life of Christ, *The Man Born to Be King*, beginning in 1942.

The Pilgrim Players were a group (really two groups) of professional actors who gave performances of plays—usually religious—all around England during the war years. E. Martin Browne was the organizing spirit behind the group that worked out of Canterbury; Ruth Spalding was the director of the Oxford Pilgrims. In an article in *School Drama*,[9] Browne announced the formation of the Pilgrim Players and gave the reason for their existence—his feeling that there was a wartime need for good plays (and religious ones) as well as for recreation. The headquarters of the Canterbury group was Kent College, where their first performance, Bridie's *Tobias and the Angel*, was given on November 13, 1939. In the beginning, they played around Kent, but after

[9] E. Martin Browne, "Religious Drama in Wartime," *School Drama*, II, 17 (December, 1939–January, 1940).

1940, when they began to receive financial and other (increased petrol rations, for instance) aid from the Council for the Encouragement of Music and the Arts, they managed to make longer tours. In 1942, they toured Scotland.[10]

Artistic control of the group was completely in the hands of the director (Browne), but all the members had a voice in the financial and labor arrangements. Each of them received a salary that was the equivalent of an army private's pay, and each was entitled to draw on the central fund, never very large, for clothes, holidays, or medicine when they were needed. The work, which involved problems of transportation and administration, was shared by all the members, each one assigned to a particular task. They played anywhere—in schools, in churches, in village halls, in prisons, in air raid shelters during the blitz (the Oxford group played more often in London), even in theaters. A turnover within the group was to be expected. Some of the men played with the Pilgrims until they were called for military service; some of the players went on to other theatrical activity. Pamela Keily, for instance, left the group in 1942 to become Religious Drama Advisor to the Council of Christian Communities in Sheffield; earlier visits from the Pilgrim Players had excited interest in the project, and a grant from the Religious Drama Society made the experiment possible. The peak of activity for the Pilgrim Players was passed by 1943. By that time, the CEMA had been active, encouraging theater work across England, and the need for an itinerant company was lessened. The Oxford group reformed itself as the Rock Theatre Company in 1943 and severed its connection with the Pilgrim Players. The Canterbury group dissolved itself in the summer of 1943, and when it reformed in the fall, it was organized differently—with closer CEMA connections.

Besides *Tobias*, the Pilgrim Players of Canterbury used, among

[10] Much of the factual information in this and the two following paragraphs may be found in Henzie Browne, *Pilgrim Story*, London, Muller, [1945].

other plays, Lawrence's *David* and Eliot's *Murder in the Cathedral.* For the most part, they avoided simple, pietistic plays on the assumption that their audiences, being mixed ones, had to be reached on dramatic rather than on religious grounds. The group concocted some potpourri shows—sketches, poems, songs—for special occasions—*Pilgrim Pie* (1940) for children and *Christmas Pie* (1941) to be played in shelters. They did introduce new works. A Nativity by Henzie Raeburn (Mrs. E. Martin Browne), *The Beginning of the Way,* was introduced for Christmas, 1940. It shows its wartime origins only in the scene in which a Roman officer tries to lure the hostess of the inn to Caesarea for a week end. The coming of Christ, among other things, saves the inn keeper from cuckoldry. The theme of the play is the contrasting of Jesus's way, the way of peace, with that of Jonathan, the young Zealot of Act I, whose way is that of the sword, by which he dies. Such an emphasis is not surprising for a Nativity play, but its vague pacifism seems a little unusual for 1940. In James Bridie, who contributed *The Dragon and the Dove* and *A Change for the Worse* to their Scottish tour, the Pilgrim Players had the services of a playwright much more professional than Mrs. Browne. Gordon Bottomley's *Kate Kennedy,* a verse comedy about the willful niece of a stern Scottish bishop, was introduced by the reorganized Pilgrim Players on their CEMA tour in 1944. The leading playwright of the Oxford group was Charles Williams, who wrote *The Death of Good Fortune, The House by the Stable,* and *Grab and Grace* for them, the first two in 1939, the last for a 1941 tour that never materialized. E. Martin Browne took *The House by the Stable* (on a bill that included Shaw's *Village Wooing*) to Belgium and Holland in 1945, in a tour of military camps that he organized for the YMCA.

Much of this chapter and the one that preceded it has been concerned with the workings of amateur and semiprofessional church-theater groups and with the writers who cater to such groups. The plays and the productions have only the most tenuous connection with the theater as an art form and the play as literature. Yet, an examination of the state of religious drama in modern England would be incomplete without some consideration of such activity. The mingling of the professional and the amateur in the lists and in the minds of the Religious Drama Society is a kind of accidental symbol of the crossing and recrossing of lines which has found the amateurs and professionals mixing in religious drama since Poel's *Everyman*. The result is an atmosphere in which both the adept and the initiate are at home. *The Cocktail Party* on the commercial stage is just one step beyond *Murder in the Cathedral* at Canterbury, and to know how either play found its footing is necessarily to know that there were once (and still are) busy, dedicated, and awkward religious drama enthusiasts, like B. C. Boulter and M. Creagh-Henry.

VII

Laurence Housman and John Masefield

Among the playwrights of the first period of the religious drama revival—that before 1929—only two—Laurence Housman and John Masefield—have an extensive body of work that demands more than a glance. Both men had acquired literary prominence before they turned to the theater. The reputations of both have suffered within the last few decades, and their limitations are as apparent in their religious plays as in the rest of their work. Still, their plays are more interesting and more attractive than most of those that were produced in the early days of the religious drama movement.

Laurence Housman's work reaches across the history of that movement from his initiatory *Bethlehem* (1902) to his collection *Old Testament Plays* (1950). For a man so involved with the growth of religious drama in England, Housman's relationship to Christianity has been a markedly ambivalent one. In *Nunc Dimittis*, the epilogue to the *Little Plays of St. Francis*, which Housman wrote and acted in at London University in 1933, Brother Juniper describes the dying Author, "he says he isn't a Christian. . . ." By putting the line into Juniper's mouth and by hedging it with Juniper's doubts about its accuracy, Housman manages both to deny his Christianity and to imply that the denial is false. His plays and his other religious writings suggest that the author considers himself a Christian, providing that he may define Christianity solely in terms of the life of Christ and providing also that he may choose the angle from which to view that life.

In *The Religious Advance Toward Rationalism*, a lecture delivered in 1929, Housman suggested that the existence of God, the possibility of immortality, the historicity of Jesus, and the resurrection might all be disproved, but that man would continue to believe in the message of Christ (love) and would go on resurrecting Christ within himself. Since Housman's faith, which is essentially a faith in man and his perfectability, depends so little on the supernatural concepts which are at the heart of Christianity, it is not surprising that he drifted away from the established church. Housman's attitude toward institutional religion can be seen in the essay "A Winking Providence": "I do believe that Christ is the best teacher the world has ever had; but I do not find that institutional Christianity makes His teaching either safe or plain."[1] For Housman, as the plays so often give evidence, the church not only fails to stimulate, it actively hampers faith, and yet, for all his distrust of and distaste for the church, he was attracted to it all his life. ". . . Religion is a real need of human nature," he once wrote, "and requires a corporate expression, if not institutionally, at all events communally."[2] Perhaps his willingness to work with groups such as the Religious Drama Society is an expression of the need for community that he is unable to find in the church itself. Certainly, at least half of his work as a religious propagandist—which he is in and out of his plays—is aimed at the reform of the institution; the other half argues for faith in man and the doctrine of love and warns the believer to beware of organization.

Some of the attitudes that were to mark Housman's later work are already apparent in *Bethlehem*. In his Nativity, which describes, in verse and song, the angels bringing the news to the shepherds, the wise men following the star and the adoration, the emphasis

[1] Laurence Housman, *The Preparation of Peace*, London, Jonathan Cape, [1941], p. 118.
[2] Laurence Housman, *The Religious Advance Toward Rationalism*, London, Watts, [1929], p. 23.

throughout is on love. In many ways—the foreshadowing of the Passion to come, the call to Mary for intercession, the interpolated miracle that cures a shepherd's blindness—*Bethlehem* is more conventionally Christian in emphasis than the later plays, yet its impact is not that of a simple celebration of the incarnation. Housman hoped that the play might "startle men's minds to a realization of whether for them Christianity is a curious relic of the past or a truth still living and central,"[3] but the nature of that truth is a matter of imagination or symbol rather than dogma. In an article on the production of *Bethlehem*, he wrote, ". . . I feel that there is working through the present day a great intellectual Catholic renaissance, a recognition not so much of the dogmatic truth as of the imaginative beauty of the Catholic presentment of Christianity."[4] The Christian view of the Nativity, the incarnation of God and of Love, would be quite at home with Housman's *Bethlehem*, but, for the author, the events do not have the historical significance that they have for the orthodox Christian.

Housman's Nativity play suffers from the kind of poetic effects —archaic language, reversed syntax—that are typical of his non-dramatic poetry and of most of the dramatic poetry of the early part of the century. The other chief defect of the play—one that Housman shares with most of the writers of modern Nativities— is the false simplicity of the shepherds. The excessively folksy and supposedly comic shepherds with the rich country dialect are the heritage that the Nativity maker of today has received from his medieval predecessor; the sheep-stealing scene is charming in the Wakefield *Second Shepherds' Play* mainly because the rough good nature of the characters is part of the essential naturalness —crudity even—of the play as a whole. A sophisticated attempt to recapture that tone is usually unsuccessful.

Between *Bethlehem* and *St. Martin's Pageant* (1921), Housman

[3] Laurence Housman, "In Spite of the Censor," *Critic*, XLII, 141 (February, 1903).
[4] *Ibid.*, p. 142.

wrote a few short plays on religious subjects. *Nazareth* (1916) shows Jesus as a child in his father's carpenter shop, but the emphasis is on the Passion to come. *The Lord of the Harvest* (1916), a muddled attack on greed, is an odd mixture of religion, politics, and economics. In *The Unknown Star* (1919), a Nativity which Housman wrote with H. M. Paull, a reluctant Jupiter is forced to abdicate in favor of the new god who has just been born.

The subject of *St. Martin's Pageant* was dictated in part by the occasion for it, the second centenary of St. Martin-in-the-Fields. Set in Amiens in 350, the pageant shows St. Martin sharing his cloak with a beggar to whom the cloak brings not only warmth, but vision. What the beggar sees is a procession of figures from the dead Caesar, who represents the passing of Rome, to modern Quakers working in prisons. Each of the characters in some way represents the idea of fellowship (St. Martin's cloak is the cloak of fellowship) working in society. Housman, typically, said of the pageant that he wrote it "with Christianity to the fore, and the church making a bad second all down the ages."[5]

One of the scenes in *St. Martin's Pageant* shows St. Francis with St. Clare, reciting the Canticle of the Sun. It is not surprising that St. Francis should appear in Housman's pageant, for the author's long-time preoccupation with the saint had by this time already resulted in the first of the *Little Plays of St. Francis*. The first series, which was published in 1922, grew out of Rutland Boughton's request for a one-act play for the 1921 Glastonbury Festival, but the first St. Francis plays did not come into being as a unit in 1921; *Sister Gold*, for instance, was published as early as 1916 under the title *As Good as Gold*. Housman's interest in St. Francis as a subject was probably given both impetus and form in 1918 when he prepared a volume, *St. Francis Poverello*, for a series called Messages of the Saints, but Housman had used Francis as early as 1899 when

[5] Laurence Housman, *The Unexpected Years*, Indianapolis, Bobbs-Merrill, [1936], p. 281.

"The New Orpheus," which tells how the saint sang to the birds and beasts, was published in his collection of poems, *The Little Land*.

The reason for Housman's attraction to St. Francis is obvious. The saint, as the playwright understands him, represents a religious point of view that the author accepts as his own. "The word 'Franciscan' carries with it a clearer, a simpler, a less adulterated meaning than the word 'Christian,'"[6] Housman wrote in *St. Francis Poverello*. In the essay "Prophets, Ancient and Modern" he says, "St. Francis of Assisi had the extraordinary notion . . . that man is more inclined to do good than to do evil. . . ."[7] The idea of man's inherent goodness might be for St. Francis the overcoming of sinfulness through a direct and simple approach to God, the attempt to emulate Christ, but the attitude of the plays—for all the talk of sin that fills them—is actually an emphasis on goodness that does away with the idea of original sin. For Francis is a symbol of man's potential perfectability through love and brotherhood. Francis's method, the simplicity that could descend (or rise) to childishness or inspired foolishness, he celebrates as early as "The New Orpheus." The idea of innocence meeting and defeating evil, violence, and power appeals to Housman in Francis and even more in Brother Juniper. Francis also represents for Housman simple faith contrasted to the worldly and complicated machinery of faith (or power) represented by the church. Housman's own doubt about many of the tenets of Christianity does not keep him from giving St. Francis his full quota of doctrinal faith, his visions, his stigmata, but the emphasis in the mystical scenes is a little distant, almost clinical, as though the playwright sees, but does not understand; Housman seems happier, more warmly drawn to his characters when Francis or Juniper come up against prejudice or pretension.

[6] Laurence Housman, *St. Francis Poverello*, London, Sidgwick and Jackson, 1918, p. 1.
[7] Housman, *The Preparation of Peace*, p. 187.

The First Series of the *Little Plays of St. Francis* has a thematic organization that is no longer apparent in the 1935 edition, the three-volume collection that covers not only the First Series but all the St. Francis plays that Housman added later. The early collection consists of eighteen short plays, divided—six each—under three headings—The Foregoing, The Following, The Finding. Each of the main parts has its own subject and its own tone. In the plays that make up The Foregoing, Francesco (the name Francis is not used until he becomes a priest) is shown as a typical Renaissance young man—drinking, reveling, gambling (no wenching, however)—who is attracted strangely to poverty and disease, but is not quite aware of the nature of his own attraction. The plays are dressed, verbally at least, in a literary courtliness that suggests other and older plays; *The Revellers* and *The Bride Feast*, for instance, strongly echo *Romeo and Juliet*. The hints of what is to come for Francis are strewn through all six of the plays. In *The Revellers*, he sings a song to Folly, a presage of his being a fool in Christ. In *Fellow-Prisoners*, he frees the caged birds and speaks to the wall of his prison cell—"Brother Wall!" The mixture of human and animal, of animate and inanimate in Francis's love is here initiated; "his prison wall has become a friend and companion. It means the birth of the Franciscan idea, on which everything else follows."[8] In the rest of the plays in this first part, Francis is haunted by the idea of death, a fear which he overcomes in *Our Lady of Poverty* when he kissed the leper. Another indication of the way Francis is going comes in *Blind Eyes* in which, to win a bet, he pretends to be a blind beggar, but, having received alms from a little girl (later St. Clare), he is moved by guilt to scourge himself.

The second group of plays, The Following, shows Francis at his strongest, his most certain and most joyful. The emphasis is

[8] Laurence Housman, *The 'Little Plays' Handbook*, London, Sidgwick and Jackson, 1927, p. 18.

on his personal following, their devotion to him and to God. In *The Builders*, in which Francis and his followers are actually and symbolically rebuilding the church of St. Damian's, Juniper is introduced. He is portrayed from the beginning as a solidly stupid man who is accidentally wise, genuinely good, and continuously funny, although the amusing things that he does and says are often more apparent to Francis and the brothers than they are likely to be to an audience. Some of the plays in this section—*Brother Sun* and *Brother Wolf*—deal with legendary stories of St. Francis—his preaching to the Sultan or his meeting with the wolf, in this case Lupe, a thief. *Sister Clare* introduces her to the Franciscan movement and *The Lepers* shows Francis overcoming his revulsion to work within a leper enclosure. A number of recurrent themes appear in this section. Juniper's "Father, you have a holy madness in you, and there's no curing you," in *Brother Wolf* is typical of the attitude toward Francis in all the plays. Francis's remark in *Sister Clare*, "God made a great fool when He made thee, Juniper—for when He gave thee foolishness, He gave thee light also, and wisdom, and understanding," is the complement of Juniper's statement. In *Sister Gold*, Juniper makes an implicit comparison between Francis and Christ; the confusion is a familiar one to Juniper, just as—or so it often seems—it is to the author as well.

In The Finding, the third group of the *Little Plays*, Housman deals a little angrily with the institutionalization of Francis. In many of these plays, the saint is a forlorn figure, no longer at home in the movement that he founded; Juniper is even more out of place. *The Chapter* deals with the meeting at Assisi at which a successor to the aging Francis—Brother Elias, an administrative type—is chosen. It is apparent that a great many new rules have been attached to the order and that Francis and his old followers—Juniper, Leo, Giles—do not approve. In *Brother Juniper*, Elias reprimands Juniper for an excess of charity, and

Francis comforts his old friend by forcing him to sing a song of praise to his foolishness. In *Brother Elias*, it is Francis himself who is reprimanded, for teaching poverty in the face of the Order's new acquisitions of property. In *Brother Sin*, Francis attempts to solve Brother Leo's problem about too great a love for Francis and not enough for Christ, and in reconciling the two loves of Leo, he helps solve his own problem in relation to Elias and the changing Order. In *Sister Death*, the concern of the Order for the retention of Francis's body, which the secular authorities also want, overshadows their concern for the dying man. The main emphasis of this last group of plays is on the growing opposition of the Order to the original idea of Francis, but they also have something to say of the personal spiritual life of the saint. In *The Seraphic Vision*, Francis receives the stigmata, and in *Sister Death* he has a deathbed vision that is a reavowal of his beliefs.

After the First Series of *Little Plays*, Housman began to add to the group, filling in corners of the St. Francis story that he had not touched originally. The first addition was *Followers of St. Francis* (1923). Aside from *Cure of Souls*, in which Francis talks Pope Honorius into giving the Brotherhood a special indulgence, this collection is made up of stories in which Juniper, Leo, and Giles face the complications of the changed Order. The tone is much like that of the last plays in the First Series. By the time *The Comments of Juniper* came out in 1926, an outside influence was working on Housman. The plays had been given at University College, London, in 1925, the first of an annual presentation, and Housman had been so impressed with Frank Heath's performance as Juniper that he wanted to give him more to do. Some of the plays in the new group—like *The Mess of Pottage*—are designed to give Juniper long, wise speeches; others—like *Brother Ass*—make wisdom of simplicity; still others—like *The Peace-Makers*—give occasion for slapstick. Two of the plays—*The Order of Release* and *Makers of Miracles*—touch again on Francis in relation to the changes within the Brotherhood. *The Last Comment*, the play of Juniper's death, offers a vision (or a dream) in which Juniper is forbidden to see Francis because he worshipped Francis instead of God; Francis and even Elias testify for him, however, and the saint comes to him. For the Second Series (1931), several new Juniper plays—*Juniper's First Sermon*, *The Temptations of Juniper*, *Juniper's Miracle*, *The Odour of Sanctity*—were added, as were some that attempt to fill in details of Housman's growing narrative. *Holy Disobedience* tells of Leo's dismissal from the Order, and *Gate of Life* shows Juniper regaining his faith after having lost it at Francis's death. *Gate of Death* goes back to Francis in the days of his strength, and *The House of Bondage* reaches back further to the Francesco days, depicting Francis's father, a farcical figure in *The Builders*, as a tyrant. *Four Plays of St. Clare* (1934) focus either on her behavior as a leader of the Little Sisters or—in *Good Beating*—on her early days, when she too is given a father as cruel and as lacking in understanding as that of Francesco. In 1935, *Naked Truth* and *Blind Heart*, two more plays of Francis's early life, and *Bond of Fellowship*, in which he kisses a blind beggar's eyes, were published separately. When all these were brought together for a final edition later that year, two more were added—*Fine Feathers*, another Francesco play, and *Sister Agnes*, which brings St. Clare's sister into the order.

The writing of the *Little Plays of St. Francis*, then, covers a period of almost twenty years. The First Series is best, both as a unit and individually. Housman's fascination with Francis's slow attraction to poverty and his finally forcing himself to touch the diseased and the corrupt is apparent in the early plays, but there is no indication that Housman approves, only that he observes. In fact, in *The Lepers* and *Our Lady of Poverty*, the physical manifestations of Francis's love are decidedly unpleasant. Housman admires Francis's view of human goodness, but he does not mask him by seeing him simply as the man who preached to the birds.

In the later plays, when Housman adds the melodramatically cruel father, the story of Francesco becoming Francis is somewhat obscured. The addition of the many Juniper plays changes the focus of the center group, those that deal with Francis at his best, and in a sense change the original impulse that produced the series. In *Nunc Dimittis*, the Author says to St. Francis, "Somebody said that when I began writing my 'Little Plays,' I wrote them for love of *you*, but that I went on writing them for love of Brother Juniper. That's quite true, Father." Often the plays in the series become undramatic—as in *The Seraphic Vision*; often they are too patently discussions or lectures. Still, the plays as a group convey an impression of St. Francis, which while it may be historically inaccurate, is fascinating both in itself and in relationship to the beliefs for which Housman speaks.

In 1932, Housman published a volume of unimpressive short plays, *Ye Fearful Saints!*, vaguely connected by the subtitle, "Plays of Creed, Custom and Credulity." Three of the plays— *The Time-Servers*, *The Gods Whom Men Love Die Old*, and *Old Bottles*—are concerned, directly or implicitly, with the concept of the evolving god. The other plays—a mixed lot—include *The New Hangman*, an attack on capital punishment; *The Waiting-Room*, a saccharine piece about a dying grandfather; *The Wrong Door*, a story of a good man who gets to hell by mistake; and *In This Sign Conquer*, a tongue-in-cheek account of Constantine's conversion. In only two sections—*Religious Difficulties* and *Promotion Cometh*— of Housman's best-known work, *Victoria Regina* (1934), is there any emphasis on religion, and both scenes are comic.

Housman wrote a series of biblical plays during the forties, all of which illustrate his distaste for the harshness of the Old Testament God and of the patriarchal figures. In *Abraham and Isaac* (1941), neither Sarah nor Isaac understand Abraham and his God; they are aware only that he is suffering from a command that he thinks his God has given. The logic that Abraham uses to grasp

God's will is a little suspect; since the one thing that he would not do for God is kill Isaac, then the sacrifice of Isaac becomes God's command. In reducing the conflict between Abraham and God to an internal one, Housman is able to make the point that his play intends—that the will of God lies in the hearts of men—but he also unfortunately weakens the character of Abraham by turning him into a somewhat silly and superstitious old man. Early in the play, remembering when Abraham finally agreed to turn Hagar out of camp, Sarah says, "That's your Father's way; when he's done something he didn't want to do he thinks 'twas God made him do it." The new concept that Abraham brings down from the mountain is the reverse of Sarah's statement: when he does something that he wants to do he thinks God made him do it.

In *Jacob's Ladder* (originally, *The Story of Jacob*, 1942), Housman again gives a personal interpretation of a biblical character and, as with Abraham, his Jacob loses some of his biblical charm. Part of the appeal of the biblical Jacob, particularly in the matter of Laban and the spotted sheep, is that of the King and the Duke in *Huckleberry Finn*; Jacob is an amusing deceiver. In Housman's hands, the fun goes out of the deceits; Jacob becomes primarily a self-deceiver. The two Voices that give a running commentary on Jacob's character emphasize the self-deception and remind Jacob and the audience that he must come to recognize himself as he is before he can realize the promise of his vision of the ladder.

Ramoth Gilead (1942), a short play designed to say that truth can be unpalatable, is unusual only in that it tells the story of Ahab's death without ever mentioning Jezebel. In *The Burden of Nineveh* (1942), Housman retells the story of the chastening of Jonah, but in his version, the whale is frankly an invention. "Is it not strange, Shemmel," says Jonah, "that to make men believe the truth, we prophets have to tell lies." The emphasis of the play, like that in the Bible, is on the mercy of God and his prophet's

distaste for it; it is through Shemmel—Housman's amusing
addition to the Bible story—that God rebukes Jonah.

In *Samuel the Kingmaker* (1944), Samuel is shown as a political
figure, striving to hold onto his power, using his God as an excuse
for his actions. "My play is written to demonstrate that on these
occasions Samuel's God was Samuel himself," Housman says of
Samuel's moments of prophecy. The play is filled with speeches
in which Samuel equates his desires with God's will: "I heard no
Voice—only in my own heart 'twas the Lord speaking; and *my*
wrath against Eli and his sons was *His* wrath." It is the Witch of
Endor, whom Housman uses, as he says, "to run Samuel down to
earth (where he properly belongs)," who defines the two gods of
the play, Samuel's and hers, which is to say Samuel's and Housman's:

You have a dangerous God, Samuel—a God of vengeance and wrath—
too much like yourself to be trusted. . . . my God is a safe God for man
to put trust in. For my God is Law; and in Law is no wrath, save
against them that, being fools, are blind to it.

In the end, Samuel dies alone, deserted by his sons and his
followers. In a final scene, the Witch of Endor comforts Saul,
making him see that he is suffering at the hands of his own fear,
not from any punishment of Samuel's God.

Housman's last biblical plays sum up most of his ideas on religion. In them, he speaks for a distant, a noninterfering God, one
that is a Law or the voice within man himself. He speaks against
violence and fear in the name of God and for love and understanding. If he returns too insistently to these ideas, if he labors
too heavily against the Old Testament patriarchs as they are and
against the miracles and wonders that are so much a part of their
stories, he does so from humanitarian motives. Many of these last
plays suffer from this insistence. They are, however, Housman's
best work in religious drama. In them, he manages to overcome

many of the faults—the sentimentality, the archaism, the cuteness even—that marks much of his earlier work, including the *Little Plays of St. Francis*. Housman's conception of the Old Testament characters is certainly not the heroic one that those figures might be given, but they are all seen sharply as individuals and they all have vitality by virtue of the contexts in which Housman places them.

John Masefield. John Masefield's religious plays—*Good Friday, The Trial of Jesus, The Coming of Christ*—probably have their origin as much in his concern for poetry and the drama as in his religious convictions. His theatrical experiments at his private theater at Boar's Hill, Oxford, and his interest in the development of verse speaking in England, which resulted in the Oxford Recitations, a series of contests that extended over seven years in the twenties, are evidence of the direction that his dedication took. Fred Eastman's description of Masefield—"He is frankly mystic and a Christian"[9]—may be of use in examining the religious plays directly; to understand how they came to be written, however, it is necessary also to emphasize that he was frankly a promoter of poetic drama, particularly for nonprofessionals, in the days before the advocates of that genre became so indigenous to the English dramatic scene.

In most of Masefield's plays, religious ideas are tangential. In the one-acters, *The Campden Wonder* (1906) and *Mrs. Harrison* (1906), the retelling of an old Gloucestershire tale of murder and misunderstanding, the surface piety of the parson and Mrs. Harrison is contrasted to the horror of the actual events. The titular tragedy of *The Tragedy of Nan* (1908) is largely the work of a stock church-going, Bible-reading villainess. These early prose plays share a distaste for the stern and narrow destructiveness of Old Testament biblical literalness. *Philip the King* (1914), an

[9] Fred Eastman, *Christ in the Drama,* New York, Macmillan, 1947, p. 72.

essentially undramatic play, written in verse that is largely a
matter of muddled syntax, depicts the king as a strange mixture
of pride and piety, who accepts the defeat of the Armada as "the
act of One/ Who chastens earthly kings. . . ." The theme of
Melloney Holtspur, or The Pangs of Love (1922), a flabbily supernatural offering, is that love is stronger than the conventional
view of sin. *A King's Daughter* (1923), like Clemence Dane's
Naboth's Vineyard, which came a few years later, is an unbiblical
telling of the story of Jezebel in which she is the bringer of peace
and freedom to Samaria, a victim of the machinations of Jehu.

The first of Masefield's religious plays, *Good Friday*, which he
called a dramatic poem, came at about the time of *Philip the King*,
but, as he explained, it "was interrupted by the war and never
completed."[10] Although the play was not in finished form, it was
performed by the Stage Society in 1917. *Good Friday* is, obviously,
the story of the crucifixion. The emphasis throughout is on the
bloodthirsty crowd and their desire for the death of Jesus. The
play contains the dream of Procula, Pilate's wife, who wants to
save Jesus (she cuts her arm to let her blood atone for His death);
Pilate's inclination to save Him, but his fear of political consequences; the report of Longinus, the centurion, who is convinced
by the crucifixion that Jesus is God's son. A madman, a blind
beggar, appears throughout the play as a representative of the
continual crucifixion of the gentle before the powers of the state
and the dogmatic church. He is the one figure who gives *Good
Friday* whatever continuity it has, and he states the play's theme in
telling that he was blinded because "I told the crowd/ That only a
bloody God would care for blood./ The crowd kill kids and
smear the lintel wood,/ To honor God, who lives in the pure
stars." As in most of Masefield's plays, the verse is too weak for
the work it has to do, and the madman is not invention enough

[10] John Masefield, *The Poems and Plays of John Masefield*, New York, Macmillan,
1918, II, vi.

to give the play real force. There is justice in Arnold Bennett's entry in his *Journal*: "Stage Society in the afternoon. *Good Friday* by Masefield. A terribly dull and portentous thing in rhyme. I was most acutely bored. I found that all the élite said they liked the damned thing."[11]

The Trial of Jesus (1925), a mixture of prose and song, is a much fuller account of the capture and crucifixion of Christ than is *Good Friday*. The emphasis here is not on Jesus as God or as Christ, but on His truth and the light that man can bring to man, the doctrine of brotherhood. The play opens with the confrontation of Jesus by Wisdom, who reminds Him that he can remain human, can pass up the cup that has been handed Him. Jesus accepts His death, and Wisdom, in a reversal of tone, a dropping of his common sense attitude, proclaims that "You will be one with Life." The change within the abstract figure of Wisdom is symptomatic of an uncertain quality that marks the characterizations within the play. Judas, for instance, is represented as a devoted follower of Jesus, sincerely sorry that his master has slipped into blasphemy, and also as the man who sells his friend for money. Caiaphas is a Jewish patriot, untainted by the use he makes of Judas, but he is also the man who says the biblical, "What is that to us?" when Judas realizes the extent of his betrayal. It is possible that Masefield intends to suggest that the men involved in the death of Christ are not simply stereotypes of villainy, but the effect is not one of depth or subtlety but of careless characterization. In this play, unlike *Good Friday*, Christ makes his own defense. The scriptural accounts of the trial limit the amount that Jesus can say, but Masefield does let Him answer Annas's "We, as priests, may only believe the revelation of God," with "Has God ceased to reveal Himself?" The concern of Procula and the conviction of Longinus about the nature of Christ are here, as they were in *Good Friday*, and the character of the decadent Herod, just hinted in the

[11] Arnold Bennett, *The Journal of Arnold Bennett*, New York, Viking, 1933, p. 617.

earlier play, is drawn to excess. Having moved through the incidents of the Passion, emphasizing Jesus as the bringer of a new message (Zadok: "that the Kingdom of God is in the heart, and that he who enters deeply into his heart, enters the Kingdom of God, where all are brothers."), Masefield ends his play by letting Jesus speak a somewhat conventional poem, "Open your hearts and let me in," and by allowing the chorus to close on a note that stresses the manhood, not the godhead of Christ.

Masefield returned to the material of the Passion in *Easter*, a Play for Singers (1929). This short play opens with The Way of the World singing his triumph over the rebels who try to bring men to God: "Now I have compasst the death of the healer and preacher/ Jesus, the Bringer of Tidings, I brought him his end." The action moves back and forth between abstractions and characters. The soldiers on guard at Christ's tomb follow The Way of the World and confirm his triumph: "This man stirred up a hell to struggle through/ And died in struggling, to what earthly end?" The perhaps accidental pun with which the speech ends expresses, somewhat wryly, that the soldiers may have misunderstood Christ's mission in thinking it a worldly one. The play is not completely clear about the matter itself. After Anima Christi breaks out of the tomb, bringing the crucified thieves with him, Mary Magdalen speaks of His coming to "make God's Kingdom here, and not a dream." She closes the play, however, with "Life's everlasting Spring/ Hath robbed Death of his sting." The play as a celebration of Easter seems unsure of whether the Resurrection is the triumph of man over death or over the world, whether Christ's kingdom is of this world or the next.

Masefield's Nativity, *The Coming of Christ* (1928), his Canterbury play, is probably his best work—religious or not—for the theater. It is unusual as a Nativity for an air of hopelessness and failure about Christ's mission on earth pervades the whole play. It ends in the usual adoration scene, but the joy of the occasion has already been marked by the action of the first scene. At the beginning, four angels—The Power ("I bring the Power of God. . . ."), The Sword ("I bring God's justice. . . ."), The Mercy ("I bring the Mercy of God. . . ."), The Light (I bring the Light of God. . . .") —attempt to convince the Anima Christi not to take flesh and go to earth. For one thing, as The Sword points out, man is not worth it: "Man will not change for one voice crying truth,/ And dying, beautiful as fire, for wisdom." For another, only three men will ever understand Christ's mission and these—John, Peter, and Judas—are, each in his way, failures. "And of your three most trusted friends, the one/ Will seek his own pre-eminence; and one/ Will sell you to your foes; one will deny you." Anima Christi decides that He has no choice: "But, the attempt, being worthy, should be made./ Having beheld man's misery, sin and death,/ Not to go on were treason." The play then becomes the familiar Nativity, but even the shepherds' closing song—"He puts on dying/ That Life have birth"—cannot quite erase (or transcend) the initial effect.

Running through all of Masefield's religious plays is the idea that is presented directly at the beginning of *The Coming of Christ*, the idea that His coming was in some sense a failure because the message of brotherhood and peace that He brought to earth did not really triumph. The idea is expressed most touchingly in a song at the end of Act I of *The Trial of Jesus* in which the quest of the three wise men is described: "But within were beast and stranger and a newborn babe/ Whom they pitied and gave gifts to and dismisst and left behind." Insofar as this attitude is a call for the rekindling of the spirit of Christ in men, Masefield is the Christian that Eastman called him. The sense of failure in some of the plays—notably *The Trial of Jesus* and *Good Friday*—extends to the crucifixion, however, as though Christ's mission were the earthly one hinted at in *Easter*. To the extent that the crucifixion is pictured as a failure, Masefield is an unconventional Christian writer, for the crucifixion, without which there could be no resurrection, is a triumph to the orthodox Christian. In *A Play of St. George* (1948), which mixes verse and prose, song and dance to describe the martyrdom of St. George, Masefield returns more cheerfully to the sacrifice. St. George defeats the Dragon (here, amusingly, a pirate) and then goes on to be executed by the forces of Rome. There is no suggestion in his martyrdom of anything but triumph; he is met at the gate of heaven by Christus who speaks John 6.54, "Whose eateth my flesh, and drinketh my blood, hath eternal life. . . ."

There is a fascination in watching Masefield vacillate in his plays between a conventional celebration of a Christian occasion such as the Nativity or the Passion and his own insistence that the world has rejected Christ. This personal element which gives the plays their interest, however, should not be confused with dramatic virtues. In calling *Good Friday* a dramatic poem and *Easter* a play for singers Masefield defined his own limitations. None of his plays is particularly effective as drama. As readings, their quality depends largely on their poetry. Masefield's dramatic verse, like all his poetry, is easy to read, but it seldom attains distinction. It is most moving and most effective in moments of extreme simplicity (as in some of the added songs) or in moments of emotional content (as in Longinus's description of the crucifixion) in which the emotional quality, by virtue of the biblical scene that suggests it, precedes the poetry instead of growing from it. In the long run, Masefield's contribution to English religious drama is not as likely to lie in the plays themselves as much as in his having written them. The attraction to religious drama of a major literary figure—and Masefield was that when he began—probably helped to draw other serious writers to the genre. *The Coming of Christ* in itself and in its relation to Canterbury, is, in a sense, the culmination of the scattered activity of the religious theater during the teens and twenties and the beginning of the new professionalism that marked the later development of the movement.

Sheila Kaye-Smith. Aside from Housman and Masefield, the novelist Sheila Kaye-Smith is the only other writer of religious plays from the period before 1930 who deserves any special attention. She wrote her two plays—*The Child Born at the Plough* (1927) and *The Shepherd of Lattenden* (1927)—after she had moved away from Sussex, partly out of "the emotion of nostalgia for the land I had left," partly to "recover the medieval simplicity which saw both the manger and the cross in its own fields"; as she herself admits, she did not quite succeed.[12]

In *The Child Born at the Plough,* the shepherds in the marshes between Rye and Winchelsea are waiting for the Christmas lambing and complaining of the new Squire (Herod). The Angel of the Lord, dressed as a parson with wings, appears to them and sends them to Udimore to the stable at the Plough, the public house. Thus begins a Nativity in which the strident modernism of the twenties (Salome is a flapper) is played against the background of Sussex rusticity. The suspension of time is apparent in the band of gypsies—all Old Testament figures—waiting at the Plough to welcome the child and in the appearance of Thomas à Becket, who has ridden cross-country to be present at the birth. Both the telescoping of time and the modern dress is evident in Mr. Stephen, the Deacon, who is being persecuted by Bishop Saul of Chichester; the presence of Christianity's first martyr also suggests the eventual death of the newborn baby. The three wise men, from Oxford and Cambridge, are determinedly contemporary; they find evidence of Christ in scientific terms.

The Shepherd of Lattenden attempts to do for the Passion what *The Child Born at the Plough* does for the Nativity. There is less imaginative fusing of time, however; Miss Kaye-Smith's Passion

[12] Sheila Kaye-Smith, *Three Ways Home,* London, Cassell, [1937], p. 157.

play simply transfers the Gospel events to Sussex. Canon Annas and Archdeacon Caiaphas are determined to stop the activities of the Shepherd of Lattenden, an unordained preacher who has gathered a following in the neighborhood. Judas ("a sullen looking country bumpkin") betrays Christ, and Mayor Pilate hesitates about the sentence. The agony of Gethsemane takes place in the Hop Garden at Doleham, and the resurrection is announced in Mr. Joseph's garden at Little Park Manor near Battle.

There are in *The Child Born at the Plough* an amusing sense of invention and a concrete communication of the idea that the Nativity is a continuous event. Miss Kaye-Smith's Passion play, however, is less successful than her Nativity. *The Shepherd of Lattenden* suffers from too great a need to set the map of Jerusalem down on the map of Sussex. The followers of the Shepherd are necessarily rustics, like the shepherds of *The Child Born at the Plough*, and so the majority of the lines are in heavy country accents. While such lines are possible in the joking or joyful scenes of the Nativity, it is difficult to accept them in the serious moments of the Passion. When Judas, aware finally of what he has done, throws down the thirty pieces of silver, he is forced to exit to his suicide's death with, "Well, reckon I'm shut of you all. I'll go and hang myself." Both Miss Kaye-Smith's plays get caught in the trap of falseness that waits for any contemporary writer who tries to catch the simplicity of an earlier age; only *The Shepherd of Lattenden* dies in that trap.

VIII
Charles Williams and Dorothy Sayers

Aside from T. S. Eliot and Christopher Fry, who will be considered in a later chapter, the second period of religious drama activity—between 1930 and the end of World War II—introduced two playwrights whose work is of sufficient stature—either in achievement or in intention—to be considered closely. These are Charles Williams and Dorothy L. Sayers. Williams, who died in 1945, wrote the bulk of his plays in the last ten years of his life. Although Miss Sayers continued her dramatic work into the post-war period, it bears the stamp of pre-war days, when indeed most of her plays were written; she did not turn to the commercial stage, as did Fry and Eliot, but remained a playwright for an occasion, a producer of festival plays.

Charles Williams. Charles Williams is the most fascinating product of the English religious drama revival. Williams, who is best known in the United States as a novelist, was an editor at Oxford University Press during most of his life and a voluminous writer in a variety of forms. Besides novels and plays, he wrote poetry, biography, criticism, and philosophical and theological essays. His plays, like all of his work, are heavily marked with idiosyncrasies of thought and style. Ideas which help to define his religious perceptions occur and recur throughout his work. Any definition of Williams's thought, however, is difficult, because he seems always to be communicating intuitions rather than exhibiting dogma. "His aim is to make you partake of a kind of experience that he has had, rather than to make you accept some dogmatic belief,"[1] T. S. Eliot writes. It is not that Williams expresses ideas that are foreign to conventional Christianity; it is simply that the expression itself is unconventional. Robert McAfee Brown, writing in *Theology Today*, says: "he does not depart from the faith, especially does he not depart from the Anglican faith . . . he never presents the Christian faith in a conventional manner."[2] The unusual quality in Williams's work lies probably in his relationship to the material with which he deals. Where another writer might present the supernatural as a construct of belief and fantasy, Williams always seems to be offering it as observed fact. In *All Hallows' Eve*, for instance, Williams describes the world of the newly dead: "It lay there, as it always does—itself offering no barriers, open to be trodden, ghostly to this world and to heaven, and in its upper reaches ghostly also to those in its lower reaches where (if at all) hell lies."[3] The casual "as it always does," as matter of fact as an "of course," is not simply stylistic; it is an example of a kind of familiarity with the occult that runs all through Williams's work.

Anne Ridler, in her introduction to *Seed of Adam and Other Plays*, attempts to characterize the dramatic theme of Williams's work as "a conflict between good and evil which, almost always, resolves itself into a state where the old terms are no longer true, and what was originally seen as evil is also part of perfection."[4] As is the case with most statements about Williams, that of Mrs. Ridler is at once true and untrue. The evil is often seen as part of the perfection in Williams's plays, as if in illustration of the idea

[1] T. S. Eliot, "Introduction," Charles Williams, *All Hallows' Eve*, New York, Pellegrini and Cudahy, 1948, p. xiv.

[2] Robert McAfee Brown, "Charles Williams: Lay Theologian," *Theology Today*, X, 217 (July, 1953). Brown's essay (pp. 212–229) is the best brief account of Williams's religious ideas.

[3] Williams, *All Hallows' Eve*, p. 77.

[4] Anne Ridler, "Introduction," Charles Williams, *Seed of Adam and Other Plays*, London, Oxford, 1948, p. viii.

from Boethius—"Then all fortune is good"[5]—which Williams uses and identifies in *The Descent of the Dove,* his history of the Holy Spirit, and on which he plays variations in most of his works. Just as true, however, is Eliot's statement that Williams sees evil "unerringly, as the contrast to Good. . . . "[6] The struggle between good and evil in Williams, which is almost always resolved in favor of good, but always doubtfully and tentatively so long as the resolution is an earthly one, is as often in terms of love (or Love) as it is in terms of Christ or God. "His is a mysticism, not of curiosity, or of the lust for power, but of Love," Eliot says, "and Love, in the meaning which it had for Williams . . . is a deity of whom most human beings seldom see more than the shadow."[7]

Robert McAfee Brown, in his attempt to isolate the ideas that recur in Williams, writes, "One such fundamental motif may be called *the interpenetration of the two worlds.* . . . The suggestion that there is a 'material' realm and a 'spiritual' realm would, I am sure, have shocked him."[8] For Williams, simply, the natural and the supernatural were both equally real and they attained their reality by being a unity. Eliot makes the point about Williams in personal terms[9]:

I have always believed that he would have been equally at ease in every kind of supernatural company; that he would never have been surprised or disconcerted by the intrusion of any visitor from another world, whether kindly or malevolent; and that he would have shown exactly the same natural ease and courtesy, with an exact awareness of how one should behave, to an angel, a demon, a human ghost, or an

---

[5] Charles Williams, *The Descent of the Dove,* New York, Pellegrini and Cudahy, [1939], p. 89. Williams cites Sedgefield's modernization of King Alfred's version, but the phrase is apparently not a quote. It is a one-sentence condensation of the idea as it appears in *King Alfred's Version of the Consolations of Boethius,* done into modern English with an Introduction by Walter John Sedgefield, Oxford, Clarendon Press, 1900, pp. 160–163.

[6] Eliot, *op. cit.,* p. xvi.   [7] *Ibid.,* p. xvii.

[8] Brown, *op. cit.,* p. 219.   [9] Eliot, *op. cit.,* p. xiii.

elemental. For him there was no frontier between the material and the spiritual world.

According to Brown, Williams's most important concept is that of "*the practice of substituted love* . . . his way of developing the meaning of the Pauline formula, 'Bear ye one another's burdens.'"[10] As Brown explains the concept, there are three levels of substitution: *exchange*, which is the ordinary sharing of services; *substitution*, which is the acceptance of a burden that rightly belongs to another; *co-inherence*, which involves raising the process of sharing from the personal to the universal. In the last instance, the crucifixion of Christ becomes the extreme manifestation of substituted love and the relationship of the persons within the Trinity its best symbol and, for Williams, its best fact. Williams describes it in *The Descent of the Dove* as "the new state of being, a state of redemption, of co-inherence, made actual by the divine substitution, 'He in us and we in him.'"[11] As Williams makes clear in that book, as in his play *Judgement at Chelmsford*, for him there is no temporal limitation to the substitution; a man today may share the burden of a medieval martyr just as that martyr, through his death, carries the load of the Christian in the future. The neatness with which Brown outlines the concept and differentiates between the three words is misleading, for Williams's cryptic style, in his philosophical writing, as in his plays, is not concrete enough for definition. The terms become interchangeable; for instance, *exchange* is frequently used in the plays to signify one of the deeper levels of substitution.

Another of Williams's ideas, that of the City, he has defined as loosely as "the sense of many relationships between men and women woven into a unity."[12] Elsewhere, he has said, "The

---

[10] Brown, *op. cit.*, p. 220. The quotation is from Galatians 6. 2.

[11] Williams, *The Descent of the Dove*, p. 10.

[12] Charles Williams, "The Image of the City in English Verse," *The Image of the City and Other Essays*, London, Oxford, 1958, p. 92.

principle of that City, and the gates of it, are the nature of Christ as the Holy Ghost exhibits it and inducts us into it; it is the doctrine that no man lives to himself or indeed *from* himself."[13] The word takes on a sliding scale of meanings. In *All Hallows' Eve*, it is and is not London, just as it is the world of the newly dead, just as it goes on to suggest the unity of souls in Christ. In *Judgement at Chelmsford*, the word is used specifically when Jerusalem says, "Christ our City . . ." but the City has already been used amorphously within that play.

Williams's use of the Ways of the Affirmation and Negation of Images is of importance to the plays chiefly by implication, as an example of a balance that he attempts to achieve in viewing life. "There are two main directions," Williams writes:[14]

The first is concerned particularly with the nature of things in God; the second with the nature of God. Neither, of course, can exist entirely without the other. It is not possible for the Christian to attend only to men and women (say) and not at all to God in Himself. But neither is it possible for him to attend only to God in Himself and not at all to men and women.

"If the way of affirmation by itself leads to idolatry," Brown says, "the way of negation by itself leads to gnosticism and the rejection of creation, God's creation."[15] In *The Descent of the Dove*, Williams writes:[16]

Rejection was to be rejection but not denial, as reception was to be reception but not subservience. Both methods, the Affirmative Way

---

[13] Charles Williams, "The Redeemed City," *The Image of the City and Other Essays*, p. 104.
[14] Charles Williams, "The Way of Affirmation," *The Image of the City and Other Essays*, p. 155.
[15] Brown, *op . cit.*, p. 227.
[16] Williams, *The Descent of the Dove*, p. 57.

and the Negative Way, were to co-exist; one might almost say, to co-inhere, since each was to be the key of the other: in intellect as in emotion, in morals as in doctrine.

The attempt to reduce Williams's thought to capsule form is self-defeating. The unique quality of Williams's mind is that it plays across its material, whether historical or fictional, and illuminates that material by personal vision. It is impossible that that vision should be shared exactly by anyone else. Insofar as it is a Christian vision, other Christians can approach it; insofar as it is poetic or artistic, it can be experienced as literature. Of all the modern religious playwrights, Williams is the least evangelical. Here, he says, is the way things are—things seen and unseen. The reader can accept or reject the vision as he wishes or as he must. It is Williams's achievement as a playwright that he can attract the unbelieving mind—in a willing suspension of disbelief—as well as the believing one; it is probably his weakness as a playwright that it is the mind, more surely than the emotions, that he attracts.

Williams's first play, *The Myth of Shakespeare* (1928), is, according to Anne Ridler, "a piece of deliberate and brilliant pastiche."[17] The first plays relevant to this study, however, are those in *Three Plays* (1931). Of the three, all of which are awkward and amateurish in comparison with Williams's work a few years later, only *The Rite of the Passion* (1929) can be considered a religious play. Williams has attempted to give the three plays—each written for a special occasion—a unity by printing with them four early Taliessin poems. The first poem, "Taliessin's Song of Logres," is a song of despair; the second, "Taliessin's Song of Byzantion," is a vision of the elect soul; the last two, "Taliessin's Song of the King's Crowning" and "Taliessin's Song of the Setting of Galahad in the King's Bed." tell of the establishment of Arthur and of

[17] Ridler, "Introduction," Williams, *Seed of Adam and Other Plays*, p. vi.

the transmutation of the Table at the coming of the prince. Supposedly, the plays make much the same kind of progression. *The Witch*, an unlikely series of disastrous events, centering on the witch Bess and her two evil children, is plainly a play of distress—in its verse as well as in its content. Bess, at the end, talks of hate —"that which first God saw when he beheld/ pure evil"—walking in the world. The second play, *The Chaste Wanton*, is mock-Elizabethan in style; its subject is Love. Vincenzo, an alchemist who teaches the Duchess the real, the Platonic meaning of Love, is forced—through a series of complications and accidents—to face death by execution; fittingly, it is the Duchess who must sign the warrant, since she is the Beatrice-like figure who is a step on his way to final love. The *Rite of the Passion* is, of course, a kind of transmutation of the Table. The equation is made. The three plays follow vaguely the direction that the Taliessin poems point out, but the plays themselves are so lacking in interest as drama and so derivative as poetry that the suggested unity seems never more than an afterthought.

The Rite of the Passion, which was written for a Good Friday service in 1929, contains many of the ideas that appear in later Williams plays. This Passion play focuses on three figures: Gabriel ("I am nothing but thy annunciation''); Satan ("I am thy shadow only known as hell/ where any linger from thy sweet accord"); and Love ("And I alone am utterly all in all."). Gabriel and Satan are identified at the beginning, "these both are He . . ." and Love comes between them. "But I am still the end and reconciling;/ I am all things driven on through hell to heaven." The play is divided into four parts, which deal with the annunciation, the betrayals, the crucifixion, and the resurrection, but there is no real attempt to tell the biblical story. Incidents in the Gospel narrative are touched on, but always symbolically. For instance, Peter's "The word is lost he gave his folk to keep,/ and we his church are fallen upon sleep" brings the sleep of the disciples during the agony in Gethsemane into conjunction with the forgetfulness of the modern church. The wedding at Cana and Mary's reminder that "They have no wine," touched on in Part I, is transformed in Part IV into a suggestion of communion, "I have given them wine for ever." The chief emphasis is on the multiple betrayals. John's request for a special seat in heaven, Peter's denial, and Judas's betrayal are lumped together, as they are in Masefield's *The Coming of Christ*. Herod is presented as desire turned to lust, Caiaphas, as the priest without fire, Pilate as service to an empty government. In Part IV, in which the resurrection is told through the song of minstrels, all the betrayers call on Christ. "Also my foes shall find in me their end;/ Caiaphas shall be lit with my new fire,/ Pilate shall have a god to be his friend,/ and Herod shall desire man's last desire." The possibility of salvation is apparently infinite.

Between the *Three Plays* and *Thomas Cranmer of Canterbury* (1936) there were important changes in Williams's writing. Anne Ridler suggests that one influence may have been Gerard Manley Hopkins,[18] whose poems Williams edited in 1930; that another may have been T. S. Eliot,[19] whose first plays had already appeared by 1936. Williams had dropped the inadequate blank verse of *The Witch* and *The Chaste Wanton* and had adopted the highly personal poetic style that was to mark the rest of his plays. Cranmer's lines at the beginning of the play indicate the new use of internal rhyme and even of end rhyme within a much looser blank-verse structure:

> But now is man's new fall: now the fresh creature,
> his second nature, nurtured by grace from the old,
> lusts to withdraw itself and withhold
> from the lawful food of God's favour; it lies
> on the sea-broad floor of the Church, and its eyes
> shut themselves on the steep sacramental way. . .

[18] Anne Ridler, "Introduction," Williams, *The Image of the City and other Essays*, pp. lxi–lxii.
[19] Ridler, "Introduction," Williams, *Seed of Adam and Other Plays*, p. vi.

The use of the lower-case letter to introduce lines of poetry that are not new sentences is one of the mannerisms of Williams.

The subject of *Thomas Cranmer of Canterbury* was dictated by the occasion for which it was written—the Canterbury Festival of 1936. The play tells the story of Cranmer in brief scenes that carry him from Cambridge in 1528 to his burning in 1556. The Figura Rerum, the Skeleton, acts as a vice, stirring up and commenting on the action. He is the voice of Cranmer's own desire, but he sees, before the archbishop does, that every worried turn of the churchman's mind is along the road to martyrdom. Sometimes he speaks as commentator; sometimes he talks to Cranmer; sometimes he addresses the audience directly ("There is this to be said for my lord of Canterbury,/he dimly believes in something outside himself—/ Which is more, I can tell you, than most of you do"). The play opens on the war of dogma in England with Cranmer on the side of the Protestants. He becomes Canterbury when he helps Henry VIII marry Anne Boleyn; reluctantly he helps Henry rid himself of Anne. At this point, in a speech which uses Anne's desire for the throne as a point of departure, the Skeleton presages the coming martyrdom: "If you had asked for the greatest conceivable things,/ as Thomas does unintentionally, they would cost no more./ The price of heaven or hell or the world is similar—/ always a broken heart, sometimes a broken neck." Part I of the play carries Cranmer past the death of his protector, Henry, and shows him at his work—the publishing of the English Bible and the Book of Common Prayer.

Part II deals with Cranmer's martyrdom. Mary's ascent to the throne causes his arrest and the Skeleton remarks, "Thomas, your heart that was double with God and the Devil/ must be choked by a heart double with the Devil and God." Cranmer, afraid of burning, unsure of his beliefs, recants, crying "where is my God?" The Skeleton picks up the cry, "Where is your God?/ When you have lost him at last you shall come into God." When it becomes plain that Cranmer is to be burned, for all the recantation, the Skeleton, who has said earlier, "I am the Judas who betrays all men to God," begins to tempt him. Before the fire, Cranmer calls back the recantation in a phrase that abjures much more—all the uses to which he has put God. He says, "all writings wherein I denied God's will,/ or made God's will but the method of my life,/ I altogether reject them." As he is being hurried away to the fire, the Skeleton stops him for one last exchange. "Friend, let us say one thing more before the world—/ I for you, you for me: let us say all:/ if the Pope had bid you live, you would have served him." Cranmer answers, "If the Pope had bid me live, I should have served him." *Thomas Cranmer of Canterbury* is probably unique among plays of martyrdom. To the end, Cranmer remains weak, confused, frightened, only accidentally a martyr. The richness of Williams's conception lies in the fact that, although Cranmer prefers life to martyrdom, his preference in no way belittles either the martyrdom or its meaning for the church.

Seed of Adam (1936), Williams's first Nativity play, is in many ways his most imaginative drama. "This Nativity is not so much a presentation of the historic facts as of their spiritual value,"[20] William says in a synopsis that he prepared for a performance of the play at Colchester. At the beginning of the play, the Tsar of Caucasia (King of Gold) and the Sultan of Bagdad (King of Frankincense) are ruling men and serving Adam through power and philosophy. Adam is aware that something is missing: "will moans and groans/ for gold of brawn and brain regain/ the way to the entry of Paradise?" He decides that his daughter Mary, whose love is indiscriminate and universal, embodying the beautiful and the ugly, the pure and the impure, should marry; he gives her to Joseph, who in this version, following an old legend, is a young warrior. Mary says, "Love is only itself,/ everywhere,

[20] Williams, *Seed of Adam and Other Plays*, p. 93.

at all times, and to all objects." Joseph, who knows that the every-where must become concrete at least for one moment, says, "Place must be because grace must be,/ and you because of glory. O blessing,/ the light in you is more than you in the light." Gabriel comes to Mary.

Adam reappears as Augustus to take the census, "to find whether anywhere it has been said/ what place or person Paradise lies behind." Then comes the Third King (King of Myrrh) followed by his slave, who is in a way his torturer, Mother Myrrh. Williams explains these characters in his synopsis: "The Third King represents the experience of man when man thinks he has gone beyond all hope of restoration to joy, and is accompanied by a negress, who is, briefly, Hell."[21] The Third King says to Adam, "did you know/ I was the core of the fruit you ate?" and he explains that Mother Myrrh grew from a worm within that core. "I came to find this mind of Rome,/ this concept, this Augustus, the new Adam," the Third King says, and then, "Why father! The old Adam, after all!" His journey was delayed, he explains, by angels "with exhortations of earnest heavenly evangels:/ but what can angels do against decaying matter?" Adam directs his soldiers to apprehend Mother Myrrh and the Third King, who says, echoing Jesus in the kind of meaningful inversion that Williams likes to make, "Are you come out with swords and staves to take us?/ We were often with you in your temples."[22] At this point, Mary cries out "in a shriek of pain and joy," and the Third King addresses the Chorus: "You desired twice—me and not me,/ the turn and the Return; the Return is here,/ take care that you do not now prefer me." Mother Myrrh acts as midwife to Mary, and the Third King, who has said earlier that she eats without killing, now adds, "my mother has taken

---

[21] Williams, *Seed of Adam and Other Plays*, p. 94.

[22] Jesus said, "Are ye come out as against a thief with swords and staves for to take me? I sat daily with you teaching in the temple. . . ." (Matthew 26. 55) Cf., Luke 22. 52–53; Mark 14. 48–49.

the taste of the new bread." The phrase suggests the bread of Christ's body, which, like the wine of *The Rite of the Passion*, is for everyone. It suggests too, since Mother Myrrh eats without killing, the crucifixion with the resurrection implicit in it, and, since she is Hell, the harrowing of Hell. The play ends in adoration in which all the characters—including the Third King and Mother Myrrh (like Judas in *The Rite of the Passion*)—take part.

Judgement at Chelmsford (1939) was written to be performed at the New Scala Theatre, London, in celebration of the twenty-fifth anniversary of the diocese of Chelmsford, but the coming of the war prevented its presentation. Essentially, it is a pageant play, but, as one would expect from Williams, it is more than the collection of incidents that make up the typical pageant. Williams describes what he hoped to do in a note at the beginning of the published play:

"Judgement at Chelmsford," unlike most pageants, combines all its Episodes into a complete whole. Each, therefore, must be understood not as a separate incident, but as an incident related to all the others and to the final climax. Each episode also has, for those who care to take it so, two sides: the historical and the spiritual. Thus the complete pageant offers a representation not only of the history of the diocese, but of the movement of the soul of man in its journey from the things of this world to the heavenly city of Almighty God.

In the play, Chelmsford comes (on her birthday) to the Gates of Heaven to join the ancient Sees (Canterbury, Rome, Constantinople, Antioch, Jerusalem), but she is stopped by The Accuser, whose job is to show the truth. St. Cedd, who first brought Christ to Essex, is called as her defender. The episodes are the evidence for and against her admission. Episode I shows the church in modern times, a priest who can offer only self-denial to a young girl who is intent on life. Much of the emphasis here is on the chatter of volunteer church workers with unlikely schemes to bring the young people back to the church. The underlying idea, which is so far underlying that it is quite invisible, is that God, too, is working through these halfhearted gestures. The idea is not presented dramatically; it exists only in St. Cedd's summary words, "God, for his reasons, did not choose to bless/ everyone with the violence of grace," and in Williams's assertion in his notes that "This episode as much as any other is therefore an assertion of Christianity."

Episode II exhibits the Chelmsford witches, denounced by Matthew Hopkins, an unsuccessful lawyer who seems to have done God's work because it paid. All of the Sees ask pardon; the persecutions are not Chelmsford's alone. Episode III turns to martyrdom and the ideas of martyrdom expressed in *Thomas Cranmer of Canterbury*. In burning the abbot, Thomas Becke, a Catholic martyr, and Rose Allen, a Prostestant martyr, at the same stake, Williams says again that it is the martyrdom and the belief that inspired it that are important to the church. "I see I was not the only one with a mission," says Rose Allen, "though indeed mine was given me by your need." St. Cedd leads into Episode IV with "perhaps the rage/ of prophets and patriarchs is no greater thing/ than in every age the mere stirring of good will." The episode shows the girls in Barking Abbey on a day of misrule practicing a play by Nicholas Udall. The Accuser enjoys the proceedings, comments that "wit/ flashes to heaven more from a full stomach . . ." and then proceeds to attack the church for failing in its earthly duty: "Where is the meat and drink meant for the poor?" Episode V, then, shows the priest John Ball leading the Peasant's Rising of 1431 and shows the hungry being driven back by the forces of the state with the tacit approval of the lords of the church. "Man finds the doctrine of exchange hard and strange," says The Accuser; once again the Sees ask pardon. Episode VI shows the martyrdom of St. Osyth, a nun killed by the Danes. About to go to beatification, Osyth describes, her vision, which expresses so many of the ideas of Williams:

> I saw the City where Love loves and is loved.
> It was striking out of earth; all the liking
> of man for man, woman for woman, man for woman
> opened outward into a glory; it ran
> out of the hidden points of the flesh and the soul
> into the whole pattern of exchange of beauty,
> and Fate free, and all luck good.

At Chelmsford's request, Osyth agrees to stay on earth, the doctrine of substitution reaching across the boundaries of time.

Episode VII brings Constantius to the court of Old King Cole (King Coel of Colchester) and to Helena. King Cole and Constantius discuss the City in a way that seems to indicate that it is Rome and again that it is greater than Rome; it is defined as Christ in the next episode. The love of Constantius and Helena, which will result in Constantine, the first Christian emperor, is in itself a portent. Constantinople says, "a million lovers/ circulate Holy Wisdom through the world,/ to be spiritual Sees of Christendom. There is/ an apostolic tradition in the blood. . . ." At this point, Chelmsford calls on Christ, "*Be quick, be quick; it is I; you love me; come,*" and The Accuser says, "Ha, sweet, have I driven you to ground at last?" In the final episode, Thomas Ken preaches of St. Helena and the Invention of the Cross; his message is that each man must make a journey to Jerusalem as St. Helena did, but not physically as she did, and that each must find the cross: "But find you the Cross within you. . . ." In the Epilogue, Chelmsford, "leaning happily on the Cross," calls on all the characters in the pageant episodes, who have been in and of Chelmsford before it was Chelmsford, "Answer then, I for you and you for me—/ all you my past, all you my present, all/ you invisible powers that shall yet be my future./ Say, shall I name the glory, in you and for you?" They agree. The Accuser, who has said of himself early in the play, "God made me to be the image of each man's desire—/ a king or a poet or a devil—and rarely Christ./ Most men when at last they see their desire,/ fall to repentance—all have that chance," now becomes The Lover. He is the Skeleton again from *Thomas Cranmer of Canterbury*—"the Judas who betrays all men to God." As The Lover, he leads Chelmsford to the Great Sees, who welcome her. Chelmsford, who has been seen at her worst in the witch hunts and in the hunger of the poor, and at her best in the martyrdoms and in the simple pleasures of Barking Abbey, must finally go beyond these events—in which, whether good or evil, Christendom operates—to call directly on Christ. "All who are in her, past, present, and to come unite themselves to her in the great exchange of mortal and divine love through the Incarnation and Atonement," Williams writes. His point is easily understandable as an historical statement of the growth of a Christian diocese; for him, it is just as simply true as a statement of the human soul's journey to salvation.

In 1939, when the Oxford University Press moved its wartime headquarters from London to Oxford, Williams began an association with Ruth Spalding's Oxford branch of the Pilgrim Players which resulted in three plays—*The Death of Good Fortune* (1939), *The House by the Stable* (1939), and *Grab and Grace* (1941). *The Death of Good Fortune*, which is called a Christmas play, is a dramatic illustration of two of Williams's favorite ideas—as Mary puts it in the play, "that all substance is love, all luck is good." Good Fortune rules briefly, on the sufferance of Mary, making the lover lucky in his love, the king in his kingdom, the old woman in her desire to escape her daughter-in-law, even the magician in his magic. He is accepted as a god, and even Mary admits that there is deity in him: "his nature is heavenly,/ but when men fell, he was half-blinded;/ he does not know himself nor do men know him." Only the Magician's daughter doubts him: "Can you, father, or your new god Good Luck/ help me in a world where despair only is true?" Good Fortune dies, for being a god he must die within the Christian framework of this play, and out of the despair of his believers, Mary bids him rise again. He comes alive by stages, stopping "Under a shape crucified and burning," and again before Mary and her child enthroned. Good Fortune, newly alive, accepts that all luck is good and asks "who moves with me to welcome all chances that may come?" The Magician follows out of knowledge ("This I know, if I do not believe: here am I.") and the Lover and the Girl out of faith ("this we believe, if we do not know: here are we."); the king and the old woman cannot accept the new definition of Good Fortune. They depart with Mary's benediction: "You have chosen your ways; be blessed; go with God." The lesson is ended; Mary has shown what she announced at the beginning of the play, that the god Good Fortune would suffer a change and that:

> Nor anywhere, for any flood of shed blood,
> sharp single anguish, or long languish of grief,
> shall any deny my work, or the great cry
> to every man upon earth of my lord your Son—
> all chance is heavenly, all luck is good.

The House by the Stable, another Nativity, is simpler in verse and story than most of Williams's plays. Man, the play's protagonist, is—for all the abstract name—Williams's most endearing character, the one with whom an audience can most easily identify. In *Judgement at Chelmsford*, the interest lies in the intellectual working-out of the soul's salvation; in *The House by the Stable* it is the struggle for Man's soul and his double allegiance to Hell and God that give the play its power. Even though an audience knows that no religious playwright is likely to allow a character called Man to be damned, *The House by the Stable* is constructed so that the outcome seems always in doubt. The comparative simplicity of the play and its genuine dramatic qualities—as well as its fondness for occasionally funny spiritual jokes—make it Williams's most popular play, the one most likely to be given by religious drama groups.

In the play, Man is the master of his house, living in sin—"You are man, the lord of this great house Earth,/ or (as its name is called in my country) Sin"—with a lovely lady named Pride. Man vacillates between an uncertain humility and a noisy braggadocio; Pride, of course, flatters him, fostering the latter: "before you came, Pride, I was half-afraid/ that someone or something had been before me, and made/ me and my house, and could ruin or cast aside." Hell, Pride's brother, comes and offers to give Man his house. In his description of his estate, Hell says, "The air provokes/ hunger often—you are so sharp-set/ you could almost eat yourself," a speech that suggests damnation as a kind of self-devouring process, but that also hints at communion, the eating of Man-God, as the escape from the hunger of Hell. Man, not wanting to accept an outright gift from Hell, decides to shoot dice with him for his estate, and, at Hell's suggestion, he puts up a small stake to make the contest interesting—an insignificant old jewel which he has not seem for a long time. The jewel is Man's soul. In the midst of the game, Joseph and Mary come to the door and Man is tempted to give them shelter in the house, but "my Pride will not stomach it." He does give them the stable and a crust of bread. Before the third, the deciding throw of the dice, Man goes out in answer to the calls of Joseph and Mary, leaving his butler (Gabriel) to finish the game; Hell is defeated. Out in the stable, Man sees the child and, wanting to give it a present, remembers that the missing jewel is on a string around his neck. He offers his soul to the child. Man's salvation in the play comes, as it should in a Nativity, through the birth, and Williams chooses to show divine intervention in the figure of a dice-shooting Gabriel. Yet, the fact that Man offers Mary shelter, however casual the offer, indicates that he half-willed his own salvation. In *Thomas Cranmer of Canterbury* and *Judgement at Chelmsford*, Williams has already dealt more specifically with instances of the attempts of such an unconscious desire to fulfill itself; in *The House by the Stable*, the idea is simply suggested.

Grab and Grace, or It's the Second Step is a sequel to *The House by the Stable*. In it, Gabriel can no longer interfere to save Man; the birth has taken place. Man must now decide to reject Hell and Pride on his own. Before the play opens, Immanuel, the baby born that night in the stable, has been killed by Man in an unfortunate incident which he would like to forget. Immanuel has left with Man two friends—Faith, a bright young woman, and Grace, a lively little boy. Pride—who now dresses simply and calls herself Self-Respect—and Hell come back, after having wandered for a hundred years, prepared to make a new assault on Man. Faith, who is Pride's opponent, is trapped and put into a sack, but Grace sees the movement within it and thus calls attention to her predicament. "Faith in a bag is Faith at her best," Grace says; she cuts her way out and then fights and defeats Pride. Man then orders Hell and Pride to go, a decision that is painful because he sincerely loves Pride. Faith promises to be at hand if he wants her, offers him the comfort that she has: "The Peace be with you,/ And Love which is all substance in all things made." The play ends on Man's last bewildered words: "A second step . . . a second step in love . . ./ What, O almighty Christ, what of the third?" Even here, where the emphasis is on the pain of Man's own rejection of Hell and Pride, he cannot take the step without the presence of Grace; it is the boy, after all, who discovers Faith in the bag. Faith is not strong enough to escape until Grace has called attention to her hidden existence.

The House of the Octopus, Williams's last play (published 1945), was written for the United Council for Missionary Education. Williams's missionary play is more typical of him than it is of the ordinary pious praise of missionary work. The play deals with a Christian community, under the direction of the missionary priest Father Anthony, on an island that is threatened by the forces of P'o-l'u, which represents spiritual rather than political power.[23] Under the pressure of events, Anthony and Assantu, a nominal Christian who really worships his tribal gods, are forced to see themselves as they are. Their unmasking is accomplished by means of a vice character like the Skeleton in *Thomas Cranmer of Canterbury*—The Flame, who is specifically identified with the Pentecostal fire. The Flame, who is sometimes seen by the characters, sometimes only heard by them, forms and controls the action. The Flame can inspire Assantu to act for his tribal gods as easily as he can inspire the Christians. For Williams, this interpretation of The Flame is more than a dramatic convention. In *The Descent of the Dove*, in describing the Church's putting-down of the Montanist heresy, he writes: "It refused (if the phrase may be allowed) the irresponsible outbreaks and the moral extremism of the Holy Ghost for the established formulae and the moral discipline of Messias."[24]

In Act I of *The House of the Octopus*, as the forces of P'o-l'u approach, the community convinces Father Anthony that he should escape. Assantu sees this moment as a chance to declare himself; he kills Anthony's intended guide and offers himself as a replacement, hoping to sell Anthony to P'o-l'u and thus to restore the tribal gods to their ancient power. Assantu's gods incidentally demand human sacrifices whose bodies they supposedly eat, and they allow the makers of the sacrifices to walk freely among them,

[23] Charles Williams, *The House of the Octopus*, London, Edinburgh House Press, 1945, p. 5. Writing during World War II, Williams wished to make clear that his play was not a political allegory, that P'o-l'u was not Nazi Germany. He also used P'o-l'u in the Taliessin poems; see "The Vision of the Empire," where the word is spelled P'o-lu. Charles Williams, *Taliessin through Logres*, London, Oxford, [1954], pp. 12–13.
[24] Williams, *The Descent of the Dove*, p. 34.

finally to become eaters; running through the play, although seldom specifically, is the suggestion of the opposition between Assantu's eating gods and the Christian God who gives Himself to be eaten. Anthony, who does not really believe that the community can stand without him, reluctantly consents to go with Assantu. When, in Act II, the conquerors arrive, only a young girl, Alayu, breaks down under the threat of being fed to the octopi of P'o-l'u; in her moment of apostasy, she is accidentally killed by one of the soldiers. The bulk of Act II deals with the spiritual struggles of Anthony. The Marshal of P'o-l'u offers him the chance to go on preaching if he substitutes the name of the P'o-l'u god for that of the Christians, and he is tempted. The Flame uses Anthony's own temptations against him, assuring him that although the name might not be of importance to God, man must still be willing to live and die by such names. Here, again is the attitude toward martyrdom that Williams uses in *Thomas Cranmer of Canterbury* and *Judgement at Chelmsford*.

Along with his struggle with himself over the Marshal's suggestion, Anthony must fight the community which cannot accept the priest's matter-of-fact dismissal of the dead Alayu as an apostate. Siru, one of the leaders of the community, argues that Alayu's death cry might have been a cry of rebirth, that mortals cannot know what moments in time are important to God. Anthony finally dismisses Siru's arguments by insisting that he is the one to decide. Here, then, is the heart of Anthony's problem. He sees himself, and not God, as the controlling force in the community. He is forced (by The Flame, for this is a dream section of the act) to admit that he does not want the community to live for God, except through him. In the same kind of self-revelatory dream, Assantu finally says that he wants to eat, not to be eaten. He and Anthony, each in terms of his own religion, are pushed by the same desire—not to serve gods, but to become them. In the last act, the spirit of Alayu saves Anthony from an attack by Assantu.

The oppressors—forced to abandon their plan to convert the Christians to P'o-l'u—decide to machine gun their captives; in the moments that remain, Anthony, who sees himself clearly now, forgives Alayu her apostasy. The only survivor of the massacre is Torna, the youngest of the community, who drags himself into the forest to live and to carry on through The Flame. *The House of the Octopus* provides more action on stage than any other of William's plays, and yet it is Anthony's struggle within himself, his dialogue with The Flame, that gives the play its best moments.

Williams also wrote two unpublished plays—the prose *Terror of Light*, which he hoped to rewrite in verse, and the radio play *The Three Temptations*—both written after the beginning of the war.[25] He is—as the descriptions of his plays indicate—a playwright whose audience is limited. Although his manipulation of ideas through symbolic figures is likely to attract an audience composed of those who are drawn to imaginative constructions of myth and image, his personal concern with abstract and abstruse spiritual concepts is just as likely to hold off the man who finds myth attractive but distrusts an author too much preoccupied with his own myth. On the other hand, those who share Williams's belief may also have trouble accepting him. R. H. Ward, himself a religious playwright, expresses something of this distrust of Williams in a generally admiring review of *Seed of Adam and Other Plays*. All four plays, Ward says,

express his curious personality as clearly, and as subjectively, as any of his writings: his individual sense of rhythm, his unusual uses of words, his tendency to exhibitionism and the difficult for its own sake, his odd quirks of thought—and indeed, belief; among which one could cite his forgetfulness . . . of the fact that the Son of God was also the son of man, and only significant as the one by reason of being the other. Whence, it may be, the curious absence of *caritas* from the work of a

[25] Both plays mentioned, Ridler, "Introduction," Williams, *Seed of Adam and Other Plays*, p. ix.

soul as little *naturaliter Christiana* as a distinguished Christian poet's could well be.[26]

On the matter of style, Ward has a valid point. Whether or not Williams is actually attracted to the unusual for its own sake— and a book like *The Descent of the Dove* seems to indicate that he is not, that his style is the natural complement of his thought— theatrical production is likely to underline the difficulty of his work, to hint at the "exhibitionism" which seems to distress Ward. His fondness for internal rhyme quite naturally turns up phrases in which he appears to be straining for effect, and such jarrings on the ear are likely to stay with the listener longer than the felicitous phrases. At their best, Williams's sentences are complicated, their rhythm unusual, his verse difficult to read; the demands that he makes on an actor are greater than those of any other modern writer of theatrical verse. Ward's own verse, for instance, overrich and rhetorical as it is, is simple by comparison —a poetry for intoning. Williams, as a dramatic poet, suffers chiefly from the fact that his verse demands attention. His rhythm does not lull and his meaning does not come simply. In this case, his limitation may well be his virtue.

The theological charge that Ward brings against Williams— that Williams has forgotten the dual nature of Christ, his manhood as well as his godhead—is interesting mainly because it is not true. In play after play, Williams celebrates Christ's double nature. In *The Rite of the Passion*, the Herald says, "God is he . . . Man is he." In *Seed of Adam*, Joseph says, "Father Adam, come in; here is your child,/ here is the Son of Man, here is Paradise." In *Judgement at Chelmsford*, St. Cedd speaks of "the work of Man's Son,/ God's Son, Christ of the double Nature. . . ." The other plays could also yield examples. In finding that Williams has forgotten Christ as Man, in insisting that he lacks *caritas* (when no

[26] R. H. Ward, "Imagination Breaks Through," *Christian Drama*, I, 5 (April, 1949).

other playwright has had so much to say about love), Ward seems to be reacting unfavorably to Williams's forbiddingly cerebral approach to religion. There is no doubt that Williams feels deeply about the relationship of man to man (witness his demand in *Judgement at Chelmsford* that the church fulfil its social duty, his insistence in the same play and in *The Death of Good Fortune* that the love of man for woman is part of a greater love, and his characterization of and obvious affection for Man in *The House by the Stable* and even of Cranmer), but since he chooses to work with abstractions, his plays obviously fail to have the direct emotional impact of a drama in which an audience can identify itself with the characters. Williams's intellectual approach to his subject does not show that he lacks *caritas*. The way in which Williams plays with ideas, manipulates them so that they form new complexes and give new understanding indicates that, for him, ideas have emotional meaning; the mind and the heart, for Williams, are not as separate as Ward implies. William's originality—as Ward's criticism indicates—may narrow the breadth of his appeal, but he remains not only the most original, but also the most exciting of the modern religious playwrights.

Dorothy L. Sayers. Dorothy L. Sayers is as intellectual in her approach to drama as Charles Williams is in the writing of his plays, yet there is nothing about her work that could possibly make R. H. Ward suspect her of doubting Christ's humanity. The intellectual attitude that is obvious in her essay "Towards a Christian Aesthetic,"[27] in which she offers a trinitarian view of the creative act (experience–expression–recognition) to place it more securely as a part of and an image of the Christian doctrine of creation, stops at the point of writing. Her religious plays, for all the supernatural framework of some of them and the dogmatic

[27] Dorothy L. Sayers, *Unpopular Opinions,* New York, Harcourt, Brace, [1947], pp. 30–47.

theology that informs all of them, are as concerned as, say, those of Laurence Housman with the human aspects of the religious experience. Unlike Housman, however, Miss Sayers is not uncertain about her belief. In fact, in the Introduction to *The Man Born to Be King*, she points out that her theology is the solid base from which she operates as a playwright: "A loose and sentimental theology begets loose and sentimental art-forms; an illogical theology lands one in illogical situations; an ill-balanced theology issues in false emphasis and absurdity."[28] Miss Sayers writes as a confirmed Anglican, in the light of a faith that is expressed most succinctly in her essay "What Do We Believe?" in which she outlines her faith in its relation to the Nicene Creed.[29]

Miss Sayers, the creator of Lord Peter Wimsey, better known for her murder mysteries than for her plays, began her career as a religious playwright with *The Zeal of Thy House*, the Canterbury Festival play of 1937. The year before with the help of M. St. Clare Byrne she had adapted one of her mystery stories, *Busman's Holiday*, [30] for the stage, but it, like the later, unpublished satirical comedy *Love All* (1940),[31] is not particularly relevant to the religious theater. Almost twenty years before *The Zeal of Thy House*, however, Miss Sayers made an attempt at a miracle play— *The Mocking of Christ* (1918). This short play, which appeared in her *Catholic Tales and Christian Songs*, a collection of religious poetry was plainly never intended for acting. Written in verse, of which the meter suggests medieval models, the play presents the Persona Dei just before the crucifixion. The mockery of the soldiers is extended to include a long parade of nominal Christians who mock Christ by insisting that He be as they imagine He should. A pope, a king, and an emperor come to turn Him into a symbol of their temporal power; a bishop gives Him gaiters, and

[28] Dorothy L. Sayers, *The Man Born to Be King*, New York, Harper, [1943], p. 3.
[29] Sayers, *Unpopular Opinions*, pp. 14–18.
[30] Reviewed, *The Times* (London), December 17, 1936, p. 14.
[31] Reviewed, *The Times* (London), April 10, 1940, p. 6.

a preacher provides Him with a black robe and a Bible; modern young curates offer Him tea cups or cricket bats; anthropological critics call Him Dionysus or Osiris. In the end the Persona Dei is left alone; he speaks, "Now that I must come to die/ Nought is left of Me, save I/ Discrownèd, stript, alone. . . ." The essential nature of the Christ, the play insists, is the incarnation and the crucifixion. Of all the figures that come to mock the Persona Dei, the one that is most interesting in relation to Miss Sayers's later work is the Sentimental Person, who wants to prettify Christ. One of the things that Miss Sayers was to try to avoid most insistently in *The Man Born to Be King* was the water-color depiction of Jesus that one finds on the covers of Sunday School lessons.

The Zeal of Thy House tells the story of William of Sens and the rebuilding of the burned Canterbury Cathedral in the twelfth century. William is presented as a dedicated craftsman ("all the truth of the craftsman is in his craft./ Where there is truth, there is God. . . .") who is indifferent to standard morality. While he is working on the cathedral, he has an affair with Ursula, a Canterbury lady of quality who has allowed her devotion to the church to be transferred to its architect. A group of archangels (Gabriel, Michael, Raphael, Cassiel), who have helped in choosing William in Part I of the play, oversee the injuring of him in Part III; he falls from a scaffold because the workman and the priest have not checked the rope carefully enough. Father Theodatus, the puritan among the Canterbury priests, imagines that William's fall is a punishment for his carnal sins, but Miss Sayers's intention is to show the audience and William that his real sin is greater. He stays, suffering, and directs the workers from a pallet, unable to conceive of the work's being completed without him, until Michael appears to him in a dream and explains that even God, as Christ, left his work for another (many others) to finish. At this point, William cries out, "Oh, I have sinned. The eldest sin of all,/ Pride, that struck down the morning star from Heaven/ Hath struck down me . . ." He accepts at last that his work is, not his, but God's—"But let my work, all that was good in me,/ All that was God, stand up and live and grow"—and goes back to France, leaving the cathedral to be finished by others. The play is designed to make Miss Sayers's point about the individual act of creativity as part of the universal act of creation and the historical fact of William's accident allows her to do so. The difficulty with the play is that William as a self-satisfied artist is more believable as a character than the repentant William at the end. The play as a whole suffers from Miss Sayers's infelicity with verse and from the presence of the archangelic commentators. The trouble with the archangels is not their function, but their speeches, which seem to be divided equally between the sententious and the playful. The depiction of the priests of Canterbury suffers, too, from an excess of cuteness.

He That Should Come (1938) is a Nativity play, written originally for broadcasting, which is designed, the playwright says, "to show the birth of Christ against its crowded social and historical background. . . ."[32] The play opens with a poetic prologue in which the wise men, following the star, seek, each for a particular thing. Caspar wants "the ultimate wisdom"; Melchior, "a religion that works . . . good government,/ A reasonable way of life, within the terms of the illusion"; Balthazar, "the assurance that I am not alone." Their search fades into a prose play, the random activity of the crowded inn-yard into which Joseph and Mary come, into which Jesus is born. "The whole idea in writing it was to show the miracle that was to change the whole course of human life enacted in a world casual, inattentive, contemptuous, absorbed in its own affairs. . . ."[33] The inn-yard is peopled with types: a merchant, a Greek sampler of religions, a young Jewish gentleman who embodies both the Jewish and the Greek tradi-

[32] Dorothy L. Sayers, *Four Sacred Plays*, London, Gollancz, 1948, p. 215.
[33] *Ibid.*, p. 218.

tions, a nationalistic Pharisee, a centurion. They argue among themselves, each indicating that he is searching for something, none of them aware that the goal of their quests is being born in the stable behind them. Yet the birth of the baby cheers them, as the birth of any baby might cheer anyone within its immediate neighborhood. The shepherds who have been in earlier for a drink come back, full of the angelic news of the birth, to offer adoration, but their message is ignored by the inn-yard. The play closes with the wise men, who define the end of their journey. Caspar says, "I looked for wisdom—and behold! the wisdom of the innocent"; Melchior, "I looked for power—and behold! the power of the helpless"; Balthazar, "I looked for the manhood of God—and behold! a God made man." As is customary with realistic Nativity plays, that of Miss Sayers is full of annoying presages of what is to come. The young Jewish Gentleman says, "But if ever your Son and I should meet again, I will have a rich gift ready for him," and, of course, the young man turns out to be Joseph of Arimathea. He also says earlier of births in general and of this one in particular, "And everytime his parents are persuaded that he's going to turn out something wonderful, whereas, if they only knew it, he's destined, as likely as not, to finish up between two thieves on Crucifixion Hill." Miss Sayers, reiterating the play's intention, says, ". . . it is of the utmost importance to remind people by every means in our power that the thing actually happened—that it is, and was from the beginning, closely in contact with real life."[34] The unfortunate fact is that the inn-yard is full of characters who speak lines full of anachronistic references to the Home Office, colleges, etc., and Jesus manages to be born, not among people, but among stage clichés. The one interesting idea in the play can be found in two songs that come in the midst of all the talk. The Greek sings of Apollo ("Immortal born of mortal birth") and Joseph of Arimathea sings of the new tree that grew from the stone of the fruit of the fall of Adam and Eve. The myths apparently become one in Jesus and the idea of Jesus as half-Greek, although familiar to scholars, is unusual to Nativity plays.

The Devil to Pay (1939), is a retelling of the Faust legend, modern in concept, but written for a pseudo-medieval stage set—Hell's mouth at one side; Heaven at the other. Miss Sayers explains her concept of Faustus in the Preface to the play:[35]

> Looking with the eyes of to-day upon that legendary figure of the man who bartered away his soul, I see in him the type of the impulsive reformer, oversensitive to suffering, impatient of the facts, eager to set the world right by a sudden overthrow, in his own strength and regardless of the ineluctable nature of things. When he finds it is not to be done, he falls into despair (or to use the current term, into "defeatism") and takes flight into phantasy.

Faustus is shown as a healer and a preacher against God and the church: "If God made all things, He made the evil that torments you, and why should you serve so cruel a master? If He made not all things, He is not God, and you may defy Him as I do." The Pope (how Marlowe's slapstick scene has been transmuted!) speaks to Faustus and attempts to show him that the world cannot be saved by a sudden act of revolution, not even spiritual revolution. Faustus refuses the message; he attempts to kill the Pope with a crucifix. His increasing knowledge that the good he has done in the world has not brought happiness causes Faust to sell his soul to Mephistopheles: "Undo the sin of Adam, turn the years/ Back to their primal innocence." Without the knowledge of good and evil, Faustus loses all moral sense and is pictured manipulating a bloody battle just for amusement. In the last scene of the play, the dead Faustus is brought before the court of Heaven, charged with selling something that was not his (his

[35] Sayers, *Four Sacred Plays,* p. 113.

soul) and with giving debased value (after twenty-four years of primal innocence his soul has become a small black dog— beastliness). He cries out to Christ, and, after much discussion of the nature of Mephistopheles ("I am the price that all things pay for being,/The shadow on the world, thrown by the world/ Standing in its own light, which light God is."), Faustus is saved. Although Miss Sayers's idea of Faustus is an interesting one, the play suffers from a failure to bring together the divergent materials that fill it. The random activity of Wagner and Lisa (this play's Margaret), who supposedly carry on Faustus's good works in the pre-Mephistophelean way, is never given the integral importance that it occasionally suggests. The eventual saving of Faustus comes about largely through the definition of Mephistopheles. Miss Sayers says, "Has Evil any real existence, viewed *sub specie aeternitatis*? I have suggested that it has not; but that it is indissolubly linked with the concept of value in the material and temporal aspect of the universe."[36] Although the end of the play may make a theological point that interests its author, it seems to be an accretion on the action of the play.

The Man Born to Be King (1942) is Miss Sayers's best-known dramatic work. It is a cycle of twelve radio plays on the life of Christ, written at the request of the B.B.C. Since the radio is not subject to the Lord Chamberlain's censorship, Jesus is allowed to take part in his own story. The primary intention of *The Man Born to Be King*, as of *He That Should Come*, is to emphasize the humanity of Christ by focusing attention on his life in its historical setting. The playwright is careful to save Christ from those who do not want to soil him with human life: "Not Herod, not Caiaphas, not Pilate, not Judas ever contrived to fasten upon Jesus Christ the reproach of insipidity; that final indignity was left for pious hands to inflict."[37] In depicting the historical Jesus, Miss Sayers

---

[36] Sayers, *Four Sacred Plays*, p. 114.
[37] Sayers, *The Man Born to Be King*, p. 21.

necessarily adopts the naturalistic approach, the simple prose play that closely follows the biblical events. Her main additions come in her ordering of events into individual plays and in the characterization that she gives biblical figures in the light of the scholar's knowledge of the political and social framework of the times.

The first play, *Kings in Judaea*, is the Nativity. The presence of the adoring kings gives this play a less naturalistic, more symbolic tone than is to be found in those that follow, for conventionally the wise men represent wisdom, power and sorrow. Herod is shown here as an aging and suspicious king who has held Judaea together for thirty years and who is beginning to collapse under the strain. *The King's Herald* brings Jesus to John the Baptist for baptism and brings John's disciples—James, John, Andrew, and Judas—to Jesus. In this play, Miss Sayers introduced Baruch the Zealot, her one important fictional character, who represents the Jewish hope of political salvation from Rome. In her notes, she describes Judas, whose few lines in this play do not indicate the character whom she describes:

He, is infinitely the most intelligent of all the disciples. . . . He can see the political possibilities of the Kingdom—but also, he can see at once (as none of the others can) the meaning of sin and repentance and the fearful paradox by which all human good is corrupted as soon as it comes to power. He is as yet only beginning to see it—but presently he will see it plainly, and be the only disciple to grasp the necessity of the crucifixion. . . . He has the greatest possibilities of them all for good, and therefore for evil.

Jesus's mission is begun in *A Certain Nobleman*, in which He cures Benjamin's son and in which He suggests His identity in a speech to His mother at the wedding in Cana: "Woman, why do you trouble me? What am I to you?" Here, too, the opposition to Jesus is first articulated in an argument which He has with the

Elders, two of whom are "the nastiest type of ecclesiastic—impervious to new ideas and resentful of new men."

The Heirs of the Kingdom centers on the disciples, presenting Matthew as a stereotyped Jewish-Cockney moneylender. The first glimpse of a concerted plan to get rid of Jesus is indicated in a meeting at the house of Caiaphas ("the complete ecclesiastical politician—a plausible and nasty piece of work"), at which Baruch, who wishes either to use Jesus for his political ends or to destroy him, suggests that Judas may be the weak link. Baruch (and Miss Sayers) dismiss the possibility that he is approachable by threat or bribery, "But, he may be led into deceiving himself with specious arguments. That is the weakness of clever people. Intellectual dishonesty springing from intellectual pride—the sin by which Adam fell." Miss Sayers's Judas is a brother to her Faustus and her William of Sens. The theme of the fifth play, *The Bread of Heaven,*

centres round a sort of suggestion that the threefold temptation of the Devil is here repeated and forced each time to a refusal and a challenge. There is a refusal to exploit (1) popularity from material benefits (healing and feeding), (2) signs and wonders (walking on the sea), (3) offers of world power (the kingship offered and rejected). All this is met by the deliberate and almost violent challenge about the living bread, which affronts everything that the common man could desire or religious tradition hold sacred. This brings the desertion of the idle curious or the timid, the searching-out of the weak and strong elements among the disciples, and the certainty that salvation will have to come by way of the cross.

The action of the play involves the familiar miracle of the loaves and the incident of Peter's attempt to walk on water. Judas begins to suspect Jesus's steady refusal to accept anything but the end for which He has come, partly because Philip has been able to perform a miracle where Judas has not and partly because

Baruch has planted the seeds of doubt in Judas's mind. When Baruch says, "on the day you see Jesus Carpenter ride into Jerusalem with palms waving and the people yelling Hosanna— remember, I told you so," Judas answers, "If I thought you were right, I would kill him with my hands while he was still uncorrupted." Judas's acceptance of Jesus's final redemptive suffering makes him doubt even Jesus's ability to hold to that purpose. The fifth play contains a good indication of the kind of unfortunate change that Miss Sayers brings to the biblical language. Her attempt to force her characters to speak ordinary, contemporary prose is a valid one in the face of so many unhappy mock-biblical plays, but the transmutation of the beatitudes into sentences beginning "Happy are . . ." is unfortunate; the familiar "blessed" has too long been associated with them.

The emphasis in the sixth play, *The Feast of Tabernacles*, is on Jesus as God; it contains, among many incidents, a description of the Transfiguration. Here, too, are the fears of Jesus's followers and the machinations which finally bring Judas to Caiaphas. *The Light and the Life* "presents two sharp contrasts: (1) That between the will to life and the will to death . . . (2) That between trust and mistrust." The first is indicated in the story of Lazarus; the second in the further development of Judas: "He has now worked himself up into a state of mind where he is quite incapable of taking Christ's word for anything." In *Royal Progress*, Baruch makes an attempt to win Jesus's support. The Zealot tells Jesus to ride a horse on His entry into Jerusalem if he wants military backing; an ass if His way is peaceful. Judas intercepts Jesus's message ("To-morrow he shall have the sign he looks for.") and takes it to mean simply that Jesus has decided to become Baruch's political Messiah. He goes to Caiaphas, who speaks prophecy when he imagines he is simply being the politically astute man, able to convince Judas of what he wants to know: "Alive, he is an ordinary demagogue with all the failings of his class; dead, he is an idea—a symbol—the spirit of martyred Jewry, purged of all human dross and frailty." Miss Sayers faces in this play the necessity of explaining away the thirty pieces of silver, since they seem unlikely to the Judas that she has portrayed. She has him demand money because "I will believe in nothing but what I can see and handle. All men are liars—only *things* cannot lie." His sin of pride begets smaller sins and less attractive ones.

The ninth play, *The King's Supper* contains the last supper, the agony in Gethsemane, and the betrayal with the kiss. *The Princes of the World* brings Jesus before the Sanhedrin, before Herod, twice before Pilate, to mockery and the crown of thorns, finally to condemnation. Throughout the play there is a running conflict between Caiaphas and Pilate that places the trial of Jesus in the ironical light of practical politics. In this play, too, Judas learns the truth from Baruch, who taunts him ("Will you testify from the cross?") and discovers the truth about himself ("I was in love with suffering, because I wanted to see him suffer."). *King of Sorrows* takes Jesus to the cross. Miss Sayers's version has a number of genuinely interesting inventions, from the inspired bit of abuse thrown at Jesus as he collapses under the weight of the cross ("Take up your cross and walk!") to the conception of Dysmas, the second thief, as a compassionate man trying to comfort a harmless madman. "I have affronted all the preachers and commentators by making his 'Lord, remember me—' an act, not of faith, but of charity," she says in her notes. The play is also in some sense an apologia for Caiaphas, who is seen as having acted for valid political reasons in an attempt to save Israel from being swallowed either by Rome or by the spiritual kingdom that Christ brought. "Be content, Jesus, my enemy," he says. "Caiaphas also will have lived in vain." The last play of the cycle, *The King Comes to His Own*, deals with the resurrection and the ascension. Miss Sayers says of her attempts to telescope nine supernatural appearances into one play, "this play contains a good deal about doors, and knocking at doors. It is, in fact, a play about the door between two worlds."

The Man Born to Be King as a complete play suffers in comparison to the cycle as a conception. The very novelistic notes that accompany the printed play give a development of character, particularly of Judas, that the plays are incapable of giving. The relationships that Miss Sayers finds between particular Bible stories which make her bring them together in one sequence is not always clear in the drama itself, although her comments on the stories are usually revelatory. The depiction of Judas, the most subtle and interesting thing in the play, is in one sense unfortunate. The reaction to *The Man Born to Be King* is not one of what will Jesus do next, but one of what will Judas do next. The villain, as he so often does in the theater, steals the limelight from the hero. This fact, although not necessarily a dramatic drawback, is certainly unfortunate from the standpoint of the religious writer.

The Just Vengeance (1946), performed in Lichfield Cathedral at the 750th Anniversary Festival, is a "miracle-play of Man's insufficiency and God's redemptive act, set against the background of contemporary crisis," [38] An airman dies, his plane crashing on Lichfield, and the action of the play takes place in the moment of his death. The airman is greeted by George Fox, who had a vision in Lichfield in 1651, with "Thou art within the city. . . . For thee it is Lichfield." It is, of course, or it will become Charles Williams's City, and Miss Sayers's chorus is out of Williams's timeless time. It is made up of Lichfielders (including Samuel Johnson) from all classes and all centuries. The Airman is looking for justification for his death: "I do not believe in all this suffering—/ I do not see the sense of a suffering God. . . ." His avowal is modern, material and temporal: "I believe in man, and in the hope of the future,/ The steady growth of knowledge and power over things,/ The equality of all labouring for the community./ And a just world

[38] Sayers, *Four Sacred Plays*, p. 280.

where everyone will be happy." He is shown images, first of Adam and Eve and of Cain's murder and then of the Persona Dei and the Passion. The first asserts the guilt of all men: "Do not you all,/ Suffer with Abel and destroy with Cain." The second reasserts that guilt by having the chorus and the Airman join in the shout, "Crucify!" The Persona Dei accepts the cry of the crowd: "Say that the guilt is Mine; give it to Me/ And I will take it away to be crucified." Only Judas, Pilate, and Caiaphas, who refuse respectively hope, faith and charity, cannot accept; they go into the desert with Cain. The Airman does accept and the Persona Dei says, "Instead of your justice, you shall have charity;/ Instead of your happiness, you shall have joy;/ Instead of your peace the emulous exchange/ Of love." The play ends as the Choir sings, "Proclaim the City! Proclaim Salvation! Proclaim Christ!" In her Introduction, Miss Sayers admits to "echoes from many other writers," particularly Williams and T. S. Eliot, whose styles she imitates.

Miss Sayers's last play is the long, tedious chronicle *The Emperor Constantine* (1951). It opens with a cryptic prophecy from King Coel of Colchester, Constantine's grandfather, and ends with a demonstration that the prophecy has come true. The last line of the prophecy, "I have seen Constantine as a swimming fish," is Constantine's dying acceptance of Christianity for himself, where before he has accepted it only for the Empire. Most of the scenes are static because Constantine is always caught at a moment that demands detailed historical exposition. Strangely, in a play full of court intrigue and war, it is the Council of Nicaea and the quarrel over "homoöusios" and "homoiousios" that generates the most dramatic power. The play is seriously marred by some terrible Cockney soldiers and by supposedly funny anachronisms like those that intrude in *He That Should Come*.

The problem with Dorothy Sayers as a playwright is that she seems incapable of moving from the experience to the expression of her own trinitarian aesthetic. Her descriptions of what she intends to do are always arresting, but the finished plays never approach the quality of the conceptions. Her difficulty is largely a literary one. Alan Fairclough has written, "As a principle the use of obtrusively modern idiomatic speech seems to have been abandoned in *The Just Vengeance*: to be replaced, unfortunately, by the echoed cadences of Mr. Eliot."[39] In that one sentence, Fairclough has caught her deficiences both as a poet and as a writer of dramatic prose. Edmund Wilson, writing about Miss Sayers as a mystery writer, says, "she is more consciously literary than most of the other detective-story writers and . . . she thus attracts attention in a field which is mostly on a subliterary level."[40] His remark is also true of Miss Sayers as a religious dramatist. Alongside the output of the average amateur religious playwright, her work looks impressive; alongside that of Charles Williams or T. S. Eliot, it appears amateurish in its own right.

Christopher Hassall. Christopher Hassall is the only playwright, other than Williams, Eliot, and Miss Sayers, to have written a play for the pre-war Canterbury Festival. *Christ's Comet* (1937), the festival play for 1938, is the story of the legendary fourth wiseman. Artaban joins the other three wise men in their journey following the star (Christ's comet), but when they learn the story of the angelic vision at Bethlehem, he sends the others ahead. He plans to wander the world (in the company of a very trying comic figure, a muleteer-poet) to make himself worthy. He comes at last to Golgotha where an angel assures him:

> His name is the Beginning and the End,
> And by enduring to the End, and winning
> Faith in your heart, you witness the Beginning.
> For those who find Truth, Truth is born in them,
> And they are witnesses at Bethlehem.

[39] Alan Fairclough, "The Just Vengeance," *Christian Drama*, I, 6 (November, 1946).
[40] Edmund Wilson, *Classics and Commercials*, New York, Farrar and Straus, 1950, p. 259.

The dying Artaban is presented with a tableau of Mary, Joseph, and the baby with the Magi. The quotation is, unfortunately, a fair sample of the verse. Twenty years later, Hassall revised the play for the 1958 Canterbury Festival. He cut three acts to two, dropped some minor characters, dropped much of the music, occasionally rewrote verse passages; although the new version is a better play than the earlier one, it is still no more than an interesting idea.

Hassall's *Devil's Dyke* (1936), his earliest attempt at religious drama, is a poem rather than a play; it is "composed of six tableaux, intended to have no greater dramatic value than six paintings hung side by side upon a wall. . . ."[41] In the play, Satan returns to earth, resolved to dig a dyke that will let the waters of the ocean in to destroy everything. The Spirit of the Neighbourhood ("the bond of union between God and Man, the voice of inspiration") comes to an old Shepherd ("that part of Everyman which suffers from a sense of inferiority") and assures him that he is to stop Satan. The Shepherd sits with a sword waiting for the approaching evil then a visitor drops in and asks for aid. He speaks in such an erudite fashion that the old Shepherd breaks into the Lord's Prayer, which reveals the visitor as Satan and routs him in the revelation. Even as dramatic poetry *Devil's Dyke* is hampered by parenthetic flights into the glories of nature; the nature poetry shares space with excessive declamation. At the end of the play, there is an Inscription from the poet in which he likens his ink to Christ's blood and asks God not to let it be shed in vain. The impression is one of a very bloodless Christ.

Hassall's only post-war religious play is *Out of the Whirlwind*, which was presented in Westminster Abbey in June, 1953. Dr. Opprobrius (the Devil) turns up in the Abbey to challenge John Protheroe (who has been commissioned to write a play for the

---

[41] Christopher Hassall, *Devil's Dyke with Compliment and Satire*, London, Heinemann, [1936], p. 3.

cathedral) and Canon Fountaine of Westminster to provide a
religious play in which evil is not counted out at the beginning,
in which the cards are not stacked for the triumph of heaven. The
play which follows, the struggle for the soul of Martha Gam, is
Protheroe's (and Hassall's) limp answer. In the course of a number
of scenes, running from 1914 to 1952, Martha loses her husband
in World War I, faces economic hardship during the depression,
loses her son and her best friend in World War II, and at last
suffers a stroke. Despite all this, she remains stoical (Christian is
the adjective that Hassall has in mind), but at the moment of
physical collapse the Devil tries to get her to curse God. She
begins to do so, but ends, "the Lord gave. The Lord hath taken
away. Blessed be the Name of the Lord." The Devil is defeated.
Canon Fountaine makes it clear during the last struggle that
Martha's sufferings come neither from the Devil nor from God,
but that they are the result of her being on the battle line between
the two forces, that suffering is part of the human condition. The
play ends as Fountaine reads the Collects for All Conditions of
Men from the Book of Common Prayer. The domestic scenes
have the look of ordinary West End sentimental drama; the
imaginative framework—which includes a whole troupe of miracle
players and some characters from *Henry V* as well as the Devil,
the playwright and the priest—is extremely cluttered. *Out of the
Whirlwind* seems a rather weak illustration of the quotation from
Job 38. 1, 4 which gives the play its title and its epigraph: "Then
the Lord answered Job out of the whirlwind, and said,/ Where
was thou when I laid the foundations of the earth?"

PART THREE

The Post-war Years

IX

T. S. Eliot and Christopher Fry

Norman Nicholson, himself a poet and religious playwright, describes a theme that runs through all of T. S. Eliot's work:

This theme occurs in three forms: firstly, the need for the purgation of the will; secondly, the need for the soul to divest "itself of the love of created beings"; thirdly, the aim to arrive at the experience of the Divine by the rejection of images, i.e., the Negative Way.[1]

Nicholson's description was written in 1943, before *The Cocktail Party* (1949) and *The Confidential Clerk* (1953); yet it is as true of the later plays as it is of *Murder in the Cathedral* (1935) and *The Family Reunion* (1939). It is an incomplete truth, however, an insufficient definition, valuable mainly as an approach to the central characters of the Eliot plays—Becket in *Murder in the Cathedral*, Harry in *The Family Reunion*, Celia in *The Cocktail Party* and Colby in *The Confidential Clerk*. If Eliot's heroes choose the Negative Way, there is at least the suggestion, particularly in the last two plays, that the Affirmative Way is a possibility, that the way of the Chamberlaynes in *The Cocktail Party* and of Lucasta and B. Kaghan in *The Confidential Clerk* is as acceptable—although the acceptability is of a different order—as that of Celia and Colby. Despite the plainly defined two ways of Eliot's plays, the tone is decidedly that of the Negative Way, a tone that distresses some critics, like John Gassner, who is annoyed to find that "the sheep are categorically divided from the goats"[2] in *The Cocktail Party*.

[1] Norman Nicholson, *Man and Literature*, London, S. C. M. Press, 1943, p. 199. The quotation within the Nicholson quotation is from St. John of the Cross, Eliot's epigraph for *Sweeney Agonistes*.
[2] John Gassner, *The Theatre in Our Times*, New York, Crown, 1954, p. 101.

Although the terms are insufficient, Charles Williams's two ways to God, the Ways of the Affirmation and the Negation of Images, are a useful method of separating the two religious playwrights who have had the greatest success on the post-war commercial stage—Eliot and Christopher Fry. In defining Williams's concept of the rejection of images, Robert McAfee Brown writes, "No created thing is more than an image, an image which can become an idol, whom to serve is to be damned. So the images must be rejected."[3] Nicholson says:[4]

this was adapted by Christian mystics as a way of arriving at experience of the Godhead by the rejection of all things which were not God, i.e., the rejection of all images, analogies, all human conceptions, and the rejection of the will, even the will to attain to that experience.

This is the way of the Eliot heroes; essentially it is the way of the Eliot plays. In defining Williams's use of the affirmation of images, Brown writes, "There are 'images,' experiences, events of human life, which can testify to us of God and witness to him."[5] This is the way of Christopher Fry, who luxuriates in "the full phantasmagoria of the commonplace. . . ."[6] Williams, who influenced both playwrights, writes, "Rejection was to be rejection but not denial, as reception was to be reception but not subservience."[7] Essentially, both playwrights try to walk with Williams along the middle ground, but where Fry finds God in the world, Eliot finds Him most surely in withdrawal—into martyrdom or into Eggerson's garden in *The Confidential Clerk*. It is not surprising then that where Eliot is often admired, Fry is enjoyed; and where Eliot is rejected

[3] Robert McAfee Brown, "Charles Williams: Lay Theologian," *Theology Today*, X, 226 (July, 1953).

[4] Nicholson, *op. cit.*, p. 202.

[5] Brown, *op. cit.*, p. 225.

[6] Christopher Fry, "A Playwright Speaks," *Listener*, XLIII, 331 (February 23, 1950).

[7] Charles Williams, *The Descent of the Dove*, New York, Pellegrini and Cudahy, [1939], p. 57.

out of hand—by those who cannot accept his theology—Fry is often accepted for a religion that can be translated—against Fry's intentions—into something secular.

T. S. Eliot. Although the bulk of Eliot's dramatic work is religious, his interest in the theater antedates his conversion. It was in the Preface to *For Lancelot Andrewes* (1928) that Eliot made his famous declaration: "The general point of view may be described as classicist in literature, royalist in politics, and anglo-catholic in religion."[8] He added, "the third term does not rest with me to define."[9] As early as *The Sacred Wood* (1920), Eliot showed his interest in the drama, for there he began the examinations of the Elizabethans that were to go on through the twenties. There, too, in "The Possibility of a Poetic Drama," he somewhat prematurely dismissed the genre. Arnold Bennett reports in his *Journal* that Eliot came to him in 1924 and said that he intended to give up the kind of poetry that went into *The Waste Land*, that he "wanted to write a drama of modern life (furnished flat sort of people) in a rhythmic prose 'perhaps with certain things in it accentuated by drum-beats.' And he wanted my advice."[10] How serious Eliot was about this prose drama is doubtful; it may have been the polite invention of the young poet who wanted to elicit the aid of the older playwright for the struggling *Criterion*.

Eliot's first experiment at drama, discounting the obviously dramatic sections of *The Waste Land* (for instance, the HURRY UP PLEASE ITS TIME section of "The Game of Chess"), was *Sweeney Agonistes* (1932). The two fragments, which date back to 1926 and 1927, before the declaration in *For Lancelot Andrewes*, bring Sweeney to the house of Doris and Dusty, party girls. Like Harry in *The Family Reunion*, he has, or perhaps has not, killed a girl: "Any man has to, needs to, wants to/ Once in a lifetime, do a girl in."

[8] T. S. Eliot, *For Lancelot Andrewes*, London, Faber and Gwyer, [1928], p. ix.
[9] *Ibid.*, p. x.
[10] Arnold Bennett, *The Journal of Arnold Bennett*, New York, Viking, 1933, p. 786.

Through its double epigraph from the *Choephori* ("You don't see them, you don't—but *I* see them: they are hunting me down, I must move on.") and from St. John of the Cross ("Hence the soul cannot be possessed by the divine union, until it has divested itself of the love of created beings."), *Sweeney Agonistes* touches on the themes of the later Eliot plays—the need for withdrawal ("I'll carry you off/To a cannibal isle") and the guilt that haunts men, presumably Original Sin, which may finally lead him or drive him to the God that he seeks. "The dripping blood our only drink,/The bloody flesh our only food,"[11] Eliot says in *East Coker*, and it is a cannibal isle that Sweeney contemplates in the fragmentary play. There is no solution in *Sweeney Agonistes*, only a suggestion. The knocks on which the play ends apparently herald the Furies that Sweeney has been expecting, that the Full Chorus sings about: "And you wait for a knock and the turning of a lock for you know the hangman's waiting for you./And perhaps you're alive/ And perhaps you're dead." The knocks are the beginning of the search for God that is the subject of Eliot's poetic journey, the beginning of the search that Harry goes on in *The Family Reunion*, the play that returns with greater concreteness to the material of *Sweeney Agonistes*. In *The Use of Poetry and the Use of Criticism*, Eliot defines one of the things he was trying to do in *Sweeney Agonistes*, although he never calls the fragments by name:[12]

My intention was to have one character whose sensibility and intelligence should be on the plane of the most sensitive and intelligent members of the audience; his speeches should be addressed to them as much as to the other personages in the play—or rather, should be addressed to the latter who were to be material, literal-minded and visionless, with the consciousness of being overheard by the former.

[11] T. S. Eliot, *The Complete Poems and Plays*, New York, Harcourt, Brace, [1952], p. 128.
[12] T. S. Eliot, *The Use of Poetry and the Use of Criticism*, Cambridge, Mass., Harvard University Press, 1933, p. 147.

There was to be an understanding between this protagonist and a small number of the audience, while the rest of the audience would share the responses of the other characters in the play.

According to M. C. Bradbrook, Eliot's later plays "are built on a contrast between the Hero and the Chorus, between the man who sees and the rest who are blind."[13] If this is true, and it seems particularly valid for *The Family Reunion*, Eliot was apparently setting the pattern in *Sweeney Agonistes*.

In "The Possibility of a Poetic Drama," Eliot wrote, "Our problem should be to take a form of entertainment and subject it to the process which would leave it a form of art. Perhaps the music-hall comedian is the best material."[14] Later, he wrote, "From one point of view, the poet aspires to the conditions of the music-hall comedian."[15] He seems, in *Sweeney Agonistes*, with its jagged, jazzy songs and its end-men (Swartz and Snow), to have made a serious effort to convert the music-hall into an art form. In his first real theater piece, *The Rock* (1934), he turned for his form to another popular theatrical genre. In answering the criticism of Derek Verschoyle in *The Spectator*, Eliot said in a letter, "The 'play' makes no pretence of being a 'contribution to English dramatic literature': it is a *revue*. My only serious dramatic aim was to show that there is a possible *rôle* for the Chorus."[16] *The Rock*, which is subtitled "A Pageant Play," was written, on commission, for the Forty-five Churches Fund of the Diocese of London. It was presented at the Sadler's Wells Theatre from May 29 to June 9, 1934. Eliot claims credit for the words alone. The scenario, he says, was prepared by E. Martin Browne, who also directed it, with some historical suggestions from the Reverend R. Webb-Odell. The Reverend Vincent Howson, who

---

[13] M. C. Bradbrook, *T. S. Eliot*, London, Longmans, Green, 1950, p. 38.

[14] T. S. Eliot, *The Sacred Wood*, London, Methuen, [1953], p. 70.

[15] Eliot, *The Use of Poetry and the Use of Criticism*, p. 22.

[16] T. S. Eliot, "The Rock," a letter to *Spectator*, CLII, 887 (June 8, 1934). Verschoyle's review appeared, *Spectator*, CLII, 851 (June 1, 1934).

played the workman Ben, did so much re-writing on the work-man's speeches, Eliot says, that "he deserves the title of joint author."[17] *The Rock*, then, was like a revue in the multiplicity of its authors; the music was by Martin Shaw.

The story of *The Rock*, if it can be said to have a story, concerns the building of a particular church which goes on despite indif-ference, financial difficulties, internal squabbles, and direct attack from outside. The action is divided among three semicomic bricklayers who deliver what Eliot considers home truths ("You can't keep people off drink by tellin' 'em it's so 'armful they mustn't 'ave it; and you can't keep 'em off religion seemin'ly, by tellin' 'em it's so old-fashioned they oughtn't to want it."); historical personages (for instance, Rahere, the builder of St. Bartholomew's Church, and Nehemia at the building of the Temple in Jerusalem) who give inspiration; the opposition (the Agitator, the Redshirts, the Blackshirts, the Plutocrat); and the Chorus, which speaks "as the voice of the Church of God." Appearing throughout the action is the character of The Rock (called also The Watcher, The Stranger, The Witness, The Critic), who is revealed at the end as Peter; he it is who sets one of the main themes of the play: "*Make perfect your will.*/ I say: take no thought of the harvest,/ But only of proper sowing." As Part I closes, the Rock speaks the note of hope, "And the Gates of Hell shall not prevail./ Darkness now, then/ Light./ /Light." At the end of the play, of course, the church is built.

The Chorus touches on a number of the ideas that reappear in Eliot's other plays. *Murder in the Cathedral* is foreshadowed in "And the Son of Man was not crucified once for all,/ The blood of the martyrs was not shed once for all,/ The lives of the Saints not given once for all:/ But the Son of Man is crucified always/ And there shall be Martyrs and Saints." All the Eliot withdrawals

[17] T. S. Eliot, *The Rock*, New York, Harcourt, Brace, [1934], p. 5. All of Eliot's sharing of credits for *The Rock* appear in a "Prefatory Note" on this page.

are hinted at in "We speak to you as individual men;/ As individuals alone with God./ Alone with God, you first learn brotherhood with men." Most of Eliot's plays deal with the aloneness, not with the brotherhood, but in *The Rock* there is more social, even political content than one is ordinarily likely to find in an Eliot play. There is the direct satiric treatment of a variety of modern panaceas of the left and right. The positive social content lies in the Builder's Song ("A Church for us all and work for us all and God's world for us all even unto this last.") which is heard intermittently throughout. "There is no life that is not in community," The Chorus says, "And no community not lived in praise of God." Eliot's concern for a Christian society, a remarkably restricted and unattractive society to those who do not share his faith, is ordinarily shown in his prose works, like *After Strange Gods* (1933), that preceded *The Rock*, and *The Idea of a Christian Society* (1939), that followed it. *The Rock* is the only one of the plays that actively embodies social ideas—except by implication—and it is probably the occasion, as much as the poet, that dictates such embodiment. The plays that followed were to focus their attention more and more on the individual and his attempt to find God.

In an interview with John Lehmann almost twenty years after *The Rock*, Eliot said, "Then I remember once more feeling I'd written myself out just before 'The Rock' was commissioned. I had to write it—I had a deadline—and working on it began to make me interested in writing drama, and led directly to 'Murder in the Cathedral.'"[18] Eliot's second play, his first real play, was written for production in 1935 at the Canterbury Festival. *Murder in the Cathedral* again offered a chance to combine the political and social with the religious, but Eliot chose to focus his attention on Thomas à Becket's spiritual preparations for martyrdom rather

[18] John Lehmann, "T. S. Eliot Talks About Himself and the Drive to Create," *New York Times Book Review*, November 29, 1953, p. 5.

than on the political situation that produced the murder of the archbishop. Eliot wrote later, "I wanted to concentrate on death and martyrdom."[19] The political background is touched on briefly in the speeches of the three priests at the beginning of the play, immediately before Becket returns from France, and political expediency is presented and satirized in the scene in which the four knights ask the audience to consider that the murder was a disinterested act on their part. Two of the four tempters who come to Thomas bring worldly, i.e., political, power—one in the old alliance with King Henry, one a in new alliance with the Barons.

The heart of the play is Becket's need to face the coming martyrdom; the tempters would either have him avoid it or embrace it. "Is there no way, in my soul's sickness,/ Does not lead to damnation in pride?" he asks. It is a simple matter for him to reject the first tempter who offers the sensual and intellectual pleasures of the world and the second and third tempters with their variant offers of worldly power, even power for good. It is the fourth, the unexpected tempter against whom he must struggle, for this one brings Becket his own longing for martyrdom: "I offer what you desire. I ask/ What you have to give. Is it too much/ For such a vision of eternal grandeur?" Becket recognizes and, supposedly, rejects the fourth tempter: "The last temptation is the greatest treason:/ To do the right deed for the wrong reason." For Becket his death must be part of a pattern which he accepts and helps to create in the acceptance, but it must not be a personal desire for eternal glory. The theme is set early in the speech in which he chides the priests for shushing the Women of Canterbury:

> They know and do not know, that acting is suffering
> And suffering is action. Neither does the actor suffer
> Nor the patient act. But both are fixed

[19] T. S. Eliot, *Poetry and Drama*, Cambridge, Mass., Harvard University Press, 1951, p. 29.

In an eternal action, an eternal patience
To which all must consent that it may be willed
And which all must suffer that they may will it,
That the pattern may subsist, for the pattern is the action
And the suffering, that the wheel may turn and still
Be forever still.

Dramatically, the play is over at the end of Part I, when Becket rejects the four tempters. The Interlude (the Archbishop's Christmas sermon) and Part II are mainly concerned with emphasizing that Becket's martyrdom was a genuine, an unselfish, an impersonal act. In his sermon Becket says:

A Christian martyrdom is no accident. Saints are not made by accident. Still less is a Christian martyrdom the effect of a man's will to become a Saint, as a man by willing and contriving may become a ruler of men. . . . A martyr, a saint is always made by the design of God, for His love of men, to warn them and to lead them, to bring them back to His ways. A martyrdom is never the design of man; for the true martyr is he who has become the instrument of God, who has lost his will in the will of God, not lost it but found it, for he has found freedom in submission to God. The martyr no longer desires anything for himself, not even the glory of martyrdom.

The sermon becomes an explanation—if a beautiful one—of the death that is to come. The comic scene with the four knights completes the idea that Becket has rejected the fourth tempter. Eliot says of the prose scene with the knights, "it is intended to *shock* the audience out of their complacency,"[20] to show them apparently that the familiar voice of common sense, of reason, of political expediency can be used to reduce a martyrdom to a banality. Structurally, however, that scene has a more important function. There is no evidence within the play, except in the words of Becket himself, that the fourth tempter has been routed. The

[20] T. S. Eliot, "The Aims of Poetic Drama," *Adam*, XVII, 12 (November, 1949).

fourth knight must be used to put the final touches to that idea. E. Martin Browne, who directed the play at Canterbury, says:[21]

the Fourth Knight, for instance, in arguing that Becket is a suicide, is repeating the suggestion put into Becket's mind by the Fourth Tempter, and thereby it unifies the whole experience of Becket, showing it as a single struggle towards Christian acceptance.

More than that, the fourth knight is treated satirically ("I may, for aught I know, have been slightly under the influence of *St. Joan*,"[22] says Eliot), and so his insistence that Becket selfishly allowed himself to be killed, his persuasive "you will unhesitatingly render a verdict of Suicide while of Unsound Mind" becomes foolish and must be rejected out of hand. The fourth knight's case, however, is not an impossible one. The play does not disprove his argument; it simply states that the martyrdom is genuine. Since *Murder in the Cathedral* was written for Canterbury, for Becket's own cathedral, a prior acceptance of Becket's martyrdom by the audience is to be assumed. Unless the political archbishop is accepted as St. Thomas à Becket before the play begins, *Murder in the Cathedral* is likely to suffer from an ambiguity that Eliot probably does not intend. The play ends with a celebration of martyrdom ("We thank Thee for Thy mercies of blood, for Thy redemption by blood. For the blood of Thy martyrs and saints/ Shall enrich the earth, shall create the holy places.") so presumably the fourth knight is to be a joke and no more. It is difficult to believe that Eliot intends that his Becket should be as amusingly ambiguous a martyr as Charles Williams's Cranmer, but one of the appealing things about the play is that it can be read again and again without quite convincing the reader of the precise nature of Becket's martyrdom.

[21] E. Martin Browne, "'Murder' Comes of Age," *Christian Drama*, III, 6 (Summer, 1956).
[22] Eliot, *Poetry and Drama*, p. 30.

The Women of Canterbury, who make up the Chorus of the play, are examples of an important element in all Eliot's dramatic writing. "Forgive us, O Lord, we acknowledge ourselves as type of the common man," they say quite specifically at one point. The refrain, "Yet we have gone on living,/ Living and partly living," runs through many of their speeches. The Women are the ordinary people, those not strong enough to be saints and martyrs, those frightened of sainthood and martyrdom because the unusual, whether greatly good or greatly evil, upsets the known routine of life. For this reason, in the opening speeches the Chorus are afraid and sorrowing at Becket's return. They know ("They know and do not know . . .") that a great event is about to take place and they are not capable of dealing with it: "In life there is not time to grieve long./ But this, this is out of life, this is out of time,/ An instant eternity of evil and wrong." For Eliot, the ordinary person, even the ordinary Christian, can never do more than glimpse "The point of intersection of the timeless/ With time . . ." as he says in *The Dry Salvages*. The Women of Canterbury cry out at Becket's death, but they will return, as they must, to the routine that they have always known. As Thomas says, using exactly the words that Eliot used the same year in *Burnt Norton*, "Human kind cannot bear very much reality."

Murder in the Cathedral became the first successful modern religious play. From Canterbury, it went to the Mercury Theatre in London and then, a year later, it was revived at the Duchess Theatre. It has become the staple of the most ambitious religious and university drama groups, in the United States as well as in England. E. Martin Browne, writing in 1956, said of it, "no serious play of our century has been played so often or in such diverse settings, from theater to boys' club, from cathedral to air-raid shelter. . . ."[23] In 1952, *Murder in the Cathedral* became a film, under the direction of George Hoellering; Eliot not only added

[23] Browne, *Christian Drama*, III, 6 (Summer, 1956).

some new lines ("if it seems inferior to that of the original play, I must ask the critic to observe that I had to imitate a style which I had abandoned as unsuitable for other purposes than that of this one play. . . ."[24]), but he also read the part of the fourth tempter, who is never seen on the screen. The Old Vic revived the play in 1953, and then issued a recording of it. *Murder in the Cathedral* is certainly the most influential and the hardiest product of the revival of religious drama in England.

In *The Family Reunion*, Eliot again takes up the theme of *Sweeney Agonistes*. When Harry comes home to Wishwood, his mother's estate, he is followed by the Furies, whom he first discovers in words that echo the Aeschylean epigraph of the earlier fragments: "Look there!/ Can't you see them? *You* don't see them, but I see them. . . ." Harry's return follows on the drowning of his wife, whom he may or may not have killed ("perhaps/ I only dreamt I pushed her"), and at Wishwood, where he thought he would be safest, he is most exposed to the Furies. He has to learn in the course of the play that his family history, like that of the *Oresteia*, on which the play is based, is full of corruption and confusion. His father had married Amy, but learned to love Agatha. He had planned to kill Amy, but in the end—at Agatha's insistence—had separated from his wife in order to save the child (Harry) in her womb, a child who spiritually is Agatha's as much as Amy's. Amy, growing old, expects (or half hopes, not quite expecting) that Harry will settle down on the estate, but Agatha, who understands what is harrowing him, tells him the ancient scandal and helps to explain why his Furies should be most active at Wishwood:

> What we have written is not a story of detection,
> Of crime and punishment, but of sin and expiation.
> It is possible that you have not known what sin

[24] T. S. Eliot, "Preface" to T. S. Eliot and George Hoellering, *The Film of Murder in the Cathedral*, New York, Harcourt, Brace, [1952], p. vi.

You shall expiate, or whose, or why. It is certain
That the knowledge of it must precede the expiation.
It is possible that sin may strain and struggle
In its dark instinctive birth, to come to consciousness
And so find expurgation. It is possible
You are the consciousness of your unhappy family.

The sin that Harry must expiate is a family curse as befits a modern version of the *Oresteia*, but it is also Original Sin. After beginning to understand the Furies, Harry is able to face them ("This time, you are real, this time, you are outside me,/ And just endurable.") and even to follow them ("my business is not to run away, but to pursue"). They are the signs pointing him to the painful journey of expiation that still lies ahead in which "The knot shall be unknotted/ And the crooked made straight."

There are three levels of understanding in *The Family Reunion*. Harry is the saint or the man on the way to special spiritual knowledge. Agatha and Mary, the cousin who has always loved Harry, are unable to follow him, but they are able to understand the nature of the journey that he must make; they, too, see the Furies. Agatha says to Mary, "We must all go, each in his own direction,/ You, and I, and Harry. You and I,/ My dear, may very likely meet again/ In our wanderings in the neutral territory/ Between two worlds." They will not meet Harry, however, for he will have gone beyond them. The rest of the aunts and uncles form an uncomprehending Chorus that prefers to focus its attention always on the little incident, the polite comfort, the known situation. Their failure to understand is partly a refusal, for near the end of the play Charles says, "there is something I *could* understand, if I were told it./ But I'm not sure that I want to know." Amy, too, is unable to comprehend Harry, except insofar as her apprehension is a comprehension. The chauffeur Downing is a special character, one who seems not quite human. He suggests Pylades in the *Choephori*, who is always at Orestes's side, who speaks only in the moment in which Orestes strikes down his mother, who may be the god Apollo and not a human comrade at all. Downing, who also has seen the Furies, says, ". . . I have a kind of feeling that his Lordship won't need me/ Very long now." His prescience is more than that of an attentive servant; his "I'll never leave him so long as he requires me" suggests that he is a kind of indeterminate guardian, like Julia and Alex in *The Cocktail Party*, perhaps even a guardian angel.

The difficulty with *The Family Reunion* lies in the unpleasantness of Harry as a person. A man in spiritual torment might certainly be indifferent to those around him, and a man who had to divest himself of the love of created beings might be a little brutal in the process, like Peter forsaking his family to follow Jesus, but it is difficult to create a sympathetic stage character out of such materials. Harry's "You can't know why I'm going. You have not seen/ What I have seen" may be accurate, but it is inescapably smug; his snappish treatment of his aunts and uncles, his laughter at his brother's accident, his apparent indifference at his mother's death seem to pave the road to salvation with other men's feelings. Agatha says at one point, "We must try to penetrate the other private worlds/ Of make-believe and fear. To rest in our own suffering/ Is evasion of suffering. We must learn to suffer more." Harry never achieves that kind of suffering in the play; his is a resolutely self-centered search. Although the guilt he is expiating may be a universal guilt, he seems to be mainly concerned with getting the Furies off his own back. The non-Christian Jean-Paul Sartre lets his Orestes, in *The Flies*, display much greater human compassion. Eliot has criticized his own play in these terms:[25]

we are left in a divided frame of mind, not knowing whether to consider the play the tragedy of the mother or the salvation of the son. The two situations are not reconciled. I find a confirmation of this in

[25] Eliot, *Poetry and Drama*, pp. 37–38.

the fact that my sympathies now have come to be all with the mother, who seems to me, except perhaps for the chauffeur, the only complete human being in the play; and my hero now strikes me as an insufferable prig.

In *The Family Reunion*, Amy, able to see Harry's journey only in practical terms, assumes that he is about to become a missionary. Harry says, "I never said that I was going to be a missionary./ I would explain, but you would none of you believe it;/ If you believed it, still you would not understand." By his next play, *The Cocktail Party*, ten years after *The Family Reunion*, Eliot has apparently accepted Amy's image of Harry's journey as a dramatically valid symbol. In *The Cocktail Party*, Celia, the play's Harry, goes as a missionary to the fictional island of Kinkanja, where she is killed. The play is Eliot's most succinct statement of the two ways of Christian living. Not only Celia, but the Chamberlaynes—Lavinia and Edward—are forced to choose, with the help of Sir Henry Harcourt-Reilly, who is more than human, less than psychiatrist. The Chamberlaynes return to the life they have known with the added knowledge, "that every moment is a fresh beginning. . . ." Celia goes on to martyrdom. The fourth troubled character, Peter Quilpe, remains unresolved at the end of the play; he is just beginning to realize "That I've only been interested in myself;/ And that isn't good enough for Celia."

Each character's choice of way depends not upon desire, but upon capability. Celia's symptoms—"An awareness of solitude" and "a sense of sin"—make her right for Harcourt-Reilly's sanatorium, which is the starting point for "a long journey," that echoes *The Family Reunion*. In explaining herself to the doctor, Celia says:

> It's not the feeling of anything I've ever *done*,
> Which I might get away from, or of anything in me
> I could get rid of—but of emptiness, of failure
> Towards someone, or something, outside of myself;
> And I feel I must . . . *atone*—is that the word?

Harcourt-Reilly explains that he "can reconcile you to the human condition," but when she rejects that possibility he explains the other way:

> The second is unknown, and so requires faith—
> The kind of faith that issues from despair.
> The destination cannot be described;
> You will know very little until you get there;
> You will journey blind. But the way leads toward possession
> Of what you have sought in the wrong place.

Celia chooses the sanatorium. A few minutes earlier in the play, the doctor has explained that the sanatorium is not for the Chamberlaynes. Edward says, comforting Lavinia (and the offered comfort is a new beginning), "we must make the best of a bad job./ That is what he means." Harcourt-Reilly answers, "When you find, Mr. Chamberlayne,/ The best of a bad job is all any of us make of it—/ Except of course, the saints—such as those who go/ To the sanatorium—you will forget this phrase,/ And in forgetting it will alter the condition."

The play really ends with the double decision, just as *Murder in the Cathedral* actually ends with Becket's rejection of the tempters; the last act, as Eliot says, "just escapes, if indeed it does escape, the accusation of being not a last act but an epilogue."[26] In it, the news of Celia's death is given to the Chamberlaynes and to Peter Quilpe and Sir Henry explains that Celia's death is the logical outcome of her free choice, "And if that is not a happy death, what death is happy?"

The trouble with the play in the theater is that an ordinary secular audience is likely to share the Chamberlaynes' suspicion that Celia's death is a waste and not a triumph. Another difficulty lies in the two ways—not in an intellectual understanding of them, but in the qualitative difference between them. It is true

---

[26] Eliot, *Poetry and Drama*, p. 40.

that Sir Henry says of the Chamberlaynes' way, "It is a good life. Though you will not know how good/ Till you come to the end," but elsewhere he worries at returning the couple "To the stale food mouldering in the larder,/ The stale thoughts mouldering in their minds." Both ways are presumably honorable ways, even honorable Christian ways, but the tone of the play operates against the assumption that the Chamberlaynes have found anything of value. There is at least some justification for the interpretation of James Thurber's intellectual butler in "*What* Cocktail Party?": "It's another variant of the prickly-pear theme, I should say, if I'm not perhaps being a bit too basic." Quoting a colleague, the butler sums up the theme of the play. "It is desolater than you think."[27]

Some attention should be given to two other aspects of the play—the supernatural framework and the play's relationship to the *Alcestis*. Occasionally Sir Henry seems to put himself into the world of the Chamberlaynes, but throughout the play, there are indications that not only he, but the gossipy Julia and the solidly suave Alex are supernatural figures whose business is with the lives of the humans around them. These indications can be as casual as Celia's "There isn't much that Julia doesn't know," or as specific as the toast that Celia makes to the Guardians: "It may be that even Julia is a guardian./ Perhaps she is *my* guardian." In the libation scene at the end of Act II, when Sir Henry, Julia and Alex speak first "The words for the building of the hearth," and then "The words for those who go upon a journey," the special nature of the three characters is emphasized. Here, too, Julia says, "But what do we know of the terrors of the journey?/ You and I don't know the process by which the human is/ Transhumanised: what do we know/ Of the kind of suffering they must undergo/ On the way of illumination?" Possibly, they do not know because they have not made the journey; more probably, given the phrasing in the speech, they do not know because they can go on no human journey. Where Downing in *The Family Reunion* only suggests a guardian angel, these three seem specifically to be guardians. That Sir Henry is more than a human character is also implied by Eliot's statement[28] that the play's source is the *Alcestis* of Euripides. Heracles was at least part god. The relationship of the *Alcestis* to *The Cocktail Party* lies apparently in the fact that Sir Henry brings Lavinia back to Edward, as Heracles brought Alcestis back from actual death, while Sir Henry brings Lavinia back only from a metaphorical one. Still he says "it is a serious matter/ To bring someone back from the dead." Aside from this, the only other likeness to the *Alcestis* is Sir Henry's drinking and singing in the first act (he sings a clean version of "What is the matter with One Eyed Riley?" which incidentally suggests the eye on the house in *The Family Reunion*).

At the end of *The Cocktail Party*, Sir Henry tells the Chamberlaynes, "Only by the acceptance/ Of the past will you alter its meaning." It is an idea that determines Harry's need to know in *The Family Reunion*, and it is a recurring theme in much of Eliot's nondramatic poetry, particularly *Four Quartets*. It is the serious substance behind the farce façade of *The Confidential Clerk*. When Colby at last finds out who he is technically—the son of Henry Guzzard, second-rate organist, deceased—he can begin to find out who he is spiritually—the son of Eggerson, the confidential clerk, who can best be described in E. Martin Browne's report from the author, "When I first talked to Eliot, he said to me 'Eggerson is the only *developed* Christian in the play.'"[29] On the surface, *The Confidential Clerk* is simply a farcical confusion of

---

[28] Eliot, *Poetry and Drama*, p. 38.
[29] Quoted, Burke Wilkinson, "A Most Serious Comedy by Eliot," *New York Times*, February 7, 1954, Section 2, p. 1.

parentage. The action of the play involves sorting out which young man is whose son: the resolution is achieved quite artificially through the appearance of Mrs. Guzzard, a *deus ex machina*, who says shortly after her entrance, "I should like to gratify everyone's wishes." She does reasonably well. She finds a son for Lady Elizabeth—not Colby, as she had hoped, but B. Kaghan: "You wished for your son, and now you have your son./ We all of us have to adapt ourselves/ To the wish that is granted." She produces the dead Henry Guzzard to supply Colby's demand: "I should like a father/ Whom I had never known and couldn't know now,/ Because he would have died before I was born. . . ." Sir Claude has already assumed for years that Colby is his son, so he has had his wish in advance; he must now be satisfied with the suggestion of a new understanding between him and Lady Elizabeth.

The division in this play is between Colby and the other two young people, Lucasta Angel, Sir Claude's illegitimate daughter, and B. Kaghan. Briefly, Lucasta is attracted to Colby, but she settles for Kaghan. They are to be the children of palpable parents, of Sir Claude and Lady Elizabeth, and are to have a marriage for themselves; they, like Sir Claude and Lady Elizabeth, must follow the way of the Chamberlaynes, "must make the best of a bad job." Colby is labeled as different from the beginning; he has his own way to go. B. Kaghan does the defining to Lucasta: "Now, I'll tell you the difference/ Between ourselves and Colby. You and me—/The one thing *we* want is security/ And respectability!" Of Colby, he says, "He's the sort of fellow who might chuck it all/ And go to live on a desert island." He might, in short, go to Sweeney's cannibal isle, on Harry's journey, to Celia's end. He does, in fact, retreat (or is it advance) to Eggerson's garden. In Act Two, Lucasta has already introduced the idea of Colby's garden: "You have your secret garden; to which you can retire/ And lock the gate behind you." Colby says, "If I were religious,

God would walk in my garden/ And that would make the world outside it real/ And acceptable, I think." At the end, when Colby decides to leave Sir Claude, to become a second-rate organist in Eggerson's parish, it is Eggerson's more fully cultivated garden, the one perhaps in which God walks, that attracts him. Eggerson, welcoming him, says, "I think you'll come to find you've another vocation. . . . You'll be thinking of reading for orders." *The Confidential Clerk* is a play about the search for vocation as well as for a father. Sir Henry is the efficient financier who wanted to be a bad potter; Lady Elizabeth is the dabbler in religions who wanted to be an inspirer of artists; Colby is the bad organist who almost became a financier, following the wrong father to the wrong vocation.

The Confidential Clerk operates without the supernatural framework of *The Cocktail Party*. There are jokes about guardians, as in the earlier play, but Kaghan's "I'm your guardian angel,/ Colby, to protect you from Lucasta," does not have the definitional force of the same kind of remark about Julia in *The Cocktail Party*. Nor is there any significance in Lucasta's name being Angel. E. Martin Browne says, "There are no onlookers—no Alex or Julia or Reilly. Even Eggerson, the clerk himself, is involved by his final-curtain acquisition of Colby as his spiritual son."[30] Mrs. Guzzard, the only character besides Eggerson who might be said to have supernatural connections, is also involved; she is the real mother of Colby. In *The Confidential Clerk*, the action is not so much metaphysical as it is metaphorical. Everyone in the play appears to be something (sometimes several things) that he is not; each one is intent on discovering his true identity. The truth of the final identity, however, is only partial. There is a suggestion throughout the play that everyone is talking about something other than what the words denote. While Colby's description of the father that he wants is an apt likeness of the dead Henry

[30] Quoted, Wilkinson, *op. cit.*, p. 1.

Guzzard, it also appears to be a longing for an unknown and unknowable father (read, Father) whom he can serve. The artificiality of the play's form, its use of the frame of farce is a stylistic insistence on the unimportance of the surface story and an emphasis on the central concern of the play—the search for the father who is God. As Phyllis McGinley, another Christian poet, says, somewhat wryly, "This is the way his farce ends,/ Not with a mot but a moral."[31]

Like *The Confidential Clerk*, Eliot's latest play, *The Elder States-man* (1958) is about self-recognition. The protagonist, Lord Claverton (who has been plain Dick Ferry and Richard Claverton-Ferry at earlier stages of his career), confronted by fragments of his past, learns, almost too late, who he is and what he has missed. If, Lord Claverton says, a man has one person from whom he has no desire to hide anything. "Then he loves that person, and his love will save him." Unlike the earlier plays, *The Elder Statesman* has no specifically religious theme, unless Eliot has finally found what he asked for in 1935, "a literature which should be *un*con-sciously, rather than deliberately and defiantly, Christian. . . ."[32] The only interesting thing about an otherwise quite bad play is that in it Eliot seems finally to have embraced, with real warmth, the idea that there is a possible human relationship which gives meaning to life, that there is really a second way to salvation, this side the saints and the martyrs.

Each one of Eliot's major plays has serious dramatic flaws. *Murder in the Cathedral* and *The Cocktail Party*, for instance, are dramatically finished long before the curtain falls. *The Family Reunion* and *The Confidential Clerk* suffer from an insufficiency of warmth, an impossibility of human identification with the hero.

---

[31] Phyllis McGinley, "Mrs. Sweeney Among the Allegories," *The Love Letters of Phyllis McGinley*, New York, Viking, 1954, p. 93.

[32] T. S. Eliot, "Religion and Literature," *Selected Essays*, New York, Harcourt, Brace, [1950], p. 346.

Just as Eliot has called Harry "a prig," he has built into *The Con-fidential Clerk* a valid criticism of Colby. Lucasta says:

> You're either above caring,
> Or else you're insensible—I don't mean insensitive!
> But you're terribly cold. Or else you've some fire
> To warm you, that isn't the same kind of fire
> That warms other people. You're either an egotist
> Or something so different from the rest of us
> That we can't judge you.

Eliot means to imply that Colby is warmed by that other fire, that he is beyond the judgment of ordinary men, but theatrically he is simply cold. Although Eliot can hardly be called an evangel-istic writer, his plays are primarily intellectual constructions, demonstrations of his theological views and, as a result, character-ization sometimes suffers.

Eliot's work for the theater—like his work in general—is, however, seldom criticized on purely aesthetic grounds. His most vocal antagonists are suspicious not of the structure of his plays, but of the theology that defines them. When William Carlos Williams speaks sharply of "T. S. Eliot with *his* new church, all spit-licked and polished . . ."[33] or when Sean O'Casey writes of Eliot's "well-fifed madrigals of deaths and desolation. . . .,"[34] they appear to be annoyed mainly because a poet of Eliot's stature should not celebrate life as they do, that he should be taking Charles Williams's way of negation. When Eliot makes the division between the Chamberlaynes and Celia in *The Cocktail Party*, it is easy to suppose that he puts himself on Celia's road. The assumption is not true. E. Martin Browne writes of that play:[35]

[33] Quoted, Dorothy Tooker, "The Editors Meet William Carlos Williams," *A.D. 1952*, III, 11 (Winter, 1952).
[34] Sean O'Casey, *Sunset and Evening Star*, New York, Macmillan, 1954, p. 124.
[35] E. Martin Browne, "Theatre Aims of T. S. Eliot," *New York Times*, January, 15, 1950, Section 2, p. 3.

Eliot has sometimes been called a pessimist because he sees no shining future on the spiritual plane for the majority of us. But this is certainly not a pessimistic play . . . there are two ways. One, the life of civilized tolerance in the natural world. . . . The other is the adventurous way of the spirit. It is for the few, who are beacons to light the paths for others.

For Eliot the Chamberlaynes' way "is a good life." It simply suffers, for him, by comparison with the other. There is, however, no evidence that he imagines himself taking any way but that of the Chamberlaynes. In *Four Quartets* he writes:

> But to apprehend
> The point of intersection of the timeless
> With time, is an occupation for the saint—
>
> .   .   .
>
> For most of us, there is only the unattended
> Moment, the moment in and out of time,
>
> .   .   .
>
> These are only hints and guesses,
> Hints followed by guesses; and the rest
> Is prayer, observance, discipline, thought and action.

It is as though he were saying again from a new vantage point what he said more than forty years ago in "The Love Song of J. Alfred Prufrock": "I am not Prince Hamlet, nor was meant to be. . . ." At best, he seems to be able to go as far as Agatha, to look longingly after Harry as he sets out on his journey. Perhaps he is trying to reach as far as Eggerson, who, as Browne says, "is at peace with himself and his God."[36]

Any criticism of Eliot's work leads inevitably to an examination of the man's beliefs and even of his personality. No such bypaths are necessary, however, in an assessment of his importance to the revival of religious drama and to its acceptance on the commercial

[36] Quoted, Wilkinson, *op. cit.*, p. 3.

stage. The continuing popularity of *Murder in the Cathedral*; the recurrent theatrical interest in *The Family Reunion*[37] and the commercial success of *The Cocktail Party* are evidence that Eliot has found a place for himself in the modern English theater. The flaws in Eliot's plays are marks on major works. Compared to the ordinary post-war English theatrical productions, Eliot's plays have great stature. He is not a playwright of Shaw's importance, but he is serious and sensitive, and the best of his plays are impressive contributions to the body of modern English drama. It is because his plays are important as plays (and as verse) that they are central to the development of post-war religious drama. They appear to be a culmination, the meeting point of the two lines that run from A. M. Buckton's *Eager Heart* and from Henry Arthur Jones's *Saints and Sinners*, a joining of the church drama with the commercial drama. T. S. Eliot is the most valuable product of the religious drama revival, and his success has made serious religious considerations more acceptable on the English stage.

Christopher Fry. Christopher Fry makes a sharp contrast to T. S. Eliot. "Reality is incredible, reality is a whirlwind. What we call reality is a false god, the dull eye of custom,"[38] Fry once said on the Third Programme. The reality of which he speaks is a natural one, as natural as the descriptions of the English countryside that fill his plays; in all of his work he celebrates the multiplicity of sensations that the world has to offer and the variety of human experience. His central theme, E. Martin Browne once said, is "the nature of human personality."[39] The cheerful excitement that Fry brings to the doings of man and the world around him is not the simple-minded optimism of Pollyanna. His plays

[37] It was revived by Peter Brook and Paul Scofield in their season at the Phoenix Theatre, London, in 1956, and by the Phoenix Theatre, New York, in 1958.
[38] Fry, *Listener,* XLIII, 331.
[39] E. Martin Browne, "From T. S. Eliot to Christopher Fry," *Adam,* XIX, 16 (No. 214–215, 1951).

deal with death, murder, war, and the gentler horrors of loneliness and advancing age. They are, however, marked with the assumption that life is a pleasure to be grasped, not a duty to be accepted. "Comedy is an escape, not from truth but from despair," he says, "a narrow escape into faith."[40] All of life leads him, by the way of the affirmation of images, to God. As Tim Meadows says in *A Sleep of Prisoners*, "Affairs are now soul size./ The enterprise/ Is exploration into God."

Part of the difference in attitude between Eliot and Fry may lie in the fact that the older playwright came to his faith across a waste land while the younger man was born to his. Fry's father, whose name was Harris (Fry took his mother's name for the sound of it), was an architect who gave up his practice to become a lay-preacher and mission-worker in Bristol. Although his father died when Fry was three years old, he has left his influence upon his son; Derek Stanford finds evidence of Fry's fondness for his father in the speeches of St. Cuthman about his dead father in *The Boy with a Cart*.[41] Fry was raised by his mother and an aunt, both religious women—Church of England, as is Fry—and he, perhaps because his mother's family had been Quaker, attended a Quaker public school. This background is probably in part responsible for Fry's refusal to treat the search for God as a painful and harrowing quest, but as a simple act of opening the eyes.

Fry's success as a playwright after World War II followed on a long and various career as a theatrical apprentice. He wrote his first verse play, *Youth and the Peregrines*, when he was seventeen; it was finally produced in 1934, when he was director of the Wells Repertory Players at Tunbridge Wells, on a bill that included the world première of Shaw's *Village Wooing*. In the late thirties he

[40] Christopher Fry, "Comedy," *Adelphi*, XXVII, 27 (November, 1950).
[41] Derek Stanford, *Christopher Fry*, London, Longmans, Green, [1954], p. 11. The biographical sections of this pamphlet (pp. 10–13) have been particularly useful in providing background on Fry, as has Derek Stanford, *Christopher Fry Album*, London, Peter Nevill, 1952.

wrote a number of plays and pageants that have never been published; they include *The Tower*, for the Tewkesbury Festival of 1939; *Thursday's Child*, which was acted at the Albert Hall in the same year; and *Open Door*, a commissioned account of the founder of Dr. Barnardo's homes. Fry has also written the music and lyrics for a standard musical about a crooner (*She Shall Have Music*— 1934), performed in night clubs, acted with various groups and directed at the Oxford Playhouse both immediately before and immediately after the war. His plays began to draw attention after the war, and following the production of *The Lady's Not for Burning* in 1948, his reputation was firmly established.[42]

Fry's published work breaks neatly into two groups—the church dramas and the theatrical comedies. The first group, most of which were written for special occasions, include *The Boy with a Cart* (1937), *The Firstborn* (1945), *Thor, with Angels* (1948), and *A Sleep of Prisoners* (1951). The second group are sometimes called the seasonal comedies, since each is set in a particular season and the action, the characters and particularly the imagery of the verse are closely related to the season during which the play takes place. In commenting on *Venus Observed* (1950), Fry uses the seasonal label; the play, he says, "was planned as one of a series of four comedies, a comedy for each of the seasons of the year, four comedies of mood."[43] The other three are *A Phoenix Too Frequent* (1946), *The Lady's Not for Burning* (1948), and *The Dark Is Light Enough* (1954). Except for the last of these, which reads at times like an elaborate Christian allegory, the comedies are religious plays only implicitly, only insofar as Fry's view of the world is a reflection of his view of God.

The Boy with a Cart, Fry's first published play, was written at the

---

[42] Stanford, *Christopher Fry*, pp. 12–13, has descriptions of Fry's unpublished plays. *The Tower* was reviewed *The Times* (London), July 19, 1939, p. 12.

[43] Christopher Fry, "Venus Considered, Notes in Preface to a Comedy," *Theatre Newsletter*, IV, 5 (March 11, 1950). Derek Stanford treats the use of the seasons in Fry's comedies in his discussion in *Christopher Fry*, pp. 21–32.

request of the vicar in the Sussex village of Colman's Hatch; in a mixture of prose and poetry, Fry tells how the boy Cuthman came to the village of Steyning and built a church. The plot is deliberately simple. Cuthman, forced to face in rapid succession the shocking news that his father is dead and that he and his mother are dispossessed, builds a cart in which he pulls his mother across South England. His destination is in God's hands for he has decided to pull until the rope of withies that binds him to the cart breaks; on that spot "The church/ And I shall be built together; and together/ Find our significance." The rope breaks in Steyning; Cuthman's mother finds neighbors to replace the ones she has left behind and, after overcoming some slight opposition, the boy founds his church. The play is suffused with miracle. When some harvesters laugh at Cuthman and his mother, when he accidentally dumps her from the cart, rain falls on them; the sun continues to shine on the boy and his mother. Cuthman is given the power to yoke and use as beasts of burden the sons of Mrs. Fipps, two bad-tempered young men who have taken the boy's oxen; when Mrs. Fipps complains, a convenient wind blows her away, "Zigzag like a paper bag, like somebody's hat!" When the king post of the nearly finished church gets out of line and cannot be moved by human means, a figure appears to Cuthman: "He stretched his hand upon it. At his touch/ It lifted to its place. There was no sound./ I cried out, and I cried at last 'Who are you?'/ I heard him say 'I was a carpenter' . . ." The play contains a chorus, the People of South England, whose chief function is to keep the not essentially dramatic narrative moving. Like Eliot's Chorus in *Murder in the Cathedral*, they are the ordinary people. They do not have Cuthman's vision, which often in this play seems too much like unbridled adolescent enthusiasm, but they do have some sense of a relationship between man and God: "We have felt the joint action of root and sky, of man/ And God, when day first risks the hills. . . ." On

at least one occasion, they express a sentiment that is familiar in
Eliot: "Between/ Our birth and death we may touch under-
standing/ As a moth brushes a window with its wing." For the
most part the chorus in *The Boy with a Cart* is derivative; the play
as a whole is interesting chiefly as a seed for the work that Fry
was to do after the war. J. C. Trewin's judgment, "a good play
for a village occasion, but not one likely to be remembered,"[44]
is perhaps a little harsh; in performance, *The Boy with a Cart* has
charm.

Fry began work on *The Firstborn* in 1938; twenty years later, he
was still revising it. The first version was finished in 1945, published in 1946, and acted at the Edinburgh Festival in 1948. The
second version was presented in London in 1952; the third, in
New York in 1958. There were extensive cuts between the first
two versions. Fry often lifted several lines out of the middle
of a long speech; that he could do so without changing the
sense of the speech indicates the verbosity of his dramatic
verse in the early plays; that he wanted to do so shows his
movement toward the sparer verse that is characteristic of *A
Sleep of Prisoners*. There were a few more cuts between the second
and third versions of the play, and some changes in emphasis,
but Fry's chief attempt was to rewrite the last scene to make
clear Moses's concern for Ramases. Essentially, the play is the
same in all three versions. It is the second edition that is being
considered here.

The Firstborn is the story of Moses, who learns something of
himself and of mankind, as he realizes the horrifying nature of
the plagues that God sends to aid his struggle against the Pharaoh.
In a "Foreword to the Second Edition" Fry says, "The character
of Moses is a movement toward maturity, toward a balancing of
life within the mystery, where the conflicts and dilemmas are the

---

[44] J. C. Trewin, "The Plays of Christopher Fry," *Adelphi*, XXVII, 41 (November,
1950).

trembling of the balance. . . ." Throughout the play, Moses remains something of a mystery to the other characters. Those at Pharaoh's court—like Anath, the now aged princess who had saved him from the Nile years before—cannot understand why he will not accept Seti's offer that would make him again an Egyptian general. His sister Miriam, who has seen so much of suffering, has settled into a weary acceptance of life that is very like death and cannot see why Moses once again wants to stir up trouble. His nephew Shendi, satisfied with saving his own skin through personal advancement in the Egyptian army, assumes that Moses is jealous of his little success.[45] Aaron, a practical revolutionary, is disconcerted by Moses's supernatural dabblings. Moses must learn in the course of the play that his use of God (or God's use of him) involves pain as well as triumph. When he confronts the Pharaoh with a dead Israelite child, thunder rolls as though God is seconding Moses's demands. When the first plague comes (the water turned to blood), Moses, without having expected it, accepts it as God's intervention. As the plagues continue, he is forced to face the words of Anath: "What is this divinity/ Which with no more dexterity than a man/ Rips up good things to make a different kind/ Of good?" The end of the play centers on Ramases, the eldest son of the Pharaoh, "the innocence, humanity, vigour, and worth which stand on the enemy side, not altering the justice or necessity of Moses' cause, but linking the ways of men and the ways of God with a deep and urgent question-mark."[46] When the final plague is due, Moses is at last fully aware of what is happening: "God is putting me back with the assassins." He runs to the palace, hoping that he and the young man's family can form a circle of life around the boy so strong that death can be overridden, but Ramases must die. The Israelites

---

[45] The conflict between Moses and Shendi is greatly reduced in the Third Edition; most of the quarrel in Act Three, Scene One has been removed.
[46] Christopher Fry, *The Firstborn*, Second Edition, London, Oxford, [1952], p. vii.

are given their freedom and a grief-stricken Moses leads them into the wilderness:

> I do not know why the necessity of God
> Should feed on grief; but it seems so. And to know it
> Is not to grieve less, but to see grief grow big
> With what has died, and in some spirit differently
> Bear it back to life.

The play ends not in simple truth, but in sorrowful affirmation: "what does eternity bear witness to/ If not at last to hope?"

In many ways Fry's most ambitious play, *The Firstborn* is less effective than his comedies. One of its weaknesses is the insufficiently realized relationship between Moses and Ramases; the other is the play's language. The climax of the play, the attempt by Moses to save Ramases, makes sense only if Moses's concern for the young Egyptian is given some dramatic explanation. Fry himself has recognized his failure to make the situation clear:[47]

The critics felt, very reasonably, that the affection between Moses and Ramases had been so barely touched on that three-quarters of the impact of Moses' realisation was lost.
. . . What I had hoped I had shown, and hadn't, was that to Moses the boy represented Moses' own boyhood when he was Prince of Egypt, represented also that love for Egypt which Moses couldn't shake off even while he was fighting her.

The structural problem with *The Firstborn* grows out of a habit of Fry's to suggest rather than to labor a point; in this case, the suggestion is too tenuous. The language difficulty is also a result of Fry's customary style of writing. His verse ordinarily is ornate and elaborate; it mirrors its author's obvious love for words, his delight in verbal jokes and bright and sometimes bizarre metaphors. In the comedies, such as *The Lady's Not for Burning*, the

---

[47] Christopher Fry, *An Experience of Critics*, London, Perpetua, 1952, p. 31.

excessive richness of the language is part of the fun; in *The First-born*, too often the phrases seem disturbingly out of place. A line like Moses's "What says the infinite eavesdropper?" which follows the roll of thunder at the end of Act One reduces God to a prying by-stander (an odd way to characterize omniscience) and robs the moment of its theatrical effectiveness. When Moses's speeches are not studded with inappropriate words such as these, they tend to be turgid and a little pompous ("I, an ambitious heart/ Needing interpretation.") For all its defects, however, *The First-born* is Fry's first serious attempt to deal with the ideas that flash in and out of all his plays, that are expressed in two of Moses's speeches: "It is the individual man/ In his individual freedom who can mature/ With his warm spirit the unripe world," and "My people shall become themselves,/ By reason of their own god who speaks within them."

In *Thor, with Angels*, the Canterbury Festival play of 1948, Fry is again concerned with man's gradual discovery of God, this time on a Jutish farm, A.D. 596. Here Cymen's new knowledge, like that of Moses in *The Firstborn*, takes its final form through the death of an innocent young man, but here the nature of Cymen's discovery is not so tentative; he learns to know the Christian God in terms of forgiveness, mercy and compassion, all weaknesses according to the old Jutish code. Cymen returns from battle with the Saxons, bringing with him Hoel, a Briton, a slave of the Saxons, whom Cymen has inexplicably saved on the battlefield. The Jute's brothers and sons consider Cymen mad and want him to sacrifice the Briton, but Cymen is keeping him in the hope that he can find out through Hoel what force is nibbling at him, weakening him, making him speak in a way that provokes his wife's "Guilt, forgiveness, humility? What next?/ Are you mad?' Hoel, who was baptized a Christian, is a remnant of the Christian Britain that preceded the invasion of the Saxons and the Jutes. He is uncertain of the nature of the God of his people ("When I was a boy I was only/ Allowed to have one, though in that One, they said/ There were three.") and he assumes that his God has long disappeared. The point of the play is that God works through Hoel without the instrument's knowing. When Cymen, goaded by his brothers, tries to kill Hoel, his sword turns toward his own son: "It seems/ All one, it seems all one. There's no distinction./ Which is my son?" In the midst of his dilemma, Cymen is called away to meet Augustine, to hear the message from Christian Rome, and he returns with the newly proclaimed religion, only to find that his brothers and his sons have killed Hoel—have tied him to a tree, his arms spread to form a cross, and stabbed him with a spear. The play ends on a kind of sermon from Cymen:

> We are afraid
> To live by rule of God, which is forgiveness,
> Mercy, and compassion, fearing that by these
> We shall be ended. And yet if we could bear
> These three through dread and terror and terror's doubt,
> Daring to return good for evil without thought
> Of what will come, I cannot think
> We should be the losers. Do we believe
> There is no strength in good or power in God?
> God give us courage to exist in God,
> And lonely flesh be welcome to creation.

The play makes its comparison between the gods of the Jutes and the new merciful God simply and effectively through the fear and impersonal cruelty of Cymen's brothers seen alongside his own doubt and growing compassion. The play's chief defect is that the death of Hoel is so completely symbolical that the audience is not given time to feel any regret for the destruction of an embryonically likable character; the death is metamorphosed too quickly into a text for Cymen's last speech. The most interesting character in the play is the aged Merlin, Joel's grandfather, King Arthur's old wizard, who makes a bridge between paganism and Christianity; it is he who states the theme of the play: "Still I observe the very obdurate pressure/ Edging men towards a shape beyond/ The shape they know."

A Sleep of Prisoners, commissioned by the Religious Drama Society for the Festival of Britain, is complicated in design, but simple in intention. It seeks to reaffirm Fry's faith in man and in God: "the play could not end in a glorious trumpeting, or even the indication of victory—we have too far to travel for that—but certainly, in hope."[48] In the play, four soldiers are imprisoned in a church, and the action, which covers one night, involves the dreams of the four in which "each, in his own dream, speaks as at heart he is, not as he believes himself to be."[49] The soldiers are Private Peter Able, who is totally incapable of anger and hate; Private David King, a man of action, who fights evil with such dedication that Peter's needling good nature finally drives him to attempt to strangle his comrade; Corporal Joe Adams, who tries to keep peace between the two of them and who finds his own strength only in army regulations; and Private Tim Meadows, an older man, almost an observer, who understands and tries to strengthen all the others. The dreams of the four men are conditioned by their prison; all are biblical. Tim Meadows dreams first. He is God, faced with the first murder. David (as Cain) kills Peter (as Abel) for the same reason that David in his own person almost strangles Peter, because Peter calmly accepts what comes, refuses to make demands on God. When the two throw dice for God's favor, David-Cain offers his strength and courage; Peter-Abel says simply, "Deal me high, deal me low./ Make my deeds/ My nameless needs./ I know I do not know." His is the winning

[48] Christopher Fry, "Drama in a House of Worship," *New York Times*, October 14, 1951, Section 2, p. 3.
[49] Christopher Fry, *A Sleep of Prisoners*, London, Oxford, 1951. Quotation is from an unpaged dedicatory letter to Robert Gittings which is printed at the beginning of the book.

throw. The Corporal (as Adam) is seen as uncertain which way to turn, insecure without the known and comforting discipline of the Garden of Eden. He seems to side with David-Cain because "The other boy/Frets for what never came his way,/ Will never reconcile us to our exile." David in his own dream appears as King David; he has Joab (Adams) kill Absalom (Peter) because he is afraid of Absalom, who refuses to see enemies everywhere that David sees them: "The indecisions/ Have to be decided. Who's against us/Reeks to God." Peter in his dream is Isaac about to be sacrificed by Abraham (David); it is the Corporal (as the Angel) who saves him, who turns Abraham's attention to the ram trapped in the thicket. As Abraham, David redefines his basic personality: "I am history's wish and must come true,/ And I shall hate so long as hate/ Is history, though, God, it drives/ My life away like a beaten dog."

The last dream, that of the Corporal, becomes a dream that all the men share. At the beginning, he is on a raft at sea, adrift actually as well as spiritually. His dream fuses with that of David and Peter and they become Shadrac, Meshac, and Abednego in the fiery furnace. They are joined by a fourth figure, Tim Meadows, who answers the Corporal's "Who are you?" with "Man" and his "Under what command?" with "God's." He is, Fry says, "human nature with hope."[50] After the three realize that they are not to be burned, that they can stand and move and face the flames, Peter discovers that the flames are people: "This/ Surely is unquenchable? It can only transform./ There's no way out. We can only stay and alter." The fourth dream ends on the words of Meadows: "The human heart can go to the lengths of God./ ... The longest stride of soul men ever took./ Affairs are now soul size./ The enterprise/ Is exploration into God." Fry sums up his intentions this way:[51]

[50] Fry, *New York Times*, October 14, 1951, Section 2, p. 4.
[51] *Ibid.*

I wanted to move from division to unity, to say that we are all souls in one sorrow, and above all to say that the answer is in ourselves, in each individual, and that each individual has in him the elements of God. What will carry the day is the belief that the good in human nature is even more powerful than the evil, if, with our whole hearts and lives, we abide by it.

The elements of God in man are apparent in the fact that Tim Meadows, who is human nature in the furnace, is God in his own dream in which "he speaks as at heart he is." The four parables of the dreams are valid dramatic statements of three approaches to life; if the play has a fault, it is that its point, by virtue of the four dreams, is too often repeated and that, even so, in the end, it needs Meadows's invocation by way of clarification. Between dreams, Fry allows himself a little muted soldierly horseplay, mainly about Meadows's inability to sleep, which becomes tiresome. As a whole, however, *A Sleep of Prisoners* is the best of Fry's church dramas.

The first of Fry's seasonal comedies, *A Phoenix Too Frequent*, is little more than an anecdote which he got from Jeremy Taylor, who had it in turn from Petronius. The action takes place in a tomb near Ephesus. Dynamene has come with her maid, Doto, to mourn her newly dead husband and to join him by means of a broken heart helped out by careful fasting. Her vigil is broken in on by Tegeus, a soldier, through whose presence, as Jeremy Taylor says, "the light returned into her eyes, and danced like boys in a festival."[52] While Tegeus lingers in the tomb, one of the hanged bodies that he is supposed to be guarding outside is stolen and, by the law of Ephesus, he is likely to put in its place. To save her new love, Dynamene offers the body of her late

[52] Jeremy Taylor, *The Rule and Exercises of Holy Dying*, p. 162, in *The Rule and Exercises of Holy Living and Dying*, London, George Routledge, 1894 (each work paged separately). Taylor tells the story, pp. 162–163. Petronius's version can be found in *The Satyricon of Petronius Arbiter,* translated by William Burnaby, New York, Modern Library, n.d., pp. 172–176.

husband: "I loved/ His life not his death. And now we can give his death/ The power of life." On the broadest comic level, Fry testifies to power of life over death, of life growing out of death. The play is slight, often very funny, often overly clever. At the time of its writing, Fry had not yet begun to label his comedies by season, but *A Phoenix Too Frequent* is set on a summer's night. The solid flowering, the lushness of that season is used against the sudden, but never tentative or spring-like love of Tegeus and Dynamene.

In *The Lady's Not for Burning*, Fry's spring comedy, the April day sees not only the renewal of nature but a kind of rebirth of faith and mystery in the rationalist Jennet Jourdemayne and of desire for life in the despairing Thomas Mendip. Mendip, an ex-soldier, tired of a life in which he can find no meaning ("Why should these omnipotent bombinations/ Go on with the deadly human anecdote, which/ From the first was never more than remotely funny?") comes to the small English town of Cool Clary (*c.* 1400) demanding to be hanged, inventing crimes to make the hanging legal. He stumbles into a witch hunt which looks as though it will take the life of Jennet, a beautiful and slightly eccentric young lady who is rumored to have turned a man into a dog. Of course, the two fall in love. The vigor of Thomas's denunciations of the world is so great and so romantic that it embodies a kind of mystery that communicates itself to Jennet. "Nothing can be seen/ In the thistle-down, but the rough-head thistle comes./ Rest in that riddle," he comforts her. Toward the end of the play, she, who has characterized herself emphatically at the beginning with ". . . I believe in the human mind," has borrowed Thomas's way of talking: "It will be enough/ If you spare me a spider, and when it spins I'll see/ The six days of Creation in a web/ And a fly caught on the seventh. And if the dew/ Should rise in the web, I may well die a Christian." He, on the other hand, has begun to find in her a reason for living, although he expresses it in terms of the April evening: "The night's a pale pastureland of peace,/ And something condones the world, incorrigibly." Skipps, the rag-and-bones man whom Thomas claims to have killed and whom Jennet is accused of transforming into a dog, is discovered, and the two candidates for death go off together. Thomas's closing line, "And God have mercy on our souls," is in character, a resignation at having been forced into an unwanted life by a greatly wanted Jennet; it is more than that, however; it is Fry's benediction on the play and the action. He says of the play, "I could see no reason . . . why I should not treat the world as I see it, a world in which we are all poised on the edge of eternity, a world which has deeps and shadows of mystery, in which God is anything but a sleeping-partner."[53] Within the play, it is the comic Chaplain, one of Fry's best creations, who echoes Fry's feelings: "When I think of myself/ I can scarcely believe my senses. But there it is,/ All my friends tell me I actually exist/ And by an act of faith I have come to believe them."

Fry's autumn comedy, *Venus Observed*, which he wrote for Laurence Olivier, concerns the Duke of Altair's decision to take a wife. He has asked three of his early loves to come to his estate, ostensibly to see an eclipse of the moon, actually so that his grown son Edgar can pick the one he should marry. Into this variation of Paris and his apple (Edgar uses an apple, too) comes Perpetua, the daughter of the Duke's estate agent, a radiant refugee from spring. Momentarily, to save her father who has been cheating the Duke for years, she contemplates marrying the older man, but a fire in the observatory (the Duke's favorite place for seductions) saves her from making the decision. She prefers Edgar; there has been an eclipse. At the end the Duke decides to marry Rosabel, the one early mistress who still wants him, the lady, in fact, who set the fire. According to Fry, the theme of the play is loneliness, and the Duke "accepts, at last, that a man's completion is not in his lifetime or in his flesh but in some distance in time, or not in time at all."[54] There is nothing in the play quite so specific as Fry's statement about the nature of the Duke's acceptance, but the loneliness is evident; the play is touched throughout with sadness, the autumn of the Duke and of the year. The fire in the observatory not only cleanses the confusions of the Duke and Perpetua, returning both to his own season, but it also offers an opportunity for the Duke's butler, a lion-tamer who has lost his nerve, to regain his courage by facing fire and for the Duke's footman, a burglar who took to stealing because he had a compulsion to climb ladders, to mount a ladder for a legitimate reason ("again the human ascent, and the need to find some conclusion to the ascent"[55]). The characters and the events do not mix as neatly in *Venus Observed* as they do in *The Lady's Not for Burning*; the butler and the footman are interesting comic inventions, but their particular quests seem to have only a tenuous relation to that of the Duke, for his, after all, is an acceptance and theirs is a triumph. The play is full of references to Fry's continuous fascination with the workings of man, for instance, Edgar's "Whatever the human mystery may be/ I am it." It is an exchange between the Duke and Jessie Dill, the most practical and most endearing of his old loves, that links *Venus Observed* most securely to the rest of Fry's work. Just before the eclipse, Jessie, remembering the surprises of her childhood, says, "And now I can't help feeling/ As if I'd just been got out of bed again/ To look at something I probably shan't see." The Duke answers, "That's the human predicament, in a nutshell."

Fry's last play to date, except for translations from Jean Anouilh and Jean Giraudoux, is *The Dark Is Light Enough*, his

[54] Fry, *Theatre Newsletter*, IV, 6.
[55] *Ibid.*, p. 5.

winter comedy. This play, which takes place in Austria during the Hungarian revolution in 1848, is, on the surface, the story of the highly civilized Countess Rosmarin, who first protects the unliked and unlikable Richard Gettner from the Hungarians (Richard has joined, then deserted the Hungarian cause) and then protects the Hungarian Janik from the victorious Austrians. All the characters in the play (except the Countess) expect something of Gettner. Her Thursday night circle, especially the acid Belmann, demand of him at least the virtues of the drawing room—politeness, gratitude—but Gettner acts as though the Countess's protection is his due. Stefan, the Countess's son, asks courage of him; Stefan goads Richard, who is a little drunk, into a duel in which Stefan is seriously injured. Gelda, the Countess's daughter, who was once, in name at least, his wife, expects love, but he cannot give the selfless love that her husband Peter gives. Despite Gettner's complete absence of virtues and even his absence of charm, the Countess protects him, although her decision means that her son-in-law must stand as hostage. In the last act, the Countess, shocked by the revolution and the wound of Stefan, is dying. She is still strong enough to hide Janik, who has come to her earlier in search of Gettner and who comes now as a fugitive. Richard, who has run away, returns at the news of the Countess's illness. In a final confrontation, in which he asks her to marry him, assuming that she must love him, the Countess reveals that she does not love him, that she does not even like him. "What in God's name was it I meant to you?" he asks, and she answers, "Simply what any life may mean." With the Austrian soldiers at the door and Janik hidden in the attic, the Countess dies. Gettner starts to leave and then returns, demanding of the dead woman, "You never showed/ Any expectations of me when you were alive,/ Why should you now?/ This isn't how I meant that you should love me!/ Very well, very well./ Be with me." He turns to face the Austrians, to protect Janik in her place, knowing that he may be facing his own death, since, for all that he was a deserter, he had taken side with the revolutionists.

The play could be taken as no more than a pacifist parable. Fry's convictions, after all, did lead him to serve in a noncombatant unit during World War II. The pacifist theme is stated quite simply in an exchange between Janik and the Countess in Act One. "Peace may go in search of the one soul/ But we are not at peace," he says, demanding the hidden Gettner, but she counters with, "*You* are not/At peace, . . ." There is ample evidence, however, that the Countess is more than simply a woman of convictions. The play is full of lines that suggest that she is God or at least the spirit of God. At the beginning, when her friends arrive for their Thursday night discussion and find their hostess gone, Belmann says of the house, "The goddess of it, in her Godlike way,/ Is God knows where." Again, he says, "You know the Countess has the qualities of true divinity./ For instance: how apparently undemandingly/ She moves among us; and yet/ Lives make and unmake themselves in her neighbourhood/ As nowhere else." Even Richard adds to the characterization with his assertion, "God's a woman." Whether or not Fry intends an equation between God and the Countess, it is evident that she represents a spirit which at the end of the play passes to Richard. The play is an illustration of an early remark of Belmann's, "She has a touching way/ Of backing a man up against eternity/ Until he hardly has the nerve to remain mortal." At the end, Richard has been backed up against eternity, and his "Be with me" is a prayer. *The Dark Is Light Enough* brings the material of the comedies close to that of the church dramas. It is about as near to allegory as the contemporary stage is likely to get.

The work of Christopher Fry, like that of T. S. Eliot, is one of the solid achievements of the religious drama revival. Not that he lacks his critics, most of whom feel that plays so filled with gaiety and verbal romping can hardly be as serious as Fry intends them.

Stephen Spender, reviewing not Fry, but Ronald Duncan and Norman Nicholson, two of the poets who imitate him, sums up for the opposition:[56]

The Fry method is to subdue the action of characters to the charm and wit of verse. The temperature of human behaviour is lowered to a point where things like robbery, fornication and murder are made to appear merely verbal, and one soon ceases to care about them. This ruthless rhyme type facetiousness is then gathered up into the poetic sermon on Sin, Grace, Boredom, etc. The general effect is as of beaded bubbles winking at the brim of a cup of cocoa.

There is some justice in Spender's criticism, which incidentally goes a little Fry-like in its last metaphor; the dancing excess of the playwright's language does sometimes seem to infect the violent moments of the plays with a cheerful unreality. The substance of Spender's complaint is suspect, however. It has some of the quality that the Shavian critics always used, those who wondered why, if Shaw were writing serious plays, he did not quit making jokes. Fry, like any original playwright, makes a demand on an audience. In his case, the demand is that they realize that his verse is not merely decoration (although it can be that), but that it is an expression of his view of the world. As the Chaplain says in *The Lady's Not for Burning*. "But life has such Diversity, I sometimes remarkably lose/ Eternity in the passing moment." Fry's strained and straining metaphors are as much a part of his approach to man and God as Eliot's increasingly spare and prose-like verse is an indication of his attitude. A word, too, is an image and Fry gathers up words, as he gathers up nature and human behavior, as sign-posts to lead him down the way of affirmation. " Joy (of a kind) has been all on the devil's side, and one of the necessities of our times is to redeem it,"[57] Fry once wrote, and, for him, the

[56] Stephen Spender, untitled review, *London Magazine*, II, 80 (December, 1955).
[57] Fry, *Adelphi*, XXVII, 29.

joy of words (occasionally for their own sake) is one of the objects of redemption. The quality of his plays may be somewhat magnified by the current interest both in religious plays and in poetic drama, but beneath the magnification there is a bedrock of worth that is evident, particularly when the work of Fry is considered in relation to that of most of the playwrights now working in the English theater.

W. H. Auden. W. H. Auden is the only other poet of reputation writing for the English stage. The bulk of his theatrical work, political, satirical, and vaguely antireligious, stems from the thirties. Since the days of *The Dog beneath the Skin*, Auden has become a Christian poet. The only theatrical evidence of his Christianity is the libretto that he and Chester Kallman wrote for Igor Stravinsky's *The Rake's Progress* (1949), unless the two dramatic poems, *The Sea and the Mirror* (1945) and *For the Time Being* (1945), be considered plays. The second of these has been performed and is included in Marvin Halverson's collection, *Religious Drama* 1.[58] Although it is not really a drama, *For the Time Being*, which he subtitles "A Christmas Oratorio," with its evocation of the mixture of yearning and rejection with which most nominal Christians approach the Nativity, is a far better piece of religious literature than most of the Nativities that have evolved from the religious drama revival.

Auden's one post-war theatrical piece, *The Rake's Progress*, is a combination of Christian morality and fairy story. In it, Tom vows his love for Anne, but is lured away by Nick Shadow (two names for the devil) to learn the pleasures of the city; Nick goes with Tom as a servant after striking a devil's agreement by which "A year and a day hence we will settle our account. . . ." Tom's adventures lead him to a comic and rather ghastly marriage to Baba, the bearded lady, whom he marries because Nick con-

[58] New York, Meridan, 1957.

vinces him that by taking Baba, whom he does not want, he will be acting in perfect freedom. When Tom begins to tire of sensuous pleasures, Nick contrives that he should dream of "An engine that converted stone to bread/ Whereby all peoples were for nothing fed./ I saw all want abolished by my skill/ And earth become an Eden of good will." This familiar temptation of the devil (he tried it on Christ in the wilderness) offers Tom the pleasure of doing good and being a hero. The machine fails, of course, and, having lost everything, Tom finds himself in a churchyard with Nick, who now claims his reward: "'Tis not your money but your soul." Anne has wandered through most of the opera singing in search of her lost love: "A love that is sworn before Thee can plunder Hell of its prey." Through the off-stage voice of Anne and a series of accidents, that are almost certainly not accidents, Tom wins a last game of chance with Nick and saves his soul. Nick causes him to go mad and, after having been comforted by the loyal Anne, Tom dies. Love cannot reclaim the fallen man as it would have done in a sentimental comedy, but, at least, it saves the man's soul. At the end the principals sing an epilogue: "So let us sing as one./ At all times in all lands/ Beneath the moon and sun,/ This proverb has proved true,/ Since Eve went out with Adam:/ For idle hands and hearts and minds/ The Devil finds/ A work to do,/ A work, dear Sir, fair Madam/ For you and you." The closing moral fits the nursery-story quality of the whole libretto, but it is a nursery moral with a difference, for the reference to Adam and Eve loads the last lines with the unmistakable suggestion of Original Sin. Auden's progress was hardly that of Tom, but there is certainly as great a distance from *The Dog beneath the Skin* to *The Rake's Progress* as there is from Anne's garden to Tom's madhouse.

X

The Mercury Poets

"He has driven more poets to drama than any man living,"[1] Christopher Fry once wrote of E. Martin Browne. Browne's most sustained driving took place between 1945 and 1948, when he and Robert Speaight operated the tiny (130 seats) Mercury Theatre for several seasons of poetic drama. Their company, called The Pilgrim Players, after the wartime group with which Browne had worked, presented not only theatrical stalwarts, such as *Murder in the Cathedral*, but introduced to the London theater Christopher Fry's *A Phoenix Too Frequent*, Anne Ridler's *The Shadow Factory*, Ronald Duncan's *This Way to the Tomb*, and Norman Nicholson's *The Old Man of the Mountains*. Fry, of course, went on to find his place in the commercial theater; the other three, particularly the prolific Duncan, continued to provide religious verse plays for specific occasions. Although the impetus of the Mercury Theatre was primarily poetic ("I invited practicing poets to write verse in the form of a play . . ."[2]), most of the plays produced were religious in fact or in intention. In an interview in *Theatre World*, Browne attempted to explain why this should be true:[3]

Because a number of productions at the Mercury have had a religious flavour, it must not be thought that we are pursuing a religious policy. Our aim is to stage plays by poets, but as poets are sensitive beings it is not surprising that they concern themselves with religious themes in time of world chaos.

[1] Christopher Fry, "Headpiece," *Christian Drama*, II, 1 (June, 1951).
[2] Quoted, Eric Johns, "Poet's Playhouse," *Theatre World*, XLIV, 28 (February, 1948).
[3] Quoted, *ibid.*, p. 31.

Browne's explanation is largely an attempt to turn a personal allegiance into an aesthetic generalization. He and Speaight were obviously drawn to poets whose religious sentiments they shared. Although the Mercury experiment was defined in poetic terms, it might as justly be identified as an attempt to establish a professional religious theater that could play to commercial audiences.

Anne Ridler. Of the three poet-playwrights introduced at the Mercury's first season of New Plays by Poets in the fall of 1945, Anne Ridler is the most interesting and original. She does not have the theatricality of Ronald Duncan; her inventiveness lies in the general conception of her plays, their special use of received myth and story. *The Shadow Factory*, her Mercury offering, was not her initiation into drama; *Cain* (1943) preceded it. In two acts of serviceable verse, Mrs. Ridler's earlier play tells again the story of the first murder. Cain's conflict with Abel rises out of his inability to accept the sin of Adam and the rejection from the garden, an acceptance which must precede a recognition that ". . . Heaven/ Is a step away, sooner or later to be taken." The final break comes when Cain's prayer is rejected by God, while Abel's is accepted. The Archangels, speaking in defense of Cain, define the two prayers: "Those who have learnt like Abel ask/ Only that what they pray may please/ Thee, yet hear also those/ Who have but learnt to speak their longing." Cain, then, almost reluctantly, kills Abel; Cain's love for Abel is one of Mrs. Ridler's best ideas in the play. Michael sums up the point of the play when he says to Cain, "Believe that the Fall in you was renewed," and, in the Epilogue, Gabriel admonishes the audience, "But in each of you again the Fall is a violence." Although *Cain* is not empty of action, it is remarkably static; its need to present the idea of the continuing renewal of Adam's fall leads too easily to long passages of explanation, often placed in the mouths of the Archangels.

The Shadow Factory is a Nativity play of which the content is as much social as religious. It is set in a factory which Spencer Harding, the Director, runs with frightening efficiency and benevolence. Harding is so intent on directing his plant in a way that will be most productive and most rewarding to the workers that he has come to control their every move. James Firbank, the Education Officer, who does a job in which he only half believes, describes his own situation and, by extension, that of all the workers: "A decent job, health, sunshine, friends,/ And—black despair at the heart of it all." The vagueness of his misgivings are made concrete by Timothy Garnish, the artist who comes to paint a mural for the canteen: "You're just shadows: puppets worked by your Director-God who pulls strings." When the mural, which Garnish has insisted on doing in secret, is unveiled at a Christmas Eve celebration, it shows the workers as puppets, their shadows as animals. The Parson, who has come to officiate at a traditional tableau of the crib (also apart of the celebration), makes the Director see that he has been acting as though he were God and convinces him to go on with the program, leaving the mural for all to see. In the tableau, the Director, as one of the wise men, offers the child gold (power) and there is apparently revelation in the action. The last scene shows the factory and it workers in a newer, lighter mood, the Director no longer the friendly oppressor. The artist, who comes back to see if his mural has been covered, decides to stay and to do another to counterbalance it.

The play centers on the Director, who has been trying to preempt God's function as creator and who must back down, but it is concerned also with the artist, who has tried to take over the role of God as judge and who must come to see differently. Mrs. Ridler's play is not simply a naïve exercise in conversion and revelation. The Director's reformation is marked with uncertainty. The Caretaker, who apparently represents older and sounder ways, offers him comfort of a kind: "We must make the best of a bad job/ Mustn't we, sir? You go on, sir,/ Stick to what you were doin' before;/ A touch of despair in it'll just put it right./ . . . / You won't look such a fool in the sight of the Lord." Supposedly the play calls for a return to Christian values, represented by the baby in the crib, but sometimes Mrs. Ridler's play hints at a nostalgia for an earlier social situation. The Parson says, "The Church must turn the world back—/ An endless task, endlessly attempted—/ Only, she works within conditions:/ Since she cannot undo the past,/ Making the best of a bad job/ She works on what she finds."[4] His speech does contain a recognition that Christianity must work within a contemporary frame, but the talk of turning the world back carries a strong element of the social conservatism that flavors the work of all the Mercury poets, whose ideas and whose verse seem to owe much to T. S. Eliot.

The plays that appear in the 1950 volume *Henry Bly and Other Plays*—*The Mask*, *Henry Bly*, *The Missing Bridegroom*—are attempts to carry a specifically Christian message in terms of fable, myth and symbol. *The Mask*, which was written originally to be broadcast, is the most complicated of the three, the least likely to communicate clearly in a theater. Based vaguely on the folksong, " Shooting of His Dear,"[5] in which a boy shoots a swan and finds that he has killed a girl, *The Mask* is concerned with the force of love that can get beyond appearances. In it, Colin, who claims to have killed a girl although the police can find only a dead swan, wanders the "park of memory" in search of the girl to kill again. Margaret, whose face Colin sees as that of the swan, is a lifeless mask to her companion Susanna. The Prompter (". . . I, whose privilege to-night was omniscience. . .") arranges one more chance for

[4] The emphasis on making the best of a bad job suggests Eliot's *The Cocktail Party*, which followed *The Shadow Factory* by five years.

[5] Mrs. Ridler quotes the song at the beginning of *The Mask*, in *Henry Bly and Other Plays*, London, Faber and Faber, [1950], p. 13.

Colin, who dares finally to touch Margaret's mask and finds that
in the touching it crumbles. Susanna, who has also never tried to
pass beyond Margaret's silence, goes off alone, having learned
(although the learning process is a little obscure) that there are
more ways of living than she has suspected: "For them, the right-
hand way of acquisition./ For me, which? Way of rejection?/
Which way, left or right?/ . . . / Only, to walk in peace down
either/ And love, is not to lose the other."[6] Another character in
the play, the Park Keeper, is hesitantly defined. He wanders
through the park and the play, attempting to get people to pay for
rental chairs—"Folks often think they can go ahead/ Before
they've settled up their debts./ Then they're surprised to find
they're haunted." In the end the characters find that they do not
have to pay the Park Keeper, whom Colin has called the devil.
The significance lies apparently in the Park Keeper's own words:
". . . I/ Your tiresome watch-dog till you die./ Or—till you live."
The haunting debt of memory represented by the park and its
keeper is finally lifted from the three figures through understanding and love, which must come from themselves but through the
machinations of the omniscient figure of The Prompter. The
suggestion is that they learn to live through some final, freeing
recognition of God.

Henry Bly owes its plot to one of Grimm's fairy tales, "Brother
Lustig." Like Brother Lustig, Henry Bly is a returned soldier who
shares his meager store of money and bread with a beggar who
appears to him three times in different disguises. In Grimm's
story, the beggar is specifically St. Peter; Mrs. Ridler does not
label him exactly (except through Henry's "Old Saint"), but his
function is the same in the play and the tale. Henry joins forces
with the Tramp, who has the power to cure, and, although the
Tramp will take no reward, Henry cheerfully accepts material
return for his friend's miracles. After the Tramp cures a stuttering

---

[6] There are echoes here of Charles Williams.

woman, she offers a cooked lamb which Henry accepts; while the Tramp prays, Henry lays out the supper, but, unable to wait, he eats the lamb's heart, only to find that that is the only piece the Tramp wants. The incident of the lamb's heart in Grimm is an example of Henry's trickiness; in the play, it serves the same function, but has an added significance. "The heart is food, martyr, servant and master/ To those who are pierced with the same banner," says the Tramp, implying that Henry has accepted the sacrifice of Christ without admitting it. The further miracles in the play, the curing of the crippled Alice and the later healing of her stricken father, which Henry attempts alone and in which he would fail except for the secret help of the Tramp, parallel similar incidents in the fairy tale, not in detail, but in function within the plot. It is the reward that Henry accepts for these two cures that leads the Tramp to break with him, presumably leaving the adventurer to shift for himself. In parting, he gives Henry a magic pack which will provide whatever he desires.

In the second part of the play, Henry is seen ten years later, a wanderer still, no nearer any satisfaction; now and again he does find something he wants in his pack, but since he is uncertain of his desires, the pack functions only occasionally. He spends the night in a haunted house where the ghosts are out of his own past ("But isn't this Hell, to meet oneself/ After years of putrefaction?"), after which he starts out for an uncertain destination. The Tramp, whom he meets but does not recognize, tells him that "there is a way to peace, if you go back,/ Right back to where you started." Henry cannot do that; he takes a short cut which brings him to Hell's gate where he is denied admission because the gate-keeper is afraid that his magic pack might swallow all of Hell. At Heaven's gate, his old friend the Tramp (so it is St. Peter) is on duty, but he turns Henry away. Angrily Henry gives him back the pack and then, remembering its power, desires himself inside the pack and thus gains entry into Heaven. In the Grimm story, the entrance is simply the crowning trick of Brother Lustig's career; Mrs. Ridler has other uses for the magic pack. As Henry enters heaven, he stops to wonder: "Was I the one to be tricked, after all?/ The pack expressly meant for this?/ . . . Just to trap me into heaven?" In Mrs. Ridler's hands, the story of Brother Lustig has become a parable on the operation of divine grace.

At the beginning of *The Missing Bridegroom*, the Verger speaks the lines that indicate what the play is to be about:

> The messengers of heaven come
> As gulls upon the tame town,
>
> . . .
>
> Yet, beaten off, they'll not return
> Except at call, nor utter twice
> Their tender, cryptic, healing cries.

Within the play, Janet Frost is waiting to be married (for the third time) and the bridegroom, whose address she does not know, fails to appear. Each of the brittle and sophisticated wedding guests reveals that the missing bridegroom has in some way tempted him and, in the last scene, when the Verger is unmasked as the bridegroom, he reveals why each felt temptation: "Because I must be all things to all men./ Did I not show you what you looked for. . . ." Each of the guests, the bride and the priest have been touched by him, but in the end they all reject him and the vision they have seen through him. The Bride, who has come closest, who has heard the birds in the church tower ("Not everyone has noticed them," says the Verger), lets him go. At that moment she sees the birds, but they fly away. "Too late, too late loved," she cries. The play ends on her cry, but the Verger's opening speech has left room for that other cry that will bring the birds back; the play suggests that the Bride may finally, in some sense, find her missing bridegroom.

Mrs. Ridler's latest play, *The Trial of Thomas Cranmer* (1956) is a chronicle verse play, commissioned by the Church of St. Mary the Virgin, Oxford; it was produced, as a radio broadcast, to celebrate the 400th anniversary of Cranmer's martyrdom. The play is an attempt to recreate the historical archbishop, with close attention to contemporary records; for dramatic purposes, however, two trials are telescoped into one, and several recantations have also become one. A character, the Witness, based on an actual witness of the burning, is used in a vain attempt to make the story a parable for us: "we who see clearly/ The tyranny of theirs, our hands are not clean." Mrs. Ridler's hands are not quite clean, for that matter, because her persecuting papists look rather like stock *agitprop* villains. All her characters, villainous or not, are uninteresting; the playwright may have tried to give them accuracy, but she fails to give them life. The real trouble with Mrs. Ridler's play is Charles Williams, to whose memory it is dedicated. His *Thomas Cranmer of Canterbury* is so complicated and fascinating a play that any verse-historical run-through of the martyr's career is bound to seem tepid in comparison, and Mrs. Ridler almost forces that comparison when, even if she does have historical justification,[7] she makes Cranmer an advocate of Williams's doctrine of exchange.

Ronald Duncan. Both Mrs. Ridler and Norman Nicholson as verse dramatists owe something to T. S. Eliot, but plainly the most derivative of the three lesser Mercury playwrights is Ronald Duncan. His debts are deeper and more varied. His pre-war plays, for instance, derive from Ezra Pound. *The Unburied Dead* (1938), a slightly obscure play about the failure of a strike in the mines, is written in verse that is reminiscent of Pound's and

---

[7] In her Introduction to Charles Williams, *The Image of the City and Other Essays*, London, Oxford, 1958, p. xlviii, Mrs. Ridler quotes a line from Cranmer's *Defence of the Sacrament*, III, 10, which seems to justify her giving the archbishop Williams's doctrine of exchange.

Pimp, Skunk and Profiteer (1939), a satirical lampoon designed supposedly for street performance, plainly owes its ideas to Pound. Bearing an epigraph from Mussolini, the short play makes the unsavory point that the impending fight against the Nazis is a plot of the international bankers. The most interesting of Duncan's early plays, all of which appeared in *The Dull Ass's Hoof* (1940), is *Ora Pro Nobis* (1939), which he calls a miracle play, written to follow the order of the mass. Actually a Nativity, it shows the figures within the church enthusiastically excusing themselves, hunting scapegoats for their own insufficiencies. The Priest asks, "Lord, how can I ask Thee to forgive their sins/ Since they do not admit any?" The congregation does admit to worshiping Chance, Money, Race, Justice, and Self and seems on the point of coming to Jesus, whose birth is announced in the course of the service, when a messenger arrives with the news that the soldiers are coming. "Whose?" asks one of the figures. "Does it matter?" comes the answer. Considered on its own, *Ora Pro Nobis* would seem to be an essay on the consequences of a refusal to face responsibility; in relation to *Pimp, Skunk and Profiteer*, it takes on a different tone. In the light of the political system for which Duncan seems to be apologizing in *Pimp, Skunk and Profiteer*, it does matter whose soldiers.

By the time of *This Way to the Tomb* (1945), Duncan seems to have forsaken the political implications of his earlier plays; he has turned to a conventional espousal of Christianity and to the attack on rationalism and materialism which so often accompanies such espousal today. The play is divided into two parts, which the author labels Masque and Anti-Masque. In the Masque Father Antony comes to the Island of Zante to overcome fear and desire, to find peace. He brings with him three novitiates, who are his tempters; the peasant Marcus represents his body; the poet Julian, his sensual appetite; the scholar Bernard, his intellectual pride. Marcus and Julian die as Antony rejects them, but

Bernard appears triumphant until in sudden humility the abbot cries out, "Dear Christ, I sink in my own misery./ For pity's sake lift me into your Mercy, Mercy!" Bernard falls, too. Having overcome pride, Antony accepts some food that Marcus brought him earlier; this act revives the novice who says, ". . . Father, we thought you were dead." Antony answers, "There is no death. . . . " The Anti-Masque brings the Astral Group to Zante to debunk the myth of Antony's yearly resurrection. Led by Father Opine ("Science is his faith, to Science he is devout/ Cynicism is his psalm, fact his creed"), the group finds the tomb empty and accepts the fact not as a sign of resurrection, but of Antony's failure to reappear. Actually Antony comes on as an Old Man in answer to a woman's cry, "Now give us back our faith in heaven and hell." He is attacked as a charlatan; he says, "I can only be Saint Antony/ When my three attributes/ Body, desire and intelligence/ Make me complete by each/ Confounding their own separate frailty." A Postcard Seller who wants to leave bread for Antony even on an empty tomb is revealed as Marcus; the Chorus is Julian; and Father Opine, who returns to argue reason over faith, is assured by Antony, "Without faith, Bernard, there is no reason." The three attributes have returned, and the play closes on a testimonial of life over death. The chief virtues of the play are the use of the three novices in their several forms—although the manipulation becomes a little too pat—and a certain amount of fun that the Anti-Masque manages to generate. The first part with its temptations of the saint suggests the temptations of Becket in *Murder in the Cathedral*; the second part is plainly the stepchild of *The Dog beneath the Skin*, although it never achieves the flashy effectiveness of the earlier play.

The plot of Duncan's libretto for Benjamin Britten's opera *The Rape of Lucretia* (1946) is dictated by the ancient story that the composer and the playwright choose to retell. Here, again, is Tarquinius's rape of the virtuous Lucretia and her suicide; there is only a suggestion of the overthrow of the Tarquins that followed the rape. Duncan's addition consists of two singers, male and female, who act as commenting choruses on the action; the angle from which they see the events is clear in their lines: "We'll view these human passions and these years/ Through eyes which once have wept with Christ's own tears." The opera offers the words of the Male Chorus as a hope that transcends the violence of the story: "In His Passion,/ Is our hope,/ Jesus Christ, Saviour, He is all! He is all!" Nevill Coghill defends Duncan's libretto by insisting that "A more senseless and disgusting story than that of Lucrece is hard to imagine, and it was suddenly put in its proper perspective by the introduction of a Christian commentary by the chorus."[8] Coghill's defense would be valid only if the unhappy story of Lucretia were sensationalism and no more; actually, it embodies a strong sense of moral outrage that predates Duncan's intrusive Christian commentary. The playwright's additions, although they offer narrative bridges, remain extraneous.

Stratton (1949) is the story of a strong and self-assured man who crumbles finally under the weight of his own self-love and pride. The Reverend John Courtenay, the rum-drinking vicar, whose vices have grown to sins under Stratton's indulgence, describes the protagonist with "His character is as secure as this house/ On its old foundations," a description that is important in light of the fact that the house is almost carried away by a flooded river in Act Three. Stratton comes to love his daughter-in-law, to kill his son, to strangle his wife. Katherine, the daughter-in-law, makes him realize that in killing young Cory he has, in fact, killed himself. Certain of Stratton's lines attempt to lift the play out of the realm of murky, psychological melodrama by trying to give his actions universal significance. "That is why Man crucifies Christ daily/ Because Man is not only on a Cross himself/ But is indeed

[8] Nevill Coghill, "Hyaena and Bone," *Christian Drama*, I, 7 (February, 1948).

the all-embracing Cross itself./ It is all endless crucifixion," he
says; and again, "And all of us betray the thing we love,/ Then
find it is our soul that we have sold/ For who is not a Judas to
himself?" Duncan's attempt to make of Stratton's story a parable
of man as crucifier and crucified, as betrayer and victim is obscured by an excess of plot complications, shifting symbols, and
loose abstractions. *The Times*, reviewing a revised version of the
play performed in 1950, quite justly sums up *Stratton*: "It is a play
that dies slowly and painfully of a surfeit of ideas, themes, and
words; above all, of words. . . . It is because he loves himself that
he becomes his own crucifier. This idea is frequently stated but
never dramatively justified. . . ."[9]

Duncan is most effective when he is less pretentious, as in *Our
Lady's Tumbler* (1950), a slight play commissioned by the Salisbury
and District Society of Arts for performance in Salisbury Cathedral. Here, Duncan tells again the twelfth-century French tale
about the novice, an ex-tumbler, who tries to please the Virgin
Mary with his only talent and who dies making his offering. The
play opens on the feast day of the Blessed Virgin, on which,
according to legend, the statue of Mary will move if she is offered
a perfect gift. Brother Gregory, the gardener, offers her a rose,
putting it into the statue's hand; Brother Justin offers her a song;
Brother Sebastian, a canzone. When Brother Andrew (once
Merry Andrew) tries to entertain her, after the others have gone,
he finds that he can no longer sing, dance, or tumble. He keeps
trying until an attempted somersault strains his weak heart and he
dies; the rose falls out of the statue's hand onto his body. Father
Marcellus speaks over the dead novice, "O Holy Mary, Virgin
Mother,/ Is there no way for love to enter/ A man's small heart/
Unless he breaks that heart?"

Duncan followed *Our Lady's Tumbler* with two Don Juan plays,
Don Juan (1953) and *The Death of Satan* (1954). The former presents

[9] *The Times* (London), May 31, 1950, p. 6.

Don Juan as the philosophical opponent of heaven ("Don Juan did evil as a matter of principle,/ Denying the very existence of God/ He hurled his sins in heaven's face/ To prove he didn't fear damnation/ And to ridicule all redemption.") who disappears in the course of the play in a bathetic story of redemption through love. At the end, the dead Juan, not yet aware that he is dead, is almost stopped by the statue of Ana's father who offers false forgiveness in place of the true redemption which can only come through Ana. Painfully, as he turns into a statue, Juan makes his way to Ana: "Those who can be parted never loved." Duncan followed his sentimental *Don Juan* with the cheaply satirical *The Death of Satan*. The play opens in hell, a comfortable, conventional club in which Shaw, Wilde, and Byron are quite content; only Don Juan, who had some intimation of God through having known Ana, is unhappy. Satan, who is a kind of parson, sends Don Juan to earth to find out why people do not suffer when they come to hell. After a little adventuring which shows the women doing the seducing, the marriages very modern and free of jealousy, the ambitions small and material, Don Juan decides that "people don't suffer in hell any more . . ./ Because they're so bored on earth they don't notice/ That ennui which is eternity." When Don Juan brings the news, Satan offers him the boon of suffering; for the rest, "There can be no suffering where there is no hope,/ Nor can there be evil where there is no virtue./ This is the death of Satan, now Christ has died in you." He makes his will: "To those agnostics on the earth, worshippers of man and mediocrity,/ I, Satan, hereby bequeath: equality, democracy and boredom,/ Together with all my chattels and effects." If there were really as many "worshippers of mediocrity" around as *The Death of Satan* implies, the play might have been taken up more enthusiastically.

The Catalyst (1958), Duncan's latest work for the theater, is apparently a triangle play which attempts to sort out conventional and real motivation in the behaviour of men, or so Bonamy Dobrée has described it.[10] Presumably there is no religious emphasis.

Norman Nicholson. Norman Nicholson's *The Old Man of the Mountains* (1945) moves Elijah to Cumberland, where he opposes Squire Ahab, who can only build by destroying, who not so much uses the land as uses it up. When the Raven, the voice of God, speaks to Elijah he predicts drought; when it comes, he helps out as he can, finding, with the help of God, trickles of water to relieve the thirsty; he even brings the boy Ben back to life. Elijah calls a meeting on Carmel Fell, at which each of the dale people receives a vision, the prophecy of rain, in a different way: one hears, one sees, one feels. When the drought continues, Elijah begins to doubt himself, but the rain finally comes. Impressed with his stature as a prophet, Elijah is a little annoyed that the rain should turn the people's thought to practical, everyday affairs, but the Raven brings him back to earth, sends him back to his farm: "In the preoccupations of day by day/ They shall find grace and a glint of glory,/ And blossom yearly like the damsons." Nicholson owes T. S. Eliot a debt in verse and in idea—particularly in the presentation of the ordinary person as capable of no more than momentary understanding of the workings of God. Nicholson's play has none of the cuteness that mars Duncan's work; the simplicity is not always effective, but it does manage to create dramatic excitement in the build-up to the rain and a certain comic dignity in Elijah's self-doubts.

Prophesy to the Wind (1949) is a philosophically ambivalent play that takes place in a primitive society built on the ruins of contemporary civilization. Icelandic settlers mine tin and raise sheep in what was once England; John, a contemporary figure, turns up miraculously alive and brings the knowledge of electricity and

[10] Bonamy Dobrée, "Some Recent London Plays," *Sewanee Review*, LXVI, 654–656 (Fall, 1958). As this footnote is being typed, the play has not been published.

a hope of rebuilding the destroyed civilization that he has known. Hallbjorn, who fears John's dreams, allows the savage Vikar to kill the visitor from another age. The death comes too late, for Hallbjorn's daughter is already pregnant with John's child; the building, Hallbjorn decides, must go on after all, through the child. Nicholson seems to lean toward a distrust of John's material civilization, but in the end he allows Hallbjorn to accept the rebuilding even if destruction again lies beyond the growth. *The Times*, reviewing a 1951 revival, caught in one sentence the play's poetic and philosophical weakness: "The stage brings out the essentially prosaic quality of the story and shows up the verse as so much drapery hanging incongruously on situations which require argument rather than poetic metaphor for the proper development."[11]

Nicholson's *A Match for the Devil* (1953) is based on Hosea 1. 2. In the play, however, Hosea's marriage to Gomer, the temple prostitute, is more than a metaphor for the sins of Israel; it is a doubtful marriage that becomes a real one as Hosea learns the nature of forgiveness. The first attempt at marriage fails because Hosea so spoils Gomer that she has nothing to do, becomes bored and returns to the temple. Her son David urges Hosea to go and bring her back; she is tempted to come but she fears that his talk of forgiveness will lead to a repetition of the earlier boredom. She comes at last because David parades past, his clothes ragged and mussed, his sandal missing. Hosea at last realizes what is wrong with his approach: "But what does this forgiveness mean?/ It asks us to be what we don't want to be—/ We resent the presumption;/ We deny the right." When Gomer returns, it is clear that they will all work together in Hosea's bakery. The play, which dips into slapstick occasionally, is genuinely amusing often and is touching in some of its characterizations—particularly that of Hosea.

[11] *The Times* (London), August 8, 1951, p. 6.

Robert Gittings. Robert Gittings is not one of the Mercury poets, but he has much in common with them. He is a professional poet who takes to the stage on occasion, and, although some of his plays are on other subjects, his orientation is religious. *The Makers of Violence*, the Canterbury play for 1951, is the story of the martyrdom of Archbishop Alphege. Alphege's presence brings a schism in the camp of the Northmen because he leads the Norwegians toward Christianity; at the end, when he is killed by a Dane, his dying plea to Olaf, the Norse leader is "No revenge! No revenge. . . ." Olaf breaks with the Danish leader, Canute, and it is clear at the end that he is going off to try to emulate Alphege's idea of a king. At some point in the proceedings, Alphege says, "I am/ Guilty of the worst fault of those who speak and preach/ Without the deed, who say and do not do./ They are the makers of violence." Supposedly, his martyrdom is the deed, and Alphege becomes a genuine maker of peace rather than one of the makers of violence. Gittings's subject is suitable for the occasion, but his play is extremely repetitious, a quality that is made particularly apparent by the pedestrian quality of the verse.

Man's Estate (1950), which Gittings wrote for performance in Chichester Cathedral, is a short play in doggerel verse which shows St. Richard of Chichester as a boy, struggling to keep his family farm together after his parents' death: "God means us to work. And it is He/ Gives us this kind of difficulty/ As a sign/ To go on working here for His glory—." It ends with his particular angel prophesying the suffering and the success that will later be his. *Parson Herrick's Parishioners* (1955) is one of five short plays that show English poets in relation to the countryside; it is a rather unsuccessful attempt to write in Herrick's style, and it is as unconcerned with Herrick's profession as parson as Herrick himself often seemed to be.

Each of the playwrights discussed in this chapter manages to retain a degree of individuality, but an air of imitation is common to all their work. T. S. Eliot is the obvious model, although Auden and Isherwood, Charles Williams, and Christopher Fry (Gittings, for instance, has a taste for inappropriate Fry-like metaphor) make their contributions as well. The plays—perhaps because they are so largely derivative, perhaps because the playwrights are not equal to Eliot, Williams, and Fry as artists—are unlikely to attract much attention outside of circles with a special interest in religious drama. Duncan, Nicholson, and Mrs. Ridler have all had commercial productions, but, unlike Eliot and Fry, they have been given an understandably tepid reception. The talents of these three poets and of Gittings place them somewhere between Eliot and those writers who turn out plays simply for amateurs; their plays are hardly important contributions to the body of English drama, but they do seem to fill a specific demand for religious verse plays.

XI

Commercial Drama: A Reprise

Except for the presence of Eliot and Fry and the occasional incursions of the Mercury poets, the post-war commercial theater in England has depended for its religious plays, as for its secular fare, on prose dramatists. For the most part, religion has taken the forms already familiar to the English stage, those examined at length in Part I of this study. Three playwrights, however, stand out from the ordinary run of post-war commercial dramatists. Graham Green and Charles Morgan have tried to bring to the stage a consideration of religious ideas that pass beyond the conventional; Nigel Dennis has provided an intellectual, satiric attack on religion.

Graham Greene. After having made a reputation as a novelist, Graham Green came to the theater in 1953 with *The Living Room*, bringing with him many of the themes that had already become part of his fiction—the insufficiency of human love, the incompatibility of love and sin, the necessary failure of the priest along with his painful need to succeed, and the dependence on God's mercy. In the play, Rose Pemberton, following the death of her mother, comes into the home which her two great aunts share with her great uncle, Father James, a crippled priest who has been forced away from his vocation by his physical condition, but who has been unable to find the contemplation that might have replaced the practical busyness of the religion of his youth. The house is a large one, but most of the rooms have been shut off because Helen, who runs the house, is so afraid of death that she will not use or let anyone else use a room in which someone has

died. The house then has dwindled into a cribbed and constrict-
ing few rooms, and Rose is forced to sleep in the makeshift
living room, the common meeting place of the household. A
respectably grieving girl might have fitted easily into the strange
house of her aunts, but Rose, who has gone from her mother's
funeral to the beginning of an affair with a non-Catholic psychologist, Michael Dennis, brings a disturbing element into Helen's
enclosed world. The play tells a double story of the girl's growing
sense of personal guilt, which leads finally to her suicide, and of
the effect of that death on the house that has for so long avoided
life.

Rose's love for Michael, at the beginning a joy, becomes
anguish. The difficulty is the hysterical wife to whom Michael is
tied in a loveless marriage and from whom he can never be
separated—at least in the eyes of Rose's Catholicism. Her sense
of sin which turns, in retrospect, each act of love into something
cheap and ugly has its counterpart in Michael, who feels "Only a
damned sense of responsibility" for his wife, a feeling that is
probably meant to suggest a lingering, unarticulated belief in the
sanctity of marriage and a distaste for adultery. The situation is
aggravated when the interfering Helen, representative of a strict
and narrow orthodoxy, summons Mrs. Dennis. Michael's wife
threatens suicide, flaunting her sleeping tablets before Rose, and
the girl, who cannot stand giving pain, can only break with her
lover. "In a case like yours we always have to choose between
suffering our own pain or suffering other people's," her uncle
tells her. "We can't *not* suffer." Although Father James can define
her situation for her, he cannot give her the comfort that she
asks in a final scene between the two in which she vacillates
between a demand for human sympathy and one for spiritual
guidance, calling him variously Uncle and Father. He can do no
more than offer the conventional comforts of his profession:
"But when I talk my tongue is heavy with the Penny Catechism."

As the scene closes, Rose, forced into hysteria by the pressure of her desire and her guilt, takes Mrs. Dennis's sleeping pills. She cries out, "I don't believe," and then breaks, involuntarily almost, into a childhood prayer.

Dramatically, the play might well end on Rose's prayer, but Greene adds a scene in which the priest and the psychologist discuss the girl's death and the mercy of God. The implication is that forgiveness may lie just beyond Rose's nominally mortal sin, that God's mercy is beyond man's understanding. As ordinarily happens in the works of Greene, however, the mercy becomes pity. In *The Heart of the Matter*, the novel that comes closest to *The Living Room* in theme, Greene says, through the character of Major Scobie, "If one knew, he wondered, the facts, would one have to feel pity even for the planets? if one reached what they called the heart of the matter?"[1] The patient discussion about the meaning of Rose's death which comes at the end of Greene's play, like the moral after a medieval story, raises a criticism that can be most easily expressed in the harsh words of Walter Kerr:[2]

He [Greene] is willing to acknowledge the human impasse at which many lives arrive. And he wishes to suggest that out of this aching un-intelligibility, God will—in the end—make sense. But as a dramatist he can only show us the impasse, the ache, the unintelligibility. He cannot complete the picture, carry us over into the supernatural understanding that will make everyting tolerable, everything just. He is, if the phrase may be allowed, writing God's play without God's talent.

Yet Kerr's accurate summation is incomplete. The last scene does have one dramatic element of importance. The weak Teresa, so long dominated by her sister, decides to sleep in the living room

[1] Graham Greene, *The Heart of the Matter*, New York, Viking, 1948, p. 128.
[2] Walter F. Kerr, "Graham Greene Play on Religious Theme," *New York Herald Tribune*, November, 28, 1954, Section 4, p. 1.

despite Rose's death; Helen's fear of death (and of life) is thus exposed, and the house comes after many years and through the death of the innocent girl to have a "living" room.

Greene's second play, *The Potting Shed* (1957), is a kind of supernatural detective story. In it, James Callifer, the bewildered son of rationalist parents, learns at the death of his father that something happened to him long ago in the potting shed. In the course of the play-long search, James discovers that, as a boy, he hanged himself in the potting shed and that he was brought back to life when his uncle, a Catholic priest, prayed over him. The secret has been kept because the dead Henry Callifer could never face a miracle that would destroy his rationalist convictions and his wife has protected him at the expense of her son. The miracle, when it is finally uncovered, gives James a sense of presence where there has been absence—"I don't want God. I don't love God, but He's there—it's no good pretending; He's in my lungs like air"—and the possibility of a happy marriage with his ex-wife Sara, with whom there has been failure before. His search leads him to his uncle, an alcoholic still going through the motions of priesthood without the faith that would give his life meaning. In the potting shed, he tells James, he offered God his faith in exchange for the boy's life. "He answered my prayer, didn't He? He took my offer," the priest says, and somehow on that realization his faith returns. Greene has explained to a *Life* reporter that the priest's bargain is "A contract made in the dark," that his faith is "a gift from God, not a merit, and therefore was not his to give away."[3]

Neither Greene in *Life* nor James in the play, however, can quite answer the doubts of Sara, "It would have been such a useless miracle. It ruined us. It gave you thirty empty years, and your uncle. . . ." James's "But I couldn't believe in a god so simple I could understand him" is no resolution in dramatic

[3] "A Spiritual Suspense Story," *Life*, XLII, 68 (April 1, 1957).

terms. Miracles are, by definition, outside the realm of natural understanding, but the one in *The Potting Shed* seems to have been wrought not by God, but by the author. It is no miracle at all; it is a device. The play not only fails in communicating its central miracle, it is even more unsuccessful in providing a reason for its plot. If Mrs. Callifer hushes up the incident in the potting shed for fear that it will hurt her husband, his death should release her to relieve the obvious distress of her son; the complicated process by which he learns the truth—the interfering niece, the dismissed gardener's widow, the psychiatrist—becomes mere contrivance. Greene is able in *The Potting Shed*, as in *The Living Room*, to suggest characters of depth and interest, but in the later play he sacrifices them—the play as a whole, in fact—to a pious lesson.

Greene's most recent play, *The Complaisant Lover* (1959), is a triangle play that he calls a comedy, not because it is particularly funny, but because its three principals decide to continue as wife, husband, and lover, because this is an age in which once tragic passions are muted, in which, as the dentist-hero says, "we're only dressed for a domestic comedy." There is no religious emphasis in the play; in fact, there is not much of a play. Greene has also been represented on the English stage at second— actually, at third—hand in *The Power and the Glory* (1956), Dennis Cannan's English adaptation of the French play that Pierre Bost made from the Greene novel. The real story of Greene's dissolute and desolate Mexican priest is an interior one and, although the adaptation makes a respectable attempt to put that struggle on stage, it fails, partly because of its fidelity to externals.

Nigel Dennis. There is something of Graham Greene's whiskey-priest in the figure of Father Golden Orfe in *Cards of Identity* (1956), Nigel Dennis's stage adaptation of his own novel. Orfe, however, is a much broader satirical catchall than that; he represents the variety of public confession that has been both popular and profitable in the past decade. His is a small part in a play which, like the novel, is mainly concerned with making the point that identity today comes from outside the individual and can be manipulated by anyone who wants to make use of him.

Dennis's extended attack on religion, one that has the feel of the thirties about it, is *The Making of Moo* (1957), which he subtitles "A History of Religion in Three Acts." In it, three Englishmen in an unidentified country, having drowned the native god while building a dam, set out to invent a new one. Frederick Compton, the engineer, very much the practical man, wants first of all a Code; his wife will write the mythology; his secretary is to "suggest a few tunes." Much of the first act is an argument over what the god should be like, whether he should be flesh or spirit. "They have one Moo who is a man of substance, sir. He is the one they put on postcards, fully dressed and walking about," says the secretary. "Then they have a spiritual Moo who is quite invisible. He is for more sophisticated people." They choose both, and in the choosing, as in most of the choices, make fun of Christianity. In the second act, the religion of Moo has taken over, the three Englishmen have become enmeshed in their own invention; Moo is at that stage in his development when he demands human sacrifice. Even the set is "expressive of the key-idea that any return to 'real' religion involves a going backwards into primitive barbarism . . . .the irrational has utterly deposed the civilized." In the third act, Moo has become respectable. The brutality of Act Two has become prettified into tradition and metaphor. The scrubbing song, for instance, which was sung in the second act while the victims were actually being scrubbed, ritual purification before the sacrifice, is now heard, meaningless and sweet on the voices of choir-boys. At the end of the play, the son of the Comptons, now a priest of Moo, is intent on going back to the first, strong faith of his parents; "Go backwards if you must," says his mother, "but stop when you come to a pool of blood." *The*

Making of Moo, like *Cards of Identity*, is often very funny; its chief weakness is that, like any evangelizing play, it occasionally makes its satiric points with too lecture-like a precision. Pious in his impiety, Nigel Dennis has the virtue of the serious satirist and, for him, "The satirist is the theologian's blood-brother."[4]

Charles Morgan. Charles Morgan, also best known as a novelist, was the author of three plays—*The Flashing Stream* (1938), *The River Line* (1952), and *The Burning Glass* (1953)—which are related through his concept of the dangers that civilization faces. It was his belief—expressed specifically in "On Power Over Nature," the essay that introduces *The Burning Glass*, and in "Mind Control," the introductory essay of his collection *Liberties of the Mind*—that the western world, the world of Christian and humanistic values, is in continual conflict with an evil force, represented by totalitarian communism in the east and by materialism in the west. That force, for Morgan, is diabolic. Speaking of Christopher Terriford, the hero of *The Burning Glass*, Morgan says, "It became clear to him then that the development of man's power over Nature, which the last decades had witnessed, implied a subversion of the natural order, and that to regard this subversion as 'devilish' was not superstitious but reasonable."[5]

In *The Burning Glass*, a strange mixture of science fiction, spy melodrama, and Christian philosophizing, Terriford, the young scientist, accidentally discovers a setting on a weather machine that will polarize the ionosphere into a lens that can focus the sun, for life-giving warmth or violent destruction, on any part of the earth. Before the play opens, he has rejected two possibilities —to hide the discovery or to offer it for peace-time use only— and has arrived at a third—to allow it to be used for war, but not

[4] Nigel Dennis, "Preface," *Two Plays and a Preface*, London, Weidenfeld and Nicolson, [1958], p. 10.
[5] Charles Morgan, *The Burning Glass,* London, Macmillan, 1953, p. xxiii.

for peace. The rationale of his position is that the power comes from the devil and that its general use would push man further into the comforting clutches of materialism. Morgan says in the introductory essay, "the daemonic forces vary their strategy from age to age; they attack us through the fashions of our thought."[6] Christopher has apparently sidestepped the devil's strategy as the play opens. The plot concerns the kidnapping of Christopher by the Russians and the dilemma of Mary his wife, who must decide whether or not to release the secret. Instead, she and Tony Lack, the weak but lovable assistant, work the weather machine, burn warning swaths across the Russian countryside, and save Christopher. Lord Henry, the Prime Minister's assistant, who represents the world at its most worldly, fails to understand Mary's reluctance. "What evil is greater than war?" he asks, when she agrees with Christopher that the machine may be used for war. "To corrupt life." she answers. Morgan's sermon against materialism, in favor of the old virtues (represented by a chess board at the edge of the stage which is upset by the spy who spirits Christopher away, momentarily disrupting the game that Mary and Christopher have been playing for months) is imbedded in an unlikely collection of stage clichés. There is, first of all, the elaborate framework of melodrama—hidden airplanes, memorized secrets, code numbers for telephone calls. The spy is a sophisticated, bright-talking foreigner, obviously a villain from the moment he comes on stage. The prime stage stereotype, however, is Tony Lack. Tony, whose talkative weakness first reveals that a secret exists, is a good-hearted young man, turned nihilist by the war. In the end, having learned the machine setting and aware of his inability to keep the information to himself, he—in the best British stiff-upper-lip tradition—goes with a joke to his suicide's death.

The Morgan hero, represented even more by Mary than by

[6] Morgan, *The Burning Glass*, p. viii.

Christopher, is a kind of well of intelligence, strength, and quiet-ness set in a world of violence, a person who is both in and above the surrounding temporality. His power comes from Christian knowledge, or, at least, from an acceptance of virtues that are ordinarily called Christian. *The Flashing Stream* is a dramatic essay on the kind of dedication that such a man is capable of. In it, Edward Ferrers and Karen Selby, two mathematicians on a naval project, forego sex, although they love and desire each other, to work on the experiment. The cold virtues of the hero and heroine of *The Flashing Stream* are only Christian by analogy; it is with *The River Line* and *The Burning Glass* that the Christianity becomes specific.

   The River Line is not primarily about the struggle against the diabolism of materialism as *The Burning Glass* is, although Morgan's unending war underlies the earlier play, too. Marie, asked to define the enemy, says, "They are those who hate God, who despise the human person, who deny the liberty of thought." Each of the characters of *The River Line* is in the struggle, on Morgan's side of the barricades, but the point of the play does not lie in the battle. It is a story of discovery and absolution. Philip comes to England to visit Julian Wyburton and his French wife Marie, not quite aware that his visit is an attempt to lay the ghost of Heron, a man whom they have killed. During the war, Philip, Julian, and Heron were passing along the river line, a secret network that smuggled allied soldiers out of occupied France, and Marie operated one point along the line. A flash-back in the second act tells how Philip discovered a German letter on Heron, how Marie ordered him killed, and how Julian did the killing. Heron, whom they all loved, who is the most complete example of Morgan's quiet man in the center of violence, was not, as they thought, a German spy. Philip must learn this and must learn too that Heron was the half-brother of Valerie, with whom he has fallen in love. In the final scene, Heron speaks through

Valerie, absolving those who had to kill him: "They bore their responsibility in the predicament of the world." Morgan's play has difficulty communicating the "interior grace" by which Heron speaks through Valerie; in his novel, on which the play is based, Morgan sets the stage for Valerie's last scene by permitting Philip his own moment of the in-dwelling of Heron, but even in the novel the resolution is not quite valid. In both the play and the novel, the closing scene is able to conjure up something of the excitement of a séance, but it is also suffused with the séance's artificiality and manipulation.

On the occasion of the early closing of *The Burning Glass* in New York, W. A. Darlington wrote from London, "It's technical shortcomings did not go unnoticed by the London critics but Mr. Morgan has a large public here which cares too much for what he has to say . . . to be put off by faulty stagecraft. . . ."[7] Morgan's technical shortcomings are great. In all three of his plays, there is an excess of philosophical exposition. Much of the dialogue reads like a patient and repetitive attempt at pedagogy; much of it seems to come almost unchanged from the essays with which he consistently introduces his plays. That there is an interested audience for Morgan's ideas does not change the fact that the plays are weak dramatically; nor, for that matter, does it mean that the ideas are particularly clear or valid. Morgan's championing of humanistic virtues sometimes took him down doubtful paths, as in *The Burning Glass* in which all science seems to be resolutely on the side of the devil. In Morgan, the distrust of materialism, which he shared with T. S. Eliot, Dorothy L. Sayers, Graham Greene—in fact, with most of the religious playwrights—reached an unfortunate state of exacerbation, and Morgan was not quite able either to clarify his ideas or to present them dramatically.

[7] W. A. Darlington, "London Letter," *New York Times*, April 11, 1954, Section 2, p. 2.

Familiar Pattern. Along with the special cases of Greene and Morgan, the post-war English commercial stage has welcomed a number of playwrights who are working in the tradition of Henry Arthur Jones. These dramatists appear to be interested in the possibility of religion on the stage, but—although some un-doubtedly have private religious convictions—the plays indicate a greater interest in stagecraft than in theology. Bridget Boland, Wynyard Browne, and William Douglas Home are good examples. Miss Boland is the best playwright of the three. Her *The Return* (1953) deals with the decision of an Anglican nun to leave her convent and return to society, and *The Prisoner* (1954) is concerned with the psychological struggle between a cardinal and his interrogator in a totalitarian country. Both plays are examina-tions of characters who imagine a religious vocation and find that their vocation is simply for living. The value of both plays lies in Miss Boland's ability to communicate the anguish of a dream lost and a reality accepted. Miss Boland could cer-tainly have written her plays in secular terms. In choosing religious figures for her protagonists, she, like Jones long before her, shows religion as one of the sources of human passion and bewilderment.

Wynyard Browne's intention in *The Holly and the Ivy* (1950) seems to be to prove that vicars are human and can face human problems. The play concerns the Reverend Martin Gregory, whose children have been afraid to confront him with their dif-ficulties. Since the fears of the children are not based on a genuine conflict of personality, there is no reason why everything could not be explained satisfactorily in the first ten minutes of the play. In Browne's earlier play, *Dark Summer* (1947), there is a more believable conflict—between the old-fashioned, religious mother and the flip, modern girl for the love of the blind veteran. Here, however, the religion is expressed only in terms of conventional morality. In both plays, there is a neatness of plot and dialogue which unintentionally emphasizes the basic superficiality of characters who are predominantly of and for the stage.

William Douglas Home is much the kind of practical craftsman that Wynyard Browne is, and his plays communicate an even greater sense of the surface rather than the substance of life. An example is *The Bad Samaritan* (1953), in which the implied conflict between the Anglican father and the two sons, one Roman Catholic, the other free-thinking, is completely lost in a conventional melodrama of seduction and salvation.

For all the new seriousness which would seem to be implicit in the productions of the works of Eliot and Fry, the more conventional uses of religion still flourish on the English stage.

XII

The Church Circuit

The slow growth of church drama from the days of William Poel's *Everyman* and A. M. Buckton's *Eager Heart* has culminated in a nation-wide flowering since the end of World War II. Where once dramatic activity by a church group would have been an exception, today it is the rule. *Christian Drama* lists in each issue pages of church drama activity that ranges from ambitious productions of the comparatively difficult works of Eliot and Williams to the presentation of the most uncomplicated amateur plays. The majority of the work written to fill the increased demand for religious plays is as simple as the ordinary church drama of the twenties and thirties, but the years during and since the war have seen a number of imaginative plays and at least one playwright with a body of unusual work.

R. H. Ward. The most original and the most influential of the new church dramatists is R. H. Ward, who is an actor as well as a writer. Through his work with the Adelphi Players in Staffordshire and later with the Century Theatre, a group under his direction that toured England in caravans, Ward developed a dramatic form which he felt allowed the audience to participate in the experience of the play. At the centre of his experimental plays—*Holy Family* (1941), *The Destiny of Man* (1943), and *The Figure on the Cross* (1944)— is a chorus which ordinarily represents average man; individuals step out of the chorus to speak lines as characters and, once a brief scene has passed, the speakers, discarding individuality, return to the whole chorus. Ideally, the blending of the particular actor into the unity of the group is indicative of the kind of identification that Ward hopes for, one that will allow the audience to become one with the chorus in its dilemma and its search for "a knowledge of God."[1] *Holy Family* is the story of the birth of Christ and of His crucifixion told through the reactions of the Chorus which "must come to think and feel itself to be, one body: humanity." The Chorus, which both fears and hopes for the coming birth, suspect that it will be unable to accept the gift of Christ's coming: "We shall betray you, we shall gainsay you." After the familiar material of the Nativity—the annunciation, the scene at the inn, the adoration— there is a sudden switch (the play is designed to be played continuously) to the crucifixion, which, in the words of the Chorus, makes ordinary man both the crucified and the crucifier: "Mine is the heart that intends the death,/ Mine is the strength that raises the cross;/ And the death on the cross is my own." After the reluctant joy of the Nativity and the guilt of the Passion, the play ends in exultation and praise with the resurrection. To give timelessness to his retelling of the coming of Christ, to illustrate his contention that "just as the place the chorus lives in is nowhere and everywhere, so the time it lives in is both never and always," Ward lets the Chorus search for the meaning of Christ by listing a catalogue of contemporary sufferings. In a Preface to *Holy Family*, Ward finds the antecedents for his break with naturalism in the Greeks, the Elizabethans, and, in modern times, Henri Ghéon; a more obvious influence on this particular play is T. S. Eliot, whose concept of the Chorus as the voice of the ordinary man in *Murder in the Cathedral* is borrowed by Ward and whose verse is echoed in the speeches of Ward's Chorus: "And now for us the season of hope,/ For us, the poor and unnoticed. . . ."

[1] R. H. Ward, *Holy Family*, London, S.P.C.K., 1950, p. xvi.

The Destiny of Man presents the life of an anonymous Man: "An ordinary life. It is your own." The main figure wavers between two choruses, one male, one female, who represent the various possibilities of his life; at the beginning they lead him to a catechism-like definition of the double nature of man. To Chorus 1's "Man, what are you?" Man answers, "A figure chained to earth"; when Chorus 2 repeats the same question, he says, "The promise of a god." The hero is seen growing away from his earthly father, taking a wife, finally reaching a point of decision—between power for himself and power within. Man is unable to choose "Sainthood, or selfhood"; there is another possibility—"the middle way." Even the middle way demands a choice, however, between the reconciliation of the opposite natures of man or the compromise of one by the other. Man chooses compromise and achieves material success, but then he begins to learn that "To live for himself is not enough for man." The Choruses call on Christ and the man starts to repent, but calls back his repentance. When danger strikes (obviously, but not specifically the war), Man curses God, but he finds his footing and begins to profit from the danger. Finally, it is the loss of all that he loves (his family) and all that he owns that brings Man to admit guilt: "I have blasphemed who made myself a God." Man dies at the end in defense of a comrade, having found Christ. The theme of the play is that Man's life is in a small way a repetition of the suffering of Christ. The Choruses say, "not for us/ After the repentance sainthood, and the cross/ Is for the destiny of destinies./ For us and him the unremembered acts./ The unremembered deaths that even so/ May be the small cross degree demands." The difficulty with *The Destiny of Man*, as with most of Ward's work, is that it operates almost exclusively in abstractions; the tentative suggestion of a palpable biography for his hero, Man—the nod toward naturalism—is never strong enough to give the character personality. Ward's attempt to achieve a universal character at the expense of the individual results in a poetic abstraction with whom it is difficult to make identification.[2]

The Figure on the Cross is a further attempt to indicate that the cross of the ordinary man is like the cross of Christ, although without its redemptive power. The play opens with a choric lament on the absence of God, the necessity for the crucifixion of Jesus, and the crucifixion of all men that it implies. The play, in which the action is continuous, as is usual with Ward, passes then to a prose section in which Christ is fastened to the cross. Then there are seven sentimental passages in which the seven speeches of the dying Christ are repeated in situations which indicate the kinds of crucifixions that men inflict on men. Typical is one in which a widow, lamenting the death of her son in war, forgives and welcomes a comrade who deserted the dead boy; the text is Jesus's words to Mary, "Woman, behold thy son!" and to John, "Behold thy mother!"[3] All of the scenes—a woman with a dying child, miners trapped underground, a priest in jail for preaching pacifism, a crashed airman, a sinking ship—are heavily strained to fit the words; the most preposterous involves an artist, sick and starving, who struggles to complete a picture, haltingly reaching that moment in which the words "It is finished"[4] will be appropriate. Throughout, the Chorus confesses that it crucifies the child, the brothers, the family, the truth, the flesh, the arts. From the seven words, the play moves to a gentle scene in which the figure is removed from the cross and ends in a choric song of hope and salvation. *The Figure on the Cross* is designed to show that men are continually crucified as Christ was, that they share His suffering as He shared theirs, but that, insofar

---

[2] In a letter to me, dated March 9, 1960, Mr. Ward indicated his own present dissatisfaction with *The Destiny of Man*, which he no longer allows to be performed. The play had been completely rewritten as *The Judgement of Adam*, which had not then been published or performed.

[3] John 19. 26–27.

[4] John 19. 30.

as He is "Lord God, Lord Christ, Creator and Redeemer," He frees men through the resurrection.

Not all of Ward's plays are written in the form that demands the shifting chorus, but even those that are more conventional—*The Prodigal Son* (1944) and *Faust in Hell* (1944)—involve the protagonist working toward rebirth. The emphasis in *The Prodigal Son* is on the nature of the journey that the son makes when he leaves his father; the father says as he leaves, "Remember, too, the journey's made within." The son finds it possible to pass beyond the demands of the flesh to suffering in the flesh (from a life of ease to the tending of the swine), but he cannot bring himself to beg: "If heaven asks that I should beg of it/ Upon my knees, be humbled to the dust,/ Let go the pride of manhood from my grasp,/ Then heaven may keep its bounty." At last, he learns to achieve the death of self and pride, to admit his guilt and finally to forgive all, even himself. He is then ready to return home. The prodigal's brother, a man with an institutional sense of right and wrong ("But the right is simple./ It's what the law demands and conscience knows."), cannot welcome the returned son because to do so would be to discount his own life. The father makes him see that "your sin lies/ In self-deception," and the prodigal is given a grudging welcome. The point is that the prodigal son is all men; his journey in the play is remarkably like that of the hero of *The Destiny of Man*. Two Presenters provide the continuity throughout the play, acting in place of Ward's usual chorus; they lead the prodigal son to his final repentance, making dramatically possible scenes that would normally be introspective.

Faust is another of Ward's figures who represent all men. A speech of Wagner's at the beginning of *Faust in Hell* makes the identification clear: "You shall see yourselves/Who see my master, and his dreadful fate—/ . . . We here, you there, when all is said and done,/ Conjointly play Faust's story out again." Like Sayers's

Faust, Ward's hero wants knowledge and power to gain "Freedom for all men, nothing for myself." Once he has bargained away his soul, however, Mephistopheles taunts him, "Where have you known a man of power whose power/ Had any other ends in his intention,/ And was not used at last but for himself?" Two words, keys in heaven, will free Faust from his bond; he learns inadvertently from Mephistopheles that one is *love*; the other he later discovers is *death*. Through Wagner he learns the meaning of the words: "Christ is your lover by his crucifixion. . . . Love that is sacrifice, death that is life." Faust learns, like the heroes of *The Destiny of Man* and *The Prodigal Son*, the courage "to expose myself/ To that self-loathing which preludes repentance." At the end, he calls on Christ, the bond falls from Mephistopheles's hand and Faust dies, free.

The Wise and the Foolish Virgins (1949) tells again the biblical parable of the wise virgins who husbanded their oil and thus had light to welcome the bridegroom, and the foolish virgins who did not. The tale is set in a frame in which a crowd of Seekers—a parson, a post-office employee, a domestic, a factory worker, a publican—come to gain entrance into heaven and are turned away because they have sought heaven only halfheartedly. The angels use the play's titular parable to teach the Seekers a lesson and then send them away: "Seek first true knowledge of this Kingdom, then/ Return to us, no longer small sad men." This play, which stoops occasionally to some overly cute angelic horseplay, is a competent presentation of the parable in modern, comic terms with the moral still at the heart of it. It is, however, unlike the bulk of Ward's religious drama.

Ward's serious plays with their recurrent theme of man's redemption are couched deliberately in a Christian idiom that makes them unlikely candidates for attention outside church circles. The repeated pattern of material reward, guilt, despair, repentance, and salvation is never given validity in dramatic terms within the plays; its success depends upon an acceptance of Ward's faith in the redemptive power of Christ. Each of the plays becomes an elaborate argument for the acceptance of death (death of pride, death of self) as the prior condition of life; the argument sometimes is specific, as in the exchange between Man and the two choruses in *The Destiny of Man* or between the son and the Presenters in *The Prodigal Son*. Although the subject of Ward's plays and the impersonal quality of its development limits the general appeal of his work, his plays are probably the best— aside from those of Charles Williams—that have been written primarily for church drama groups. Not that his plays are without fault. Ward is aware of the limitations of his verse for he has said of his plays, "their poetry is designed to be effective in the theatre and not elsewhere."[5] For all that the verse is excessive and repetitious, achieving at time a high-flown flatulence, it is generally speakable—or rather chantable—and so likely to provide the weight of choric abstraction that Ward's kind of play demands. At their weakest—as in the scenes based on Christ's seven last words in *The Figure on the Cross*—Ward's plays approach the sentimentality of ordinary pious naturalism. His imaginative use of the chorus, which continually indentifies the protagonist with the observer, has a practical as well as a symbolic value. It keeps casts small and its stylization reduces the need for extensive props and scenery; the small producer—and most church groups are small producers—is likely to appreciate Ward's plays for their practicality as much as for their artistry.

Ward has his imitators. Among those who have been most successful with Ward's use of the chorus are two clerical playwrights—Philip J. Lamb and Philip W. Turner. In *Sons of Adam* (1944) and *Go Down Moses* (1954), Lamb adopts Ward's method to biblical plays. In *Sons of Adam*, which the author subtitles, "A Meditation on Our Lord's Nativity in Four Movements," Lamb

[5] Ward, *Holy Family*, p. xi.

shows the eviction from the Garden of Eden, Abraham's near sacrifice of Isaac, and a kind of biblical montage that shows David doubting his power, Jeremiah predicting the Babylonian captivity, and the suffering of the captivity itself. In each of the three scenes, the promise, "There will be a second Adam," is reaffirmed in some form. The last scene is the Nativity. In Scene I, Adam looks into the future far enough to let Lamb bring in contemporary material, as Ward did in *Holy Family*. *Go Down Moses* is a conflict between Satan and Michael for the soul of Moses. Satan tempts him to desert the Jews in Egypt, but he at last leads them to freedom. "Moses by his own choice/ Shall hold the place God's plan appoints for him," says Michael. In the last scene, Satan feeds the doubts of Moses, who regrets not having been able to enter the Promised Land, but in the end Moses refuses to curse God. When he prays, he sees a vision of the living Christ which counteracts the scenes that Satan has shown him of future wars, of the Jewish diaspora, of the crucifixion. Michael wins, but it is clear that the choice was always Moses's, that he has allied himself with God by an effort of free will.

Philip Turner, who acknowledges his debt to Ward in the Preface of *The Christ in the Concrete City* (1953), hopes to show in that play that "the Crucifixion and Resurrection are events of personal significance speaking intimately to the individual in the secret places of his own soul, and urging him to action here and now,"[6] or, as one of the chorus puts it, to show "The Calvary in your backyard." The events of the Passion are given, always in the light of the Chorus who cannot understand what is happening; their fear of knowing the truth of the Passion, their refusal to understand it implies throughout the play that Christ was crucified because he made everyone uncomfortable and that he is continually crucified for the same reason. The sins of Pilate ("Cowardice and political time-serving"), of Caiaphas ("Spiritual

6 [Philip W. Turner], *The Christ in the Concrete City*, London, S.P.C.K., 1956, p. v.

pride and ecclesiastic time-serving"), of the crowds and the soldiers ("Brutality") are shown as everyday sins, all part of the greater sin that tries "To raise up a God in the image of self . . .," the worship of man. As the crucifixion is made contemporary (and timeless), so is the resurrection. "For Christ is risen indeed, and goes before you into Galilee. . . . Your Galilee,/ The Galilee of the modern industrial city,/ Of the neon lights, and the multiple store." Both Lamb and Turner have attempted to use the method of Ward for their own purposes. Turner, for instance, has framed his Nativity in terms of the kind of life that would be familiar to his own parishioners in Leeds, to the inhabitants of any modern industrial city. The plays of both Lamb and Turner are less successful than those of Ward because, although they have mastered his technique, they are not as facile with words as he is; their verse does not have the flow that Ward's has, and, perhaps as a result, the commonplaces that fill their plays, particularly Turner's, are more obvious.

Three of Many. A handful of plays—E. R. Hougham's *Sensation on Budleigh Beacon* (1947), Tom Fleming's *Miracle at Midnight* (1952), and Dorothy Wright's *A Cradle of Willow* (1952)— stand out among the ordinary run of church drama. Reverend Hougham's play, written in jagged doggerel, finds the Rector of St. Saviour's, Budleigh, living in a cave at the top of Budleigh Beacon. He has gone there to contemplate, and his bizarre behaviour has turned Budleigh into one of England's biggest tourist towns. In the play, he comes down to report the results of his contemplation—his advance from despair at the misery and hate in the world ("Then swiftly came the call of CRUCIFY!") to a kind of naturalistic acceptance brought on by the sight of a scarlet pimpernel ("I heard the pulse beats of eternity") to a final resting in the resurrection of Christ. He returns to the empty pews of St. Saviour's to preach to the few who may hear. The initial idea of Hougham's play and some of the incidental material, particularly the slightly acid treatment of the profiteering mayor, are clever, and the play escapes the weakness of too naïve a message by balancing the rector with a soldier, also a seeker, who goes off only partially convinced by the word that the clergyman brings back from his cave.

Miracle at Midnight and *A Cradle of Willow* are both Christmas plays. Fleming's play introduces three symbolic figures—a man with a derby and a rolled umbrella, a girl who is a displaced person, and a snowman—who represent various aspects of the world. The man is the world too busy to notice or to love anyone, the girl is "The vagrant world . . . ," and the snowman is the transcience of human life. Each of them becomes a child, finds a present—their longing fulfilled—beneath the Christmas tree, and takes part in the adoration. Fleming's imaginative play uses a variety of kinds of verse, decorated occasionally with rhyme, which are generally effective; sometimes his choice of words becomes too clever, as though he had been infected with too much Fry—as when he calls the morning rooster the "alarm cock"— but the play as a whole has charm. Miss Wright's more conventional Nativity is set in England during the days when crafts flourished. Wisely it focuses attention not on biblical characters, but on a group of basket-makers whose lives are changed by the birth of Christ. Occasionally, the attempt to achieve the simplicity of life among the basket-weavers becomes strained, but the characterization in the play is generally good and, particularly in the scene at the end of Act Two when the blind man senses that the animals and the flowers are proclaiming the Messiah, it achieves a lyric quality which is unusual in the run of Nativities.

The majority of the post-war church plays can (and do) make little claim to literary stature. The tendency seems to be toward a slightly more subtle, more suggestive play than the early efforts at religious drama generally produced, although few of the post-war players with symbols have gone at it so enthusiastically as Mabel Dearmer did before World War I. The growth of a more consciously literary religious drama, represented happily by T. S. Eliot, Charles Williams, and Christopher Fry, has had its influence. The church drama movement has produced the plays of R. H. Ward, which, for all their limitations, make a genuine effort to achieve a theatrically effective form suitable for church production, and individual plays, such as Tom Fleming's *Miracle at Midnight*, which manage to be more appealing than the more pretentious efforts of, say, Ronald Duncan.

XIII

The Division and the Prospect

When Henry Arthur Jones wrote his defense of the use of religion on the stage, he added the warning that "In no case could it be profitable for the stage to become the backer or antagonist of any doctrine or creed."[1] Since 1885, when that statement was written, the number of religious plays (or plays dealing with religious subjects) has grown almost beyond the counting. At the same time, a division of opinion has appeared in the ranks of the religious drama movement, a difference that might be expressed in Jones's words, an argument about whether or not and to what extent the religious playwright should become a "backer or antagonist of any doctrine or creed." Playwrights like Jones, those who approach religion simply as a possible source of dramatic material, are not involved in the division. The quarrel is among believing playwrights, directors, and critics—all of whom are backers of a creed—who cannot agree about the nature and intention of religious drama. The differences were stated formally at the first international Interdenominational Conference of Religious Drama, held in 1955. In summing up the work of the conference, the Bishop of Chichester pointed out that three kinds of religious drama had been discussed—drama as evangelization, drama in church, and religious drama in the theater—the last of which he carefully labeled "not propaganda."[2]

[1] Henry Arthur Jones, *Saints and Sinners*, London, Macmillan, 1891, p. 129.
[2] Bishop of Chichester, "Summing Up," *Christian Drama*, III, 53–55 (Autumn, 1955).

Hugh Ross Williamson, whose historical plays would not be Christian by his own definition, used the phrase, "Christian (that is, converting) drama,"[3] in an essay "What Is Christian Drama?" His casual equation of Christian and converting represents a kind of thinking within the religious drama movement which makes a firm separation between the play as an art form and the play as a tool of conversion. T. S. Eliot made such the same kind of division in "Religion and Literature," although he was not speaking of drama when he wrote:[4]

the literary works of men who are sincerely desirous of forwarding the cause of religion: that which may come under the heading of Propaganda. . . . my point is that such writings do not enter into any serious consideration of the relation of Religion and Literature. . . .

The advocates of the religious propaganda play would seem to agree. Their concern, however, is with conversion not with literature and they would prefer to sacrifice the aesthetic to the evangelical. One of the most explicit statements comes from the Reverend Cyril J. Thomas, a director of religious plays who has acted as technical adviser for the Methodist Drama Society: "So the value of Christian drama lies, not in its aesthetic appeal, though this must not be despised, but in its propaganda, or, if you prefer the term, its evangelical content—its ability to win people for Jesus Christ."[5] The Reverend Philip W. Turner, whose *The Christ in the Concrete City* was written specifically in the hope that it could aid conversion in industrial areas, such as Leeds, where Turner has his parish, or Sheffield, where the play was first presented by Pamela Keily, has discussed evangelical drama in terms rather like the practical manuals prepared for the use of Sunday

---

[3] Hugh Ross Williamson, "What Is Christian Drama?" *Christian Drama*, I, 3 (July, 1950).

[4] T. S. Eliot, *Selected Essays*, New York, Harcourt, Brace, [1950], p. 346.

[5] Cyril J. Thomas, "The Value of Religious Drama to the Methodist Church," *London Quarterly and Holborn Review*, CLXXIX, 268 (October, 1954).

school teachers. After listing hints for the writing of effective propaganda plays—simplicity, shortness, speed—Turner goes on to dismiss aesthetic concerns with "Such plays may be crude, like the comic strip."[6] Both the advocate of the evangelical play and the Christian playwright who, like Dorothy L. Sayers, begins by "ridding himself of all edificatory and theological intentions,"[7] are in basic agreement with George K. A. Bell, who accepted evangelical activity as one function of religious drama, when he said, "The question arises as to whether these plays are works of art."[8]

Drama in the church is more closely allied to the propaganda play than it is sometimes taken to be. The difference lies in the audience rather than in the hoped-for effect. Except for plays that are put on in churches as entertainment—which must include many festival plays—the drama in the church is envisaged as an extension of the religious service. Just as the converting play hopes to bring the unbelieving to faith, the drama in the church hopes to lead the believing in an act of faith. The Reverend F. N. Davey, of the Society for Promoting Christian Knowledge, has summed up this attitude with, "when drama is employed in Church, as it ought to be employed, in close conjunction with liturgical acts, there must, I believe, always be a point at which drama gives way to liturgy and what has hitherto been *an* audience becomes *the* congregation."[9] Many religious plays, particularly Nativities and Passion plays, are designed to achieve this effect. Freda Collins's *Redemption* is an example; of it, the Reverend Gilbert Shaw says, "The audience is not being asked to enjoy, or to be excited by some stirring of emotion or intellectual con-

---

[6] P. W. Turner, "Drama as Medium of Evangelism," *Christian Drama*, III, 47 (Autumn, 1955).

[7] Dorothy L. Sayers, *The Man Born to Be King*, New York, Harper, [1943], pp. 3-4.

[8] Bishop of Chichester, *op. cit.*, p. 55.

[9] F. N. Davey, "The Christian Religion and Drama," *Christian Drama*, I, 2 (July, 1947).

ceit, but in its conclusion are invited to recite the Creed, which is the epitome of their faith."[10] E. Martin Browne pointed to the success of plays as incentives to worship, "Players will long remember how after a play given in the Bishop's garden at Chichester the whole audience, numbering some 600 people, followed the procession of the actors into the Cathedral to join in a service. Many a Passion Play has ended in a spontaneous impulse to silent prayer."[11]

The third kind of religious play, that which the Bishop of Chichester designated as religious drama in the theater, would seem to differ from the propaganda play and the church play by the way in which it is judged. The evangelical play must be judged by its ability to make converts; the church play by its power in drawing the audience into an attitude of worship. The more ambitious religious play demands aesthetic judgment, requires that it be considered primarily as a play. Dorothy L. Sayers wrote in the introduction to *The Man Born to Be King*:[12]

The idea that religious plays are not to be judged by the proper standard of drama derives from a narrow and lop-sided theology which will not allow that all truth—including the artist's truth—is in Christ, but persists in excluding the Lord of Truth from His own dominions.

Despite her protestations that her play, that any religious play, should be judged by the standards of secular drama, her introduction takes away as much as it gives. Her statement that "at no point have I yet found artistic truth and theological truth at variance"[13] suggests that theological truth leads to artistic

---

[10] Gilbert Shaw, "Introduction," Freda Collins, *Redemption*, London, Mowbray, [1952], p. 6.

[11] E. Martin Browne, *The Production of Religious Plays*, London, Philip Allan, [1932], p. 80.

[12] Sayers, *op. cit.*, p. 4.

[13] *Ibid.*, p. 3.

truth. Nevill Coghill in an essay in *Christian Drama* has written:[14]

A Christian play, therefore, resembles a socialist or other politically governed play; it is *parti pris*, and committed to propaganda. It is a weapon of conversion, and makes an assault on the will. In other words, it is something more than, and in a sense something hostile to, a work of art. This may be the reason why there are so few good ones.

Coghill is not talking of the propaganda plays for which Philip Turner called or the church plays that F. N. Davey discussed; for Coghill, any religious play is automatically a propaganda play by virtue of the author's faith. For that reason the aesthetic judgment of religious plays becomes confused. The theological truth of a playwright—whatever his particular truth may be— inevitably dictates the direction that his play takes.

Cyril J. Thomas may have put the preconception of the religious dramatist crudely, but there is no religious play discussed in this study (from *Eager Heart* to *The Confidential Clerk*) that does not conform in some sense to his dictum that "In religious drama this conflict will be between Good and Evil, . . . with Good triumphant in the end."[15] Gilbert Shaw has said the same thing differently: "it may instruct in morality, or point to questions that are insoluble by fallen man's unaided thought, yet just because it instructs or questions it must bring in the certainty of judgment and manifest the God-given solution of the human problem."[16] Although R. H. Ward has written, "I am not advocating propaganda plays and I am not suggesting that it is the duty of religious drama specifically to make converts to the churches by offering to the public the churches' dogmas as the only possible expression of truth,"[17] he has, on another occasion, echoed Thomas and Shaw

[14] Nevill Coghill, "Hyaena and Bone," *Christian Drama*, I, 6 (February, 1948).
[15] Thomas, *op. cit.,* p. 268.
[16] Gilbert Shaw, *op. cit.,* p. 3.
[17] R. H. Ward, "Elements of Religious Drama, Part II," *Christian Drama*, I, 5 (July, 1947).

with greater sophistication: "Ultimately, too, the message borne by the religious dramatist is always one of hope. . . . The climax of all religious drama'is the great scene in which transfigured son and eternal father meet and embrace."[18]

The specific assumption of Thomas, Shaw, and Ward that every religious play leads to a happy, a hopeful, a God-given solution is implicit in E. Martin Browne's more general statement that "it is God-centered, and treats of God's action in human lives and their responses to it,"[19] and in Pamela Keily's contention that it is "concerned in some way with the relationship between God and Man."[20] The apparently broad definitions of Browne and Miss Keily are limited by the fact that Christianity does suppose a particular relationship between God and man. The exact nature of that relationship is always in doubt, since there is a continuing difference of opinion on theological matters within the body of Christian thought. J. Alan Kay, editor of the Methodist *The London Quarterly and Holborn Review*, has written, "It may seem superfluous to say that the writer must express a sense of God that is not only real but true; but there are religious plays, and good ones, that say things about Him that are false."[21] Accepting that one playwright's truth may be Kay's falsity, there is still a common ground of belief among Christians, and it is inevitable that the Christian playwright should be directed by his faith in God; his acceptance of the incarnation, death, and resurrection of Christ; and the possibility of salvation through that resurrection. "Short of damnation, it seems, there can be no Christian tragedy,"[22] Dorothy L. Sayers once wrote. It is apparent from the

[18] R. H. Ward, "The Nature of Religious Drama," *London Quarterly and Holborn Review*, CLXXIX, 255–256 (October, 1954).

[19] E. Martin Browne, "Function of Religious Drama and Its Present Needs," *Christian Drama*, III, 7 (Autumn, 1955).

[20] Pamela Keily, "Bring It Alive," *Christian Drama*, I, 13 (July, 1950).

[21] J. Alan Kay, "Editorial Comments," *London Quarterly and Holborn Review*, CLXXIX, 246 (October, 1954).

[22] Sayers, *op. cit.*, p. 11.

examination of plays in this study that the religious playwright is not interested in depicting damnation. The playwrights may differ among themselves in intention—may be writing a tract, an addition to the worship service or a genuine play that attempts to carry religious ideas in dramatic terms. They may differ in tone —from the mawkishly pietistic plays for amateurs to the subtle and sophisticated plays of Eliot and Williams. All of them, however, are bound by beliefs which are not necessarily shared by secular audiences.

The Prospects. By now, the revival of religious drama has become so entrenched in England, dramatic production has become so much an activity of the churches of most denominations that the number of plays is likely to continue to grow. The quality of the majority of these plays is low, however, and is unlikely to improve. In 1931, E. Martin Browne wrote:[23]

Much pious writing is impious art; and too many of the earnest souls who produce plays without technical knowledge cannot tell the difference. There are those who deny the importance of the artistic standard, prostituting the art of the theatre to pious sentimentality with a smug face. It would be well for them to realize that the picture of God which they present causes many sensitive souls to curse rather than to love Him.

Since that date, the work of men like Browne has been directed toward the injection of professionalism into the production and writing of religious plays. The activity of the Religious Drama Society, the example of Canterbury and other festivals, the attraction of such men as Eliot, Williams, and Fry to religious drama has had an effect, of course, but the level of the average religious play has not lifted greatly. In 1947, R. H. Ward, almost echoing Browne's statement of 1931, wrote:[24]

[23] E. Martin Browne, "The Church and Drama," *Church Quarterly Review*, CXIII, 70 (October, 1931).
[24] R. H. Ward, "Elements of Religious Drama, Part I," *Christian Drama*, I, 5 (April, 1947).

I have in my time watched and read a great many religious plays. Few of them have been of a kind to move the deeper centres of my being, few of them have given me any incentive to live a better life, many of them have disgusted me as an artist, bored me as a human being, and given me the impression of belittling, rather than glorifying, the beauty and grandeur of the personality and life of Jesus, of the truths inherent in the Christian religion and of the nature and history of the Church. In a word, far from being of service to religion and to man, they have done both man and religion a disservice.

The quality of the average religious drama may offend the artistic sensibilities of men like Browne and Ward, but the advocate of the evangelical play asks only that it attract possible converts and the producer of the ordinary Nativity or Passion play asks only that it express sentiments suitable to the occasion. The aesthetic value of a play is ordinarily no more a consideration of the church audience than the intellectual value of a sermon is of the congregation. As a result of the undemanding nature of the audiences, inept and awkward plays continue to provide the bulk of the religious drama repertory. Most of those on the Religious Drama Society's selected list would fit the harried descriptions of Ward and Browne quoted above.

The more ambitious plays, those written for festivals or other special church occasions, are subject to the same dampening demands of the audience. T. S. Eliot, explaining the feeling that he hoped to counteract with *Murder in the Cathedral*, wrote, "people who go deliberately to a religious play at a religious festival expect to be patiently bored and to satisfy themselves with the feeling that they have done something meritorious."[25] For the most part the special plays are one of two kinds. They are laborious lumbering jobs, such as Dorothy L. Sayers's *The Zeal of Thy House*, or painful attempts to escape the pompous which,

[25] T. S. Eliot, *Poetry and Drama*, Cambridge, Mass., Harvard University Press, 1951, p. 26.

like Ronald Duncan's *The Death of Satan*, are likely to lapse into cuteness. The chief value of the festivals is that they provide an opportunity and an incentive for the playwright who is religious and wishes to be professional as well. That special events provided the occasion for the early dramatic work of Eliot, about half the plays of Fry, and all the dramas of Charles Williams indicates the aesthetic potential of church drama.

The future of religious drama in the English commercial theater is still problematic. The appeal of religious dramatists to secular audiences remains limited. It is true that the post-war commercial theater has opened its doors to serious religious plays, but the number of playwrights who have come through those doors is small. Only Eliot and Fry among the poets, and, to a lesser extent, Charles Morgan and Graham Greene among the prose dramatists have made successful entrances. In the cases of Eliot, Morgan, and Greene, moreover, the playwright has brought with him a literary reputation which assures critical attention and, to some extent, an interested audience. Fry's success has come through his comedies, like *The Lady's Not for Burning*, which can be accepted comfortably in secular terms. The plays of Charles Williams, who is one of the best of the modern religious playwrights, have never commanded an audience outside of religious circles. Although Williams's supernatural novels achieved a certain popularity, the richness of theological ideas and the manipulation of Christian symbol that inform his dramas have limited their potential audience. Even Eliot, Greene, and Fry at his most specifically religious—*The Dark Is Light Enough*—have held audiences in spite of rather than because of their ideas.

There is little doubt that playwrights such as Bridget Boland and Wynyard Browne, who are in the tradition of Henry Arthur Jones, will continue to hold the stage, will continue to use religious experience and clerical figures as dramatic material so long as such experience and figures are part of English life. For the playwright who writes out of religious commitment, however, the problem is one of learning to express his ideas in genuinely dramatic terms, of learning to write plays that embody ideas rather than vehicles that illustrate them. None of the postwar religious playwrights has been as successful as George Bernard Shaw, or even as James Bridie—both religious playwrights after their fashion—in juggling ideas and drama. The last act of *The Cocktail Party* and the last scene of *The Living Room* hang like warnings over the writers of religious plays. If the preconception of the playwright is so great that he comes to believe that his idea is intrinsically so powerful that the play can stand aside and let the idea speak for itself—and religious faith seems in the case of many playwrights to have led to that preconception—then he had better be writing tracts rather than plays. All religious playwrights, as Nevill Coghill has suggested, are to some extent tract writers; most of them are tract writers and no more. Eliot, Fry, and Williams occasionally become preachers, but primarily they are playwrights.

For more than half a century, since Jones's *Saints and Sinners*, professional playwrights have shown that English audiences will accept plays that deal with religion so long as the plays bear some resemblance to popular forms. The amateur church drama movement has shown that there are specialized audiences who cheerfully accept plays so long as they have some practical relation to the faith to which the audience adheres. These two kinds of audiences still exist and generally remain separate, although occasionally they do coalesce. At the point of coalescence, religious drama is most likely to produce plays that are more interesting than mechanical stage pieces, such as Wynyard Browne's *The Holly and the Ivy*, and more validly dramatic than the festival plays of Dorothy L. Sayers or Christopher Hassall. The busy religious drama activity of more than half a century, which has provided a great number of plays with a wide range of quality, has also produced a climate which makes the production of religious dramas likely. It is such a situation, as much as a personal attraction to drama, that has drawn artists like Eliot to the theater. The work of Eliot and Fry is evidence that the English commercial theater is willing to accept serious religious plays but the brief and unsuccessful gesture of the Mercury poets— Ronald Duncan, Anne Ridler, Norman Nicholson—toward the commercial stage indicates that only a playwright of exceptional talent has much of a chance of bringing religious plays to a wide audience. The prospect for the religious playwright in the commercial theater has now become the same as the prospect for any other playwright of ideas. Religious ideas are as acceptable as any other ideas in the commercial theater, but no more acceptable. Eliot and Fry have made the break-through, have joined the streams that flow from Henry Arthur Jones and A. M. Buckton, but the English theater must now wait for playwrights who— like Eliot and Fry—are able to frame religious ideas in dramatic form.

Appendix

So many plays make some claim, however tangential, for consideration in a study of religion in modern English drama that I have had to limit the number of those discussed in the body of the work. I have here added a list of plays which may be useful to any reader who wishes to pursue the subject further. In each case I have given a very brief description and a bibliographical reference. I have divided the list into two sections, to conform with the division into commercial and church drama that was used in the study itself; within each division, the listing is chronological on the double assumption that readers interested in a particular author will approach the appendix (and the book) by way of the index and that there may be some readers who are interested in a particular period. This list is not exhaustive, of course; anyone especially interested in church drama would do well to consult *A Catalogue of Selected Plays*, edited by Jessie Powell and Kathleen Bainbridge-Bell, London, The Religious Drama Society, 1951.

COMMERCIAL DRAMA

1879   Henry Arthur Jones. *A Clerical Error*, New York, Samuel French, n.d. An early comedy in which a clergyman guardian imagines that his ward loves him.

1887   Arthur Wing Pinero. *Dandy Dick,* Boston, Baker, [1893]. Funny farce about an Anglican dean who becomes involved with a race horse.

1890   Henry Arthur Jones. *The Deacon,* London, Samuel French, n.d. A saccharine comedy in which a Dissenter comes to London to denounce the theater and stays to praise.

1891   Henry Arthur Jones. *The Crusaders,* in *Representative Plays,* Boston, Little, Brown, 1925, II, 1–89. A satire on a do-gooder, uncomfortably like Jones's serious good men, in which there is a typical timid comic curate.

1891   Oscar Wilde. *Salomé,* in *Five Famous Plays,* London, Duckworth, 1952, pp. 317–383. John the Baptist loses his head to a Salomé who is the epitome of *fin-de-siècle* exoticism.

1892   Bernard Shaw. *Widower's Houses,* in *Plays Unpleasant,* Standard Edition, London, Constable, 1931, pp. 1–65. The reforming clergyman who never appears is the real opponent of the slum landlords and the silent owners whom they represent.

1894   Bernard Shaw. *Mrs. Warren's Profession,* in *Plays Unpleasant,* pp. 145–247. A mildly satiric portrait of a clergyman in an examination of the economic and social complications of prostitution.

1895   Bernard Shaw. *Candida,* in *Selected Plays with Prefaces,* New York, Dodd, Mead, [1948–1949], III, 197–268. A Shavian triangle play in which the clergyman husband might as well be in any profession in which public strength might mask his private dependence.

1895   Oscar Wilde. *The Importance of Being Earnest,* in *Five Famous Plays,* London, Duckworth, 1952, pp. 251–316. A fantastic inversion of social conventions in which Canon Chasuble, an unctuous comic cleric, figures on the periphery of the action.

1896   Bernard Shaw. *Man of Destiny,* in *Selected Plays with Prefaces,* New York, Dodd, Mead, [1948–1949], I, 695–745. A comedy about Napoleon with incidental, even gratuitous attacks on the Englishman for the hypocrisy of his morality and religion.

1897   James M. Barrie. *The Little Minister,* in *The Works of J. M. Barrie,* New York, Scribner, 1940, XV, 267–376. Barrie's dramatization of his own novel in which the suggestion of intolerance among Scotch Presbyterians never gets in the way of the pretty little romance.

1899   Granville Barker. *The Marrying of Ann Leete,* in *Three Plays,* New York, Mitchell Kennerley, [1911], pp. 1–79. Two satiric clerics, a casuist and a drunk, tangential to the story of a nineteenth-century New Woman in the eighteenth century.

1899   Bernard Shaw. *Captain Brassbound's Conversion,* in *Selected Plays with Prefaces,* New York, Dodd, Mead, [1948–1949], I, 599–694. Lady Cicely's conversion of Captain Brassbound is contrasted to the rice-Christian conversion of the cockney Drinkwater.

1902   James M. Barrie. *The Admirable Crichton,* in *The Plays of J. M. Barrie,* New York, Scribner, 1929, pp. 165–246. A clergyman figures in Barrie's famous shipwreck, probably because the author preferred not to conceive even of a projected marriage without the cloth at hand.

1904 W. S. Gilbert. *The Fairy's Dilemma*, in *Original Plays*, Fourth Series, London, Chatto and Windus, 1926, pp. 1–42. A youthful vicar is part of a *A Midsummer Night's Dream* confusion of lovers, which parodies both pantomime and the romantic play.

1904 St. John Hankin. *The Return of the Prodigal*, in *The Dramatic Works of St. John Hankin*, London, Martin Secker, 1912, I, 115–213. A clergyman figures in this play about a ne'er-do-well who prefers not to reform only because a Gloucestershire village needs its rector.

1905 John Davidson. *The Theatrocrat*, London, E. Grant Richards, 1905. A bishop, newly converted to a materialistic religion, is killed in a riot as he expounds his new doctrine from the stage of a theater.

1906 Hall Caine. *The Bondman Play*, London, The Daily Mail, 1906. A Sicilian confusion "intended to illustrate the conflict of the Pagan ideal of vengeance with the Christian ideal of love."

1907 Wilfred T. Coleby. *The Truants*, London, Samuel French, 1913. Dated comedy in which a one-time emancipated woman uses her return to conventional religion to save a girl who admires her discarded ideas.

1907 St. John Hankin. *The Last of the De Mullins*, in *The Dramatic Works of St. John Hankin*, London, Martin Secker, 1912, III, 1–87. The conservative sister of the rebellious Janet fails to catch the curate she wants to marry in the subplot of a play that is chiefly concerned with the most typical of the English emancipated women.

1907 W. Somerset Maugham. *Jack Straw*, in *The Collected Plays of W. Somerset Maugham*, London, Heinemann, 1952, I, 185–271, 1st half. A standard athletic young clergyman, "a modern nice sort of saint, who plays cricket," appears briefly in a play in which a parvenu family is given its come-uppance.

1908 Hall Caine and Louis N. Parker. *Pete*, London, Collins, 1908. Play version of *The Manxman*, which contrasts Pete's quiet Christianity with the harshness of Kate Cregeen's religionist father.

1908 Henry Arthur Jones. *Dolly Reforming Herself*, in *Representative Plays*, Boston, Little, Brown, 1925, IV, 1–102. A mild comedy about a quarreling couple in which a reforming clergyman sets off the action.

1908   Arthur Wing Pinero. *The Thunderbolt,* in *The Social Plays of Arthur Wing Pinero,* New York, Dutton, 1922, IV, 31–276. The bastard heiress of a rich old man finally agrees to share the wealth with her grasping relatives, perhaps under the influence of her clergyman suitor.

1908   Bernard Shaw. *Getting Married,* in *The Doctor's Dilemma, Getting Married, & The Shewing-up of Blanco Posnet,* Standard Edition, London, Constable, 1932, pp. 179–352. Several Shavian attitudes toward religion in a play that is primarily a discussion of the secular problems of marriage.

1909   Hall Caine. *The Eternal City,* MS, New York Public Library. An incredible business of love and revolution in a mythical Rome in which the Pope turns out to be the hero's father.

1909   Arthur Conan Doyle. *The Fires of Fate,* MS, New York Public Library. A treatise on spiritualism that collapses into derring-do involving the Dervishes and Archer's Camel Corps.

1909   John Galsworthy. *The Eldest Son,* London, Duckworth, 1913. The plot of Henry Arthur Jones's *The Hypocrites* with the crusading minister replaced by a clergyman whose sentiments are clichés of the horsy society in which he moves.

1910   James M. Barrie. *Old Friends,* in *The Plays of J. M. Barrie,* New York, Scribner, 1929, pp. 667–680. A bad one-act play about inherited alcoholism in which a clergyman appears as an amiable but ineffectual family friend.

1910   Hall Caine. *The Bishop's Son,* London, 1910. Privately printed. Play version of *The Deemster,* in which a banished murderer returns, in the disguise of a dead priest, to bring cures to plague-stricken Isle of Man.

1910   W. Somerset Maugham. *The Tenth Man,* London, Heinemann, 1913. A Nonconformist minister, a canting advocate of personal virtue, is one of the men involved in a shaky stock deal.

1911   Granville Barker. *Rococo,* in *Three Short Plays,* Boston, Little, Brown, 1917, pp. 1–29. A family group, including a vicar, in a slapstick quarrel over who should inherit a vase.

1911   Maurice Hewlett. *The Agonists,* New York, Scribner, 1911. A revision of an early trilogy in which the author, using figures from Greek legend, tries for "a tragic story of the failure of God to implant himself in man."

1911   Bernard Shaw. *Fanny's First Play*, in *Selected Plays with Prefaces*, New York, Dodd, Mead, [1948–1949], III, 745–827. Before the play within the play opens, its heroine has become so excited by a prayer meeting that she has gone to a theater, been picked up by a Frenchman, gone to a dance hall, mixed in a riot and gone to jail.

1911   Israel Zangwill. *The War God*, New York, Macmillan, 1912. A court intrigue, in lamentable verse, in which a Tolstoy-like prophet of peace finally triumphs over the apostles of violence.

1912   Lascelles Abercrombie. *Judith*, in *Emblems of Love*, London, John Lane, 1912, pp. 127–187. One of the poet's "discourses," obviously never intended for the stage.

1912   Cosmo Hamilton. *The Blindness of Virtue*, New York, George H. Doran, 1913. A plea for sex education in which a stock clergyman saves a stock misunderstood wastrel.

1912   Basil Macdonald Hastings. *Love—and What Then?*, London, Sidgwick and Jackson, 1912. A gallery of clerical types in an ambiguous comedy about a clergyman's wife with a wandering eye.

1912   Arthur Wing Pinero. *Preserving Mr. Panmure*, Chicago, The Dramatic Publishing Co., n.d. Much ado about the hero's attempt to kiss the governess in a comedy that lightly kids organized piety.

1912   Githa Sowerby. *Rutherford and Son*, London, Sidgwick and Jackson, 1912. Quarrel between generations in which the son's weakness lies in his having deserted the family business to become a clergyman.

1912   Israel Zangwill. *The Next Religion*, London, Heinemann, 1912. Hall Caine in reverse; a clergyman, having lost his faith, sets out to preach religion-cum-science.

1913   St. John Ervine. *Jane Clegg*, New York, Holt, 1915. A philandering husband and his mother use conventional Christian reasons to persuade the emancipated wife not to walk out; they fail.

1913   John Galsworthy. *Hall-marked*, in *The Works of John Galsworthy*, Manaton Edition, New York, Scribner, 1923–1928, XXI, 447–466. One-act play in which the Rector, like the Squire, is a stock figure representing conventionality.

1914   John Galsworthy. *The Mob*, in *The Works of John Galsworthy*, Manaton Edition, New York, Scribner, 1923–1928, XX, 1–96.

Pacifist play in which a conventional churchman appears briefly voicing patriotic sentiments.

1914   Israel Zangwill. *Plaster Saints,* London, Heinemann, 1914. A "high comedy" about an erring clergyman which reads liką a parody of Henry Arthur Jones and Hall Caine, and of Zangwill when he tries to be serious.

1918   Algernon Blackwood and Violet Pearn. *Karma,* New York, Dutton, [1918]. A reincarnation play.

1918   Eden Phillpotts. *St. George and the Dragons,* London, Duckworth, 1919. An unlikely comedy in which a bishop breaks up two socially unsuitable love matches.

1919   Ian Hay. *Tilly of Bloomsbury,* London, Samuel French, 1922. A comic clergyman, clumsy variation, stumbles around the tea things in a comedy about marriage between classes.

1920   James M. Barrie. *Mary Rose,* in *The Plays of J. M. Barrie,* New York, Scribner, 1929, pp. 543–611. The mysterious island on which Mary Rose disappears is tentatively if pointlessly compared to Heaven.

1920   E. Temple Thurston. *The Wandering Jew,* New York, Putnam, 1921. Pageantry, excess, and archaic language carry the Jew who spat on Christ across the centuries to death at the hands of the Inquisition.

1921   Clemence Dane. *A Bill of Divorcement,* New York, Macmillan, 1921. The possibility of hereditary insanity and the impossibility of English divorce law with a clergyman to express conventional church views on the latter.

1921   John Drinkwater. *Oliver Cromwell,* London, Sidgwick and Jackson, 1921. Stilted historical play in which Cromwell is presented primarily as a fighter for freedom, secondarily as a religious figure.

1923   St. John Ervine. *Mary, Mary, Quite Contrary,* New York, Macmillan, 1923. A comic clergyman and some clerical jokes on the edge of a foolish comedy about a fluffy actress.

1923   J. O. Francis. *Birds of a Feather,* in *Twenty One-Act Plays,* ed. John Hampden, London, Dent, [1938], pp. 105–124. A bishop saves some poachers in a brief, pleasant anecdote of a play.

1925   C. K. Munro. *The Mountain,* London, Collins, [1926]. An Elder of the Church, perhaps a supernatural figure, initiates the train of events that moves the hero from personal tyranny, to public power, to sacrifices of self for a greater good.

1926 Mrs. Cecil Chesteron and Ralph Neale. *The Man Who Was Thursday*, London, Benn, 1926. An adaptation of G. K. Chesterton's novel about the conspirators who are unmasked as friends ᵗand the arch-conspirator who is revealed as God.

1926 Clemence Dane. *Granite*, London, Heinemann, 1926. Three acts of passion and murder among the salvagers of Lundy in which the mysterious stranger is apparently the Devil.

1926 Clemence Dane. *Mariners*, New York, Macmillan, 1927. The love of a clichéd country clergyman for his slattern wife finally inspires a young girl to marry the worthless young man she loves.

1926 John Galsworthy. *Escape*, in *The Works of John Galsworthy*, Manaton Edition, New York, Scribner, 1923–1928, XXII, 357–461. Episodic nonsense about an escaped criminal in which a parson, choosing Christianity over convention, gives him shelter.

1927 Noel Coward. *Sirocco*, in *The Collected Plays of Noel Coward*, London, Heinemann, 1950, III, 271–354. A pompous parson serves as part of the English background to a tiresome play of grand passion in Italy.

1930 Noel Coward. *Post Mortem*, in *Play Parade*, Garden City, New York, Doubleday, Doran, 1933, pp. 349–423. Antiwar play in which one of the targets is the use of Christian slogans in support of the war.

1930 Campbell Dixon. *This Way to Paradise*, London, Chatto and Windus, 1930. Play version of Aldous Huxley's *Point Counter Point*, which fails to achieve the novel's monumental picture of a spiritual vaccum.

1931 Lionel Hale. *She Passed Through Lorraine*, London, Deane, [1932]. A comedy about a bogus reincarnated Joan of Arc, who leads a fantastic French household on a new crusade.

1932 James Bridie. *The Amazed Evangelist*, in *A Sleeping Clergyman and Other Plays*, London, Constable, 1934, pp. 339–363. The joke of this short play is that the hero, faced with the forces of Hell, begins to read from "A Popular Synopsis of the Views of the Neo-Mechanists," the scientist playing at bell, book, and candle.

1932 Alfred Sangster. *The Brontës*, London, Constable, 1933. The effects of a father's "narrow, bigoted Evangelical mind," this time in a historical, literary setting.

1933 A. A. Milne. *Other People's Lives,* London, Samuel French, 1935. An interfering clergyman joins some Cowardish bright young things in wrecking the lives of a harmless family.

1933 Mordaunt Shairp. *The Green Bay Tree,* in *Sixteen Famous British Plays,* ed. Bennett A. Cerf and Van H. Cartmell, New York, Modern Library, 1943, pp. 799–864. Good vs. evil in a homosexual setting in which a chapel preacher fails to save his son even when he kills the effete influence.

1934 James Bridie. *Marriage Is No Joke,* in *Moral Plays,* London, Constable, [1949]. Separate pagination for each play. One of Bridie's hard-drinking divinity students becomes, first, the Shah of Jangalistan, and, finally, a crusading clergyman in the London slums in a play which hints that a man cannot escape his religion.

1934 John Drinkwater. *A Man's House,* London, Samuel French, 1935. Essentially a social play, the account of a man whose world is shattered by the growth of a new concept, in this case the appearance of Jesus Christ.

1934 Eric Linklater. *The Devil's in the News,* London, Jonathan Cape, [1934]. A satirical fantasy about contemporary journalism in which the Devil appears and in which the diabolic framework is simply the author's way of saying "to hell with it."

1937 Kenneth Horne. *Yes and No,* New York, Samuel French, 1938. Comic clergyman, forgetful variation, in a gimmick play in which what results from both answers is presented.

1938 James Bridie. *The Last Trump,* London, Constable, [1938]. Some conventional religious types and some others wait for the end of the world.

1938 J. B. Priestley. *When We Are Married,* in *The Plays of J. B. Priestley,* London, Heinemann, [1948–1950], II, 139–201. Three acts of complication and clowning follow when three couples of staunch chapel folk discover, on their thirtieth anniversary, that the minister who married them did not have the power to do so.

1939 Gordon Daviot. *The Stars Bow Down,* London, Duckworth, 1939. The Biblical success story of Joseph in Egypt.

1945 James Bridie. *Paradise Enow,* in *Tedious and Brief,* London, Constable, [1945], pp. 175–185. Short play in which a Syrian quickly tires of his houri-filled heaven and enquires after the harp-playing heaven of the English missionary.

1945 Emlyn Williams. *The Wind of Heaven*, London, Heinemann, 1945. Christ is reborn in Wales in 1856.

1947 Gordon Daviot. *The Little Dry Thorn*, in *Plays I*, London, Peter Davies, [1953], pp. 1–74. Biblical play, quite well done, about Sara and the faith that finally brings her a child. Earlier one-act version, *Sara*, in *Leith Sands and Other Short Plays*, London, Duckworth, [1946], pp. 56–68.

1947 William Douglas Home. "*Now Barabbas . . .*", London, Longmans, Green, 1947. Cluttered prison play in which the bitter condemned man finally consents to the prayers of a conventional chaplain.

1947 Hugh Ross Williamson. *Queen Elizabeth*, London, Constable, 1947. Historical doings which touch on religion in the Protestant opposition to the queen's proposed marriage to the Duc d'Anjou.

1948 Peter Ustinov. *The Indifferent Shepherd*, in *Plays About People*, London, Jonathan Cape, [1950], pp. 227–306. A parable of compassion involving a tolerant clergyman, his bitter wife and his narrow-minded brother-in-law.

1949 Charlotte Hastings. *Bonaventure*, in *Plays of the Year*, Vol. 3, ed. J. C. Trewin, London, Elek, [1950], pp. 203–318. A mystery—murder not spiritual—in a convent; called *High Ground* (New York, Samuel French, [1951]) in the United States.

1950 James Bridie. *Mr. Gillie*, London, Constable, [1950]. The straightforward story of a schoolmaster placed in a supernatural framework of judgment after death.

1950 Tyrone Guthrie. *Top of the Ladder*, in *Plays of the Year*, Vol. 3, ed. J. C. Trewin, London, Elek, [1950], pp. 521–662. Expressionistic account of an ordinary man in which the voice at the top of the ladder is a multiple symbol—his father, his heroes, and God.

1950 Benn W. Levy. *Return To Tyassi*, London, Gollancz, 1951. The author tries to give wider significance to the quite specific problems of his heroine—the failed marriage and lost love that leads to suicide—by sprinkling the play with speeches about God and the universe.

1950 Peter Ustinov. *The Tragedy of Good Intentions*, in *Plays About People*, London, Jonathan Cape, [1950], pp. 33–139. An ambitious play about the Crusades in which the leading character, who embodies compassion and common sense, is contrasted to and a victim of the political maneuvering of the churchmen and the fanaticism of Peter the Hermit.

1951   Yvonne Mitchell. *The Same Sky,* in *Plays of the Year,* Vol. 6, ed. J. C. Trewin, London, Elek, [1952], pp. 233–311. Sentimental play in which the stern Jewish father finally forgives his daughter for having married a Gentile.

1951   John Whiting. *Saint's Day,* in *Plays of the Year,* Vol. 6, ed. J. C. Trewin, London, Elek, [1952], pp. 19–139. The murder of a recluse poet and a recluse clergyman at the hands of three madmen and a fashionable critic in a confused play that seems to be saying that when religion and art retreat from life, violence triumphs.

1955   Philip King. *Serious Charge,* London, Samuel French, [1956]. Conventional problem play in which a young clergyman is accused and cleared of a charge of homosexuality.

1955   Philip King and Falkland L. Cary. *Sailor, Beware,* in *Plays of the Year,* Vol. 12, ed. J. C. Trewin, London, Elek, [1955], pp. 331–475. A clergyman wanders in unnecessarily to solve the marital difficulties of a young sailor.

CHURCH DRAMA

1903   Dora Greenwell McChesney. *Outside the Gate,* in *Fortnightly Review,* N.S., LXXIV, 1035–1040 (December, 1903). Nativity in doggerel verse in which the angelic chorus teaches the shepherds not to expect a king in political terms.

1908   Edith Lyttleton. *A Christmas Morality Play,* London, Elkin Mathews, 1908. A starving family shares its bread with a gathering of abstractions and receives spiritual and material rewards.

1910   Robert Hugh Benson. *The Cost of a Crown,* London, Longmans, Green, 1910. Account of John Bost, Catholic martyr in Elizabethan England.

1911   Clifford Bax. *The Marriage of the Soul,* in *Poems Dramatic and Lyrical,* London, The Orpheus Press, 1911, pp. 98–128. A mystical Egyptian business in which we learn that any love is a form of the love of Osiris.

1911   Robert Hugh Benson. *The Maid of Orleans,* London, Longmans, Green, 1911. A villainous Bishop of Beauvais hurries Joan to her martyrdom, in rhymed verse.

1911   Charles Rann Kennedy. *The Terrible Meek,* in *A Repertory of Plays for a Company of Seven Players and Two Short Plays for Smaller Casts,* Chicago, University of Chicago Press, 1930, pp. 607–636. One-act play about the crucifixion.

1912   Edith Lyttleton. *Peter's Chance,* London, Duckworth, 1912. Three acts of conventional West End realism in the cause of the mission movement in London.

1913   Edith Lyttleton. *Dame Julian's Window,* in *Nineteenth Century,* LXXIII, 435–449 (February, 1913). The anchoress of Norwich presides over the familiar story of a girl too pure for this world.

1914   Robert Hugh Benson. *The Upper Room,* New York, Longmans, Green, [1914]. Blank verse Passion play, strongly Marian in tone.

1916   John Drinkwater. *The God of Quiet,* in *Pawns,* Boston, Houghton Mifflin, [1920], pp. 22–45. Antiwar play in verse.

1920   Margaret Cropper. *The Next-Door House,* London, S.P.C.K., 1920. Chatty Christmas play in which Down in the Dust and Evil Life are saved by the traditional appearance of the Virgin and the Child.

1921   H. M. Paull. *The Vision,* in *Nineteenth Century and After,* LXXXIX, 175–188 (January, 1921). The titular vision is a gentle joke in a play that is otherwise interested in attacking self-righteousness.

1922   M. Creagh-Henry. *The Gate of Vision,* in *Four Mystical Plays,* London, S.P.C.K., 1924, pp. 71–122. "Love opens wide the starry Gate of Vision" to several standard characters preoccupied with self.

1922   Cicely Hamilton. *The Child in Flanders,* in *One-Act Plays of To-day,* Second Series, New York, Dodd, Mead, 1929, pp. 247–280. Nativity involving the tableau-dreams of three soldiers.

1922   Laurence Housman. *Possession,* in *Angels and Ministers,* New York, Harcourt, Brace, 1922, pp. 89–150. A comedy about one man's heaven being another's hell, in which the after life is the setting for some kidding of Victorian ideas.

1923   B. C. Boulter. *Paul and Silas,* London, S.P.C.K., [1923]. Drama in crude verse, based on incidents in Acts, Chapter 16.

1924   M. Creagh-Henry. *The Gardener,* London, Samuel French, [1924].
Mystical figure teaches charity to the proud Lady Croesus.

1924   M. Creagh-Henry. *"Greater Love Hath No Man,"* in *Four
Mystical Plays,* London, S.P.C.K., 1924, pp. 19–38. Passion
play in which the B.V.M. forgives Peter the betrayal.

1924   M. Creagh-Henry. *The Star,* in *Four Mystical Plays,* pp. 39–70.
Some modern types learn the true meaning of Christmas.

1924   A. O. Roberts. *Cloudbreak,* in *Three One-Act Plays,* New York,
Samuel French, 1925, pp. 51–75. Judas appears as a beggar and
begs back the last of the scattered thirty pieces of silver.

1925   Margaret Cropper. *Two Sides of the Door,* in *Religious Drama,*
Vol. 2, ed. Committee on Drama of the Federal Council of
Churches of Christ in America, New York, Century, [1926],
pp. 133–148. Simple, saccharine Christmas play in which The
Householder, opening his door to all, opens it to the Christ
child.

1927   Laurence Binyon. *Boadicea,* London, Benn, 1927. A mixture of
prose and poetry in which the emphasis is as much on freedom
and England as it is on Boadicea's search for a new God.

1928   Stéphanie Cotton. *The Legend of Baboushka,* London, Deane,
1928. Nativity based on two Russian legends, one about
Baboushka, the Russian Father Christmas, and the other, the
tradition that St. Andrew preached there.

1928   Mona Swann. *At the Well of Bethlehem,* London, 1930. Privately
printed. Three playlets—on Ruth, David, and Mary—joined
by the narration of the women at the well, arranged from the
words of the Bible.

1929   M. Creagh-Henry. *The Stray Sheep,* London, Samuel French,
1929. A Shepherd saves a sick baby and brings three despairing
adults to belief in good, in tiresome dialect.

1930   Margaret Cropper. *The Legend of St. Christopher,* London, St.
Christopher Press, 1932. A straightforward telling of the story
of the strong man who wants to serve the strongest king in the
world.

1932   Henzie Browne. *Disarm!,* London, S.P.C.K., 1932. Pacifist
play written for performance in a church.

1932   H. D. C. Pepler. *The Rosary,* in *Mimes Sacred and Profane,* London,
Samuel French, [1932], pp. 23–54. Miming of the five joyful, the
five sorrowful, and the five glorious mysteries.

1932   H. D. C. Pepler. *The Stations of the Cross,* in *Mimes Sacred and Profane,* pp. 55–67. Miming of the Stations.

1932   Mona Swann. *Jerusalem,* London, Gerald Home, 1933. Three Biblical stories arranged from the Authorized Version.

1933   M. Creagh-Henry. *Alban of Verulamium,* London, S.P.C.K., [1933]. Legendary account of the conversion and martyrdom of Alban.

1934   Nora Ratcliff. *Pedlar's Progress,* in *Eastward in Eden and Other Plays,* London, Nelson, [1937], pp. 89–120. A self-conscious folk play in which a pedlar poses as the devil to gull the villagers.

1935   Nora Ratcliff. *Eastward in Eden,* in *Eastward in Eden and Other Plays,* pp. 31–58. Eve's temptation and fall depicted as an act of great dignity.

1936   Margaret Cropper. *The Pageant of Peace,* in *A Book of One-Act Plays,* by John Drinkwater, etc., London, Allenson, [1936], pp. 51–66. Abstractions—Peace, Truth, Valour, etc.—carry the pacifist message in free verse.

1936   Dermot Morrah. *Chorus Angelorum,* London, Samuel French, [1936]. A Nativity full of tiresomely cute child angels.

1936   I. P. Rawkins Jeffers. *The Pageant of Saint Alban,* Goodmayes, Essex, The ·Holmsbury Press, [1936]. A play with music first performed at the Church of St. Alban, Dagenham, by the 12th and 12thA Barking Girl Guides (St. Alban's Own).

1936   H. F. Rubinstein. *All Things Are Possible,* in *Hated Servants,* London, Gollancz, 1944, pp. 139–157. A play about Roman Christians under Nero, in which the characters speak as their counterparts would today.

1936   Horace Shipp. *The Charlady and the Angel,* in *Ten New One-Acters,* ed. Herman Ould, London, Longmans, Green, [1936], pp. 151–181. The charlady's seeing the angel is the occasion for a mild satire on fashionable religious affectation.

1938   Vera I. Arlett. *The Door Was Closed,* in *Ten Peace Plays,* ed. R. H. Ward, London, Dent, [1938], pp. 63–83. Pacifist play.

1938   Vera I. Arlett. *Water Party,* in *Eight New One-Act Plays of 1938,* ed. William Armstrong, London, Lovat Dickson, [1938], pp. 9–31. One-act of Romans crossing the Styx in which the protagonist gets a hint of the meaning of Christianity.

1938   E. Martin Browne. *The Story of Christmas in Mime,* London, The

Sheldon Press, [1952]. Directions for mimed actions to accompany the reading of the Nativity story.

1938 Neil Grant. *The Last War,* in *Ten Peace Plays,* ed. R. H. Ward, London, Dent, [1938], pp. 105–126. Pacifist play.

1938 H. F. Rubinstein. *First Corinthians,* in *Hated Servants,* London, Gollancz, 1944, pp. 97–116. A typical congregation receives Paul's letter of exhortation.

1938 F. Sladen-Smith. *The Man Who Wouldn't Go to Heaven,* in *Twenty One-Act Plays,* ed. John Hampden, London, Dent, [1938], pp. 171–195. A professional rebel finds himself in Heaven when, without realizing it, he acts simply and naturally like a child.

1938 Mona Swann. *The Invisible One,* Boston, Baker, [1938]. The retelling, for children, of an Algonquin legend about a mighty hunter (God) who transforms an ugly girl into a beauty.

1939 H. F. Rubinstein. *London Stone,* London, Nelson, 1939. Boadicea as a fanatic, contrasted to the dignity of a Roman matron and the calm faith of a religious mystic.

1942 Rodney Bennett. *The Real St. George,* London, University of London Press, [1942]. Radio play that contrasts the real to the legendary St. George.

1944 T. B. Morris. *I Will Arise!,* in *I Will Arise! and Other Plays,* London, Muller, [1948], pp. 1–40. A play of faith wavering and restored written to be acted in the ruins of Coventry Cathedral.

1944 H. F. Rubinstein. *Chosen People,* in *Hated Servants,* London, Gollancz, 1944, pp. 73–96. The disagreement between Paul and Peter over preaching to the Gentiles.

1944 H. F Rubinstein *Holyest Erth,* in *Hated Servants,* pp. 117–138. Joseph of Arimathea, as the first Christian missionary in England, gives a rational explanation of the empty tomb on Easter morning, but he makes his conversions all the same.

1944 H. F. Rubinstein. *Ohad's Woman,* in *Hated Servants,* pp. 55–72. The Samaritan woman who gave Jesus a drink of water (John 4) and the effect on her, seen from her family.

1944 H. F. Rubinstein. *Rahab of Jericho,* in *Hated Servants,* pp. 7–32. Israelite spies in Jericho, from Joshua 2.

1945 Jessie Powell. *In Him Is Life,* London, S.P.C.K., [1945]. A play for women and children in which Christ's mission is described at second hand through Mary and Martha and the mothers of the disciples.

1945 Hugh Ross Williamson. *Paul, a Bond Slave,* London, S.C.M. Press, 1945. Chatty extension of the biblical story.

1946 H. F. Rubinstein. *The Fifth Gospel,* London, Gollancz, 1946. A play about a Nazarene family in the early years of Christianity.

1947 T. B. Morris. *The White Horseman,* in *I Will Arise! and Other Plays,* London, Muller, [1948], pp. 121–163. Murky philosophical doings in bad verse about the end of the world.

1947 Hugh Ross Williamson. *The Story without an End,* London, Mowbray, [1947]. Radio playlets about Christ and the disciples used as part of the B.B.C. school-devotional system.

1948 Vera I. Arlett. *Saint Alban,* London, Gollancz, 1948. The British martyr in a play in which the emphasis is on freedom.

1948 Michael Burn. *The Modern Everyman,* London, Rupert Hart-Davis, 1948. The voice of Conscience, not the voice of God, calls Everyman, and he goes not to Heaven, but into the world to work for mankind.

1948 E. R. Hougham. *Dead End,* in *Plays of Perplexity,* London, published for the Religious Drama Society by S.P.C.K., 1948, pp. 39–83. Sentimental supernatural play about a group at the Dead End Hotel, some of whom see a vision of life rising out of destruction.

1948 V. D. Peareth. *The Prince of Peace,* London, Oxford, 1955. Conventional Nativity that recounts the biblical story in simple language.

1948 Jessie Powell. *Living Water,* London, Edinburgh House Press, 1948. A supposedly true story about how a New Testament, torn apart, passes its message, page by page, through an Arab village.

1948 Lesbia Scott. *Then Will She Return,* London, published for the Religious Drama Society by S.P.C.K., 1948. Three acts designed to show that the parson's life is difficult and that the English layman is indifferent.

1949 Rodney Bennett. *The Pilgrim's Progress,* London, published for the Religious Drama Society by S.P.C.K., 1949. An adaptation of John Bunyan's novel in which Bunyan tells the story to a garrulous gaoler.

1949 Freda Collins. *The Blind Witness,* London, The Edinburgh House Press, 1949. In one busy act a Christian blind girl saves her mother-in-law from suicide by telling her the story of Christ.

1949   Freda Collins. *Cyprian,* London, published for the Religious
       Drama Society by S.P.C.K., 1949. A three-act chronicle in
       which the hero finally gets the martyr's death he wants.

1949   *The Journey,* London, The Religious Drama Society, 1949. Play
       about Paul's imprisonment in Philippi, unusual only in that it was
       group-written through a series of discussions—at the Community
       House in Glasgow, under Oliver M. Wilkinson's direction.

1949   H. D. C. Pepler. *The Ox and the Ass* and *Christmas Gifts,* in
       Plays for Christmas, ed. Rosalind Vallance, [London], Oxford,
       [1949], pp. 7–20. Nativity plays originally designed for puppets.

1949   Hugh Ross Williamson. *The Cardinal's Learning,* in *The Best One-
       Act Plays of 1948-49,* ed. J. W. Marriott, London, George G.
       Harrap, [1950], pp. 161–186. A very political Wolsey learns how
       to solve the royal marital problems by watching a microcosm of
       them acted out in a rural inn.

1951   K. M. Baxter. *Pull Devil—Pull Baker,* London, published for the
       Religious Drama Society by S.P.C.K., 1951. An amusing use of
       mime, nursery rhyme, and folk song to describe the struggle
       for Bo-Peep's soul.

1951   Jessie Powell, *The Sandals of Rama,* London, United Society for
       Christian Literature, [1951]. A melodramatic (if earnest) attempt
       to show the practical good that Christian schools have done in
       India.

1951   Lesbia Scott. *The Window,* London, S.P.C.K., 1951. A collection
       of incidents from church history, joined by interludes which
       illustrate that the ordinary man cannot know that he is part of
       an important historical moment.

1952   James Forsyth. *Emmanuel,* London, Heinemann, [1952]. Nativity,
       in prose and verse, unusual only in that it ends not with the
       adoration but with the slaughter of the innocents.

1953   Viscount Duncannon. *Like Stars Appearing,* London, Heine-
       mann, [1953]. Chronicle of the life of Richard of Wyche, detail-
       ing his troubles, as Bishop of Chichester, with Henry III.

1953   Leo Lehman. *Saint Chad of the Seven Wells,* in *Two Saints' Plays,*
       by Leo Lehman and Robert Gittings, London, Heinemann,
       1954, pp. 1–62. An account, in stilted prose, of how Bishop
       Chad brought King Wulfhere to Christianity and later had his
       own faith restored by the king—with a symbolic white hart in
       the underbrush.

1953   Hugh Ross Williamson. *His Eminence of England,* London, Heinemann, 1953. Canterbury play about Reginald Pole's attempt to bring moderation to England's return to Catholicism under Mary.

1953   Lesbia Scott. *Wherefore This Waste?,* London, published for the Religious Drama Society by S.P.C.K., 1953. Three acts designed to show that the missionary's lot is even more difficult than the parson's and that the English layman is still indifferent.

BIBLIOGRAPHY

The bibliography lists only the plays discussed; the editions are those that I used in preparing the text. Secondary references are fully identified in the footnotes and need not be repeated here.

Arlett, Vera I., *The Gardener,* in *Poet Lore,* XL, 305–313 (Summer, 1930).
———, *The Last Man In,* in *Poet Lore,* XL, 410–418 (Autumn, 1930).
———, *This Is the Gate,* in *School Drama,* II, 20–22 (May–September, 1939).
Auden, W. H., *The Dance of Death,* London, Faber and Faber, n.d.
———, *For the Time Being,* in *The Collected Poetry of W. H. Auden,* New York, Random House, [1945], pp. 405–466.
———, *The Sea and the Mirror,* in *The Collected Poetry of W. H. Auden,* pp. 349–404.
——— and Christopher Isherwood, *The Ascent of F6,* London, Faber and Faber, 1946.
———, *The Dog beneath the Skin, or Where Is Francis?,* New York, Random House, 1935.
———, *On the Frontier,* New York, Random House, 1938.
——— and Chester Kallman, *The Rake's Progress,* London, Boosey and Hawkes, [1951].
Barker, Granville, *The Voysey Inheritance,* in *Three Plays,* New York, Mitchell Kennerley, [1911], pp. 81–212.
———, *Waste,* in *Three Plays,* pp. 213–345.
Barrie, James M., *The Boy David,* New York, Scribner, 1938.
———, *Dear Brutus,* in *The Plays of J. M. Barrie,* New York, Scribner, 1929, pp. 473–542.
———, *A Well-Remembered Voice,* in *The Plays of J. M. Barrie,* pp. 781–802.
Bennett, Arnold, *Judith,* New York, George H. Doran, [1919].
Benson, Robert Hugh, *A Mystery Play in Honour of the Nativity of Our Lord,* London, Longmans, Green, 1908.
Besier, Rudolf, *Don,* London, T. Fisher Unwin, 1912.
Binyon, Laurence, *The Young King,* London, Macmillan, 1935.
Boland, Bridget, *The Prisoner,* in *Plays of the Year,* Vol. 10, ed. J. C. Trewin, London, Elek, [1954], pp. 17–108.
———, *The Return,* in *Plays of the Year,* Vol. 9, ed. J. C. Trewin, London, Elek, [1954], pp. 255–356.

Bottomley, Gordon, *The Acts of Saint Peter,* London, Constable, 1933.
———, *Kate Kennedy,* London, Constable, [1945].
Boucicault, Dion, *The Long Strike,* New York, Samuel French, n.d.
Name is spelled *Baucicault* on title page.
Boughton, Rutland, *Bethlehem,* London, J. Curwen and Sons, 1920.
Boulter, B. C., *The Mystery of the Passion,* London, S.P.C.K., 1923.
Bridie, James, *The Baikie Charivari, or The Seven Prophets,* London, Constable, [1953].
———, *A Change for the Worse,* in *Tedious and Brief,* London, Constable, [1945], pp. 22–42.
———, *The Dragon and the Dove,* in *Plays for Plain People,* London, Constable, [1945], pp. 299–342.
———, *Holy Isle,* in *Plays for Plain People,* pp. 79–154.
———, *John Knox,* in *John Knox and Other Plays,* London, Constable, [1949], pp. 1–80.
———, *Jonah and the Whale,* in *A Sleeping Clerygman and Other Plays,* London, Constable, 1934, pp. 189–255.
———, *Jonah 3,* in *Plays for Plain People,* pp. 219–276.
———, *Mr. Bolfry,* in *Plays for Plain People,* pp. 155–218.
———, *The Queen's Comedy,* London, Constable, [1950].
———, *The Sign of the Prophet Jonah,* in *Plays for Plain People,* pp. 277–298.
———, *A Sleeping Clergyman,* in *A Sleeping Clergyman and Other Plays,* pp. 1 98.
———, *The Sunlight Sonata,* in *The Switchback, The Pardoner's Tale, The Sunlight Sonata,* London, Constable, 1930, pp. 95–156.
———, *Susannah and the Elders,* in *Susannah and the Elders and Other Plays,* London, Constable, [1943]. Separate pagination for each play.
———, *Tobias and the Angel,* in *A Sleeping Clergyman and Other Plays,* pp. 99–188.
Browne, E. Martin, ed., *The York Nativity Play,* London, S.P.C.K., 1952.
Browne, Wynyard, *Dark Summer,* London, Evan Brothers, [1950].
———, *The Holly and the Ivy,* in *Plays of the Year,* Vol. 3, ed. J. C. Trewin, London, Elek, [1950], pp. 17–104.
Buckton, A. M., *Eager Heart,* New York, Chappell, n.d.
Caine, Hall, *The Christian,* MS, New York Public Library.
———, *The Prodigal Son,* London, 1905. Privately printed.

Cannan, Dennis, and Pierre Bost, *The Power and the Glory*, MS, New York Public Library.

Chesterton, G. K., *Magic*, New York, Putnam, 1913.

———, *The Surprise*, New York, Sheed and Ward, [1952].

Collins, Freda, *The Centurion*, London, Nelson, 1940.

———, "*The Foolishness of God . . .*", New Edition, London, Samuel French, 1939.

———, *The Fortieth Man*, London, Frederick Muller, [1938].

———, *Redemption*, London, Mowbray, [1952].

Creagh-Henry, M., *Outcasts*, in *Four Mystical Plays*, London, S.P.C.K., 1924, pp. 5–18.

Cropper, Margaret, *Christ Crucified*, London, The Sheldon Press, [1951].

———, *A Great and Mighty Wonder*, London, Oxford, 1938.

———, *The Nativity with Angels*, London, Oxford, 1934.

Dane, Clemence, *Naboth's Vineyard*, New York, Macmillan, 1926.

Dearmer, Mabel, *The Dreamer*, in *Three Plays*, London, Erskine Macdonald, 1916, pp. 103–201.

———, *The Soul of the World*, in *Three Plays*, pp. 203–255.

Dennis, Nigel, *Cards of Identity*, in *Two Plays and a Preface*, London, Weidenfeld and Nicolson, [1958], pp. 55–154.

———, *The Making of Moo*, in *Two Plays and a Preface*, pp. 155–224.

Dixon, Campbell, and Dermot Morrah, *Caesar's Friend*, London, Samuel French, 1933.

Duncan, Ronald, *The Death of Satan*, London, Faber and Faber, [1955].

———, *Don Juan*, London, Faber and Faber, [1954].

———, *A Masque, This Way to the Tomb, and Anti-Masque*, London, Faber and Faber, [1946].

———, *Ora Pro Nobis*, in *The Dull Ass's Hoof*, London, Fortune Press, [1940], pp. 79–108.

———, *Our Lady's Tumbler*, London, Faber and Faber, [1951].

———, *Pimp, Skunk and Profiteer*, in *The Dull Ass's Hoof*, pp. 109–136.

———, *The Rape of Lucretia*, London, Faber and Faber, [1953].

———, *Stratton*, London, Faber and Faber, [1950].

———, *The Unburied Dead*, in *The Dull Ass's Hoof*, pp. 7–77.

Eliot, T. S., *The Cocktail Party*, in *The Complete Poems and Plays*, New York, Harcourt, Brace, [1952], pp. 295–388.

———, *The Confidential Clerk*, London, Faber and Faber, [1954].

———, *The Elder Statesman*, New York, Farrar, Straus and Cudahy, [1959].

Eliot, T. S., *The Family Reunion,* in *The Complete Poems and Plays,* pp. 223–293.

————, *Murder in the Cathedral,* in *The Complete Poems and Plays,* pp. 173–221.

————, *The Rock,* New York, Harcourt, Brace, [1934].

————, *Sweeney Agonistes,* in *The Complete Poems and Plays,* pp. 74–85.

Ervine, St. John, *John Ferguson,* New York, Macmillan, 1920.

————, *Mixed Marriage,* in *Four Irish Plays,* London, Maunsel, 1914, pp. 1–55.

————, *Robert's Wife,* London, Allen and Unwin, 1938.

Fleming, Tom, *Miracle at Midnight,* London, The Epworth Press, [1954].

Fogerty, Elsie, *The Harrying of the Dove,* London, Allen and Unwin, n.d.

Francis, J. O., *Change,* New York, Doubleday, Page, 1915.

Fry, Christopher, *The Boy with a Cart,* London, Muller, [1945].

————, *The Dark Is Light Enough,* New York, Oxford, 1954.

————, *The Firstborn,* London, Oxford, [1950].

————, *The Firstborn,* Second Edition, London, Oxford, [1952].

————, *The Firstborn,* Third Edition, London, Oxford, 1958.

————, *The Lady's Not for Burning,* New York, Oxford, 1950.

————, *A Phoenix Too Frequent,* London, Oxford, [1949].

————, *A Sleep of Prisoners,* London, Oxford, 1951.

————, *Thor, with Angels,* London, Oxford, [1949].

————, *Venus Observed,* London, Oxford, [1950].

Galsworthy, John, *A Bit O' Love,* in *The Works of John Galsworthy,* Manaton Edition, New York, Scribner, 1923–1928, XX, 97–195.

————, *Justice,* in *Works,* XIX, 1–127.

————, *The Little Dream,* in *Works,* XIX, 129–165.

————, *The Little Man,* in *Works,* XXI, 411–445.

————, *Loyalties,* in *Works,* XXI, 129–257.

————, *The Pigeon,* in *Works,* XIX, 167–266.

————, *Strife,* in *Works,* XVIII, 211–336.

Gittings, Robert, *The Makers of Violence,* London, Heinemann, 1951.

————, *Man's Estate,* in *Two Saint's Plays,* by Leo Lehman and Robert Gittings, London, Heinemann, 1954, pp. 63–79.

————, *Parson Herrick's Parishioners,* in *Out of This Wood,* London, Heinemann, [1955]. Separate pagination for each play.

Greene, Graham, *The Complaisant Lover,* London, Heinemann, [1959].

————, *The Living Room,* New York, Viking, 1954.

————, *The Potting Shed,* New York, Viking, 1957.

Hankin, St. John, *The Charity That Began at Home,* in *The Dramatic Works of St. John Hankin,* London, Martin Secker, 1912, II, 1–116.

Hassall, Christopher, *Christ's Comet,* London, Heinemann, 1937.

———, *Christ's Comet,* Revised edition, London, Heinemann, 1958.

———, *Devil's Dyke,* in *Devil's Dyke with Compliment and Satire,* London, Heinemann, [1936], pp. 3–75.

———, *Out of the Whirlwind,* London, Heinemann, 1953.

Hole, W. G., *The Master,* London, Erskine Macdonald, 1913.

Home, William Douglas, *The Bad Samaritan,* London, Evan Brothers, 1954.

Hougham, E. R., *Sensation on Budleigh Beacon,* in *Plays of Perplexity,* London, published for the Religious Drama Society by S.P.C.K., 1948, pp. 9–38.

Housman, Laurence, *Abraham and Isaac,* in *Old Testament Plays,* London, Jonathan Cape, [1950], pp. 9–36.

———, *As Good as Gold,* New York, Samuel French, [1916].

———, *Bethlehem,* New York, Macmillan, 1902.

———, *The Burden of Nineveh,* in *Old Testament Plays,* pp. 139–159.

———, *The Gods Whom Men Love Die Old,* in *Ye Fearful Saints!,* London, Sidgwick and Jackson, 1932, pp. 53–64.

———, *In This Sign Conquer,* in *Ye Fearful Saints!,* pp. 147–158.

———, *Jacob's Ladder,* in *Old Testament Plays,* pp. 37–126.

———, *Little Plays of St. Francis,* 3 vols., London, Sidgwick and Jackson, 1935.

———, *The Lord of the Harvest,* New York, Samuel French, [1916].

———, *Nazareth,* New York, Samuel French, [1916].

———, *The New Hangman,* in *Ye Fearful Saints!,* pp. 65–79.

———, *Nunc Dimittis,* London, printed for the use and benefit of the Dramatic Society of University College, 1933.

———, *Old Bottles,* in *Ye Fearful Saints!,* pp. 101–118.

———, *Ramoth Gilead,* in *Old Testament Plays,* pp. 127–137.

———, *St. Martin's Pageant,* Commemoration Week Supplement, *St. Martin-in-the-Fields Review,* No. 369, November, 1921.

———, *Samuel the Kingmaker,* in *Old Testament Plays,* pp. 161–280.

———, *The Story of Jacob,* in *Palestine Plays,* New York, Scribner, 1943, pp. 29–120.

———, *The Time-Servers,* in *Ye Fearful Saints!,* pp. 23–36.

———, *Victoria Regina,* New York, Scribner, [1937].

———, *The Waiting-Room,* in *Ye Fearful Saints!,* pp. 81–100.

Housman, Laurence, *The Wrong Door*, in *Ye Fearful Saints!*, pp. 119–145.

Hughes, Richard, *A Comedy of Good and Evil*, in *A Rabbit and a Leg*, New York, Knopf, 1924, pp. 51–140.

Huxley, Aldous, *The World of Light*, Garden City, New York, Doubleday, Doran, 1931.

Jerome, Jerome, K., *The Passing of the Third Floor Back*, New York, Dodd, Mead, 1925.

————, *The Soul of Nicholas Snyders*, London, Hodder and Stoughton, [1925].

Jones, Henry Arthur, *The Dancing Girl*, in *Representative Plays*, ed. Clayton Hamilton, Boston, Little, Brown, 1925, I, 279–357.

————, *The Galilean's Victory*, London, 1907. Privately printed.

————, *The Hypocrites*, in *Representative Plays*, III, 275–371.

————, *Judah*, in *Representative Plays*, I, 197–278.

————, *Michael and His Lost Angel*, in *Representative Plays*, III, 1–85.

————, *Mrs. Dane's Defense*, in *Representative Plays*, III, 179–273.

————, *The Physician*, New York, Macmillan, 1899.

————, *Saints and Sinners*, London, Macmillan, 1891.

————, *The Silver King*, in *Representative Plays*, I, 1–109.

————, *The Tempter*, in *Representative Plays*, II, 91–182.

————, *The Triumph of the Philistines*, London, Macmillan, 1891.

Kaye-Smith, Sheila, *The Child Born at the Plough*, in *Saints in Sussex*, New York, Dutton, [1927], pp. 33–82.

————, *The Shepherd of Lattenden*, in *Saints in Sussex*, pp. 83–136.

Kennedy, Charles Rann, *The Servant in the House*, in *A Repertory of Plays for a Company of Seven Players and Two Short Plays for Smaller Casts*, Chicago, University of Chicago Press, 1930, pp. 111–216.

Lamb, Philip J., *Go Down Moses*, London, published for the Religious Drama Society by S.P.C.K., 1954.

————, *Sons of Adam*, London, The Sheldon Press, 1944.

Lawrence, D. H., *David*, London, Martin Secker, 1926.

Levy, Benn W., *The Devil Passes*, New York, Samuel French, 1932.

Masefield, John, *The Campden Wonder*, in *The Poems and Plays of John Masefield*, New York, Macmillan, 1918, II, 1–40.

————, *The Coming of Christ*, New York, Macmillan, 1928.

————, *Easter*, London, Heinemann, [1929].

————, *Good Friday*, in *The Poems and Plays*, II, 581–640.

————, *A King's Daughter*, London, Heinemann, n.d.

Masefield, John, *Melloney Holtspur, or The Pangs of Love*, New York, Macmillan, 1922.

——, *Mrs. Harrison*, in *The Poems and Plays*, II, 41–59.

——, *Philip the King*, in *The Poems and Plays*, II, 529–580.

——, *A Play of St. George*, New York, Macmillan, 1948.

——, *The Tragedy of Nan*, in *The Poems and Plays*, II, 143–260.

——, *The Trial of Jesus*, New York, Macmillan, 1925.

Maugham, W. Somerset, *Loaves and Fishes*, London, Heinemann, 1924.

——, *Sheppey*, in *The Collected Plays of W. Somerset Maugham*, London, Heinemann, 1952, III, 183–304, 2nd half. Pagination begins again with p. 1 in the middle of the volume.

——, *The Unknown*, in *The Collected Plays*, III, 1–89, 2nd half.

Morgan, Charles, *The Burning Glass*, London, Macmillan, 1953.

——, *The Flashing Stream*, New York, Macmillan, 1938.

——, *The River Line*, London, Macmillan, 1952.

Nicholson, Norman, *A Match for the Devil*, London, Faber and Faber, [1955].

——, *The Old Man of the Mountains*, London, Faber and Faber, [1946].

——, *Prophesy to the Wind*, London, Faber and Faber, [1950].

Parker, Louis N., *The Cardinal*, New York, Samuel French, 1923.

——, *Joseph and His Brethren*, New York, John Lane, 1913.

Paull, H. M., and Laurence Housman, *The Unknown Star*, in *Nineteenth Century and After*, LXXXVI, 1065–1095 (December, 1919).

Phillips, Stephen, *Armageddon*, London, John Lane, 1915.

——, *Aylmer's Secret*, in *Collected Plays*, New York, Macmillan, 1921. Separate pagination for each play.

——, *Herod*, New York, John Lane, 1905.

——, *Nero*, New York, Macmillan, 1906.

——, *Paolo and Francesca*, New York, Dodd, Mead, 1924.

——, *The Sin of David*, in *Collected Plays*.

—— and J. Comyns Carr, *Faust*, in *Collected Plays*.

Pinero, Arthur Wing, *The Benefit of the Doubt*, Chicago, The Dramatic Publishing Co., n.d.

——, *The Notorious Mrs. Ebbsmith*, in *The Social Plays of Arthur Wing Pinero*, ed. Clayton Hamilton, New York, Dutton, 1917–1922, I, 205–362.

——, *The Second Mrs. Tanqueray*, in *The Social Plays*, I, 47–195.

Potter, Phyllis M., *From the Nursery of Heaven*, London, University of London Press, [1949].

Priestley, J. B., *Dangerous Corner*, in *The Plays of J. B. Priestley*, London, Heinemann, [1948–1950], I, 1–54.

————, *Desert Highway*, in *The Plays*, III, 203–261.

————, *I Have Been Here Before*, in *The Plays*, I, 199–268.

————, *An Inspector Calls*, in *The Plays*, III, 263–323.

————, *Johnson Over Jordan*, in *The Plays*, I, 269–338.

————, *They Came to a City*, in *The Plays*, III, 139–201.

————, *Time and the Conways*, in *The Plays*, I, 127–197.

Purvis, J. S., ed., *The York Cycle of Mystery Plays*, London, S.P.C.K., 1951.

Raeburn, Henzie, *The Beginning of the Way*, London, The Religious Drama Society, n.d.

Ridler, Anne, *Cain*, [London], Nicholson and Watson, [1943].

————, *Henry Bly*, in *Henry Bly and Other Plays*, London, Faber and Faber, [1950], pp. 35–88.

————, *The Mask*, in *Henry Bly and Other Plays*, pp. 11–34.

————, *The Missing Bridegroom*, in *Henry Bly and Other Plays*, pp. 89–119.

————, *The Shadow Factory*, London, Faber and Faber, [1946].

————, *The Trial of Thomas Cranmer*, London, Faber and Faber, 1956.

Sayers, Dorothy L., *The Devil to Pay*, in *Four Sacred Plays*, London, Gollancz, 1948, pp. 105–212.

————, *The Emperor Constantine*, New York, Harper, [1951].

————, *He That Should Come*, in *Four Sacred Plays*, pp. 213–274.

————, *The Just Vengeance*, in *Four Sacred Plays*, pp. 275–352.

————, *The Man Born to Be King*, New York, Harper, [1943].

————, *The Mocking of Christ*, in *Catholic Tales and Christian Songs*, Oxford, B. H. Blackwell, 1918, pp. 43–53.

————, *The Zeal of Thy House*, in *Four Sacred Plays*, pp. 7–103.

Scott, Lesbia, *That Fell Arrest*, London, Deane, [1937].

Shaw, Bernard, *Androcles and the Lion*, in *Selected Plays with Prefaces*, New York, Dodd, Mead, [1948–1949], I, 747–898.

————, *The Apple Cart*, London, Constable, 1930.

————, *Arms and the Man*, in *Selected Plays*, III, 108–196.

————, *Back to Methuselah*, in *Selected Plays*, II, 1–262.

————, *Caesar and Cleopatra*, in *Selected Plays*, III, 355–481.

————, *The Devil's Disciple*, in *Selected Plays*, III, 269–354.

————, *Farfetched Fables*, in *Buoyant Billions, Farfetched Fables, & Shakes Versus Shav*, New York, Dodd, Mead, [1951], pp. 59–127.

————, *Geneva*, in *Geneva, Cymbeline Refinished, & Good King Charles*, Standard Edition, London, Constable, 1946, pp. 1–150.

Shaw, Bernard, *Heartbreak House*, in *Selected Plays*, I, 447–598.
———, *"In Good King Charles's Golden Days"*, in *Selected Plays*, II, 723–806.
———, *John Bull's Other Island*, in *Selected Plays*, II, 431–611.
———, *Major Barbara*, in *Selected Plays*, I, 297–446.
———, *Man and Superman*, in *Selected Plays*, III, 483–743.
———, *On the Rocks*, in *Too True to Be Good, Village Wooing, & On the Rocks, Three Plays*, Standard Edition, London, Constable, 1934, pp. 141–274.
———, *Saint Joan*, in *Selected Plays*, II, 263–429.
———, *The Shewing-up of Blanco Posnet*, in *The Doctor's Dilemma, Getting Married, & The Shewing-up of Blanco Posnet*, Standard Edition, London, Constable, 1932, pp. 353–457.
———, *The Simpleton of the Unexpected Isles*, in *The Simpleton, The Six, and The Millionairess*, Standard Edition, London, Constable, 1936, pp. 1–81.
———, *Too True to Be Good*, in *Too True to Be Good*, pp. 1–108.
Sheriff, R. C., *Journey's End*, London, Gollancz, 1929.
Tennyson, Alfred, *Becket*, in *The Complete Poetic Works of Tennyson*, Cambridge Edition, Boston, Houghton Mifflin, 1898, pp. 659–708.
———, *Becket*, as arranged for the stage by Henry Irving, New York, Macmillan, 1893.
Thurston, E. Temple, *Judas Iscariot*, London, Putnam, [1923].
[Turner, Philip W.], *The Christ in the Concrete City*, London, published for the Religious Drama Society, by S.P.C.K., 1956.
Vane, Sutton, *Outward Bound*, New York, Liveright, [1939].
———, *Overture*, London, Chatto and Windus, 1925.
Vollmoeller, Karl, *Das Mirakel*, Berlin, Bote and Bock, 1912. English edition: *The Miracle*, in *Max Reinhardt and His Theatre*, ed. Oliver M. Sayler, New York, Brentano, [1926], pp. 249–322. This version is the revision of Vollmoeller's original by Friedrich Schirmer for the New York production at the Century Theatre, 1924, from the *Regie* book of Max Reinhardt.
Ward, R. H., *The Destiny of Man*, Ilkley, Yorks., published for "The Theatre of Persons" by The Adelphi Players, 1943.
———, *Faust in Hell*, London, published for "The Theatre of Persons" by The Adelphi Players, 1945.
———, *The Figure on the Cross*, London, published for the Religious Drama Society by S.P.C.K., 1952.

Ward, R. H., *Holy Family,* London, published for the Religious Drama Society by S.P.C.K., 1950.

————, *The Prodigal Son,* London, published for the Religious Drama Society by S.P.C.K., 1952.

————, *The Wise and the Foolish Virgins,* London, The Religious Drama Society, 1949.

Williams, Charles, *The Chaste Wanton,* in *Three Plays,* London, Oxford, 1931, pp. 69–133.

————, *The Death of Good Fortune,* in *Seed of Adam and Other Plays,* London, Oxford, 1948, pp. 25–42.

————, *Grab and Grace, or It's the Second Step,* in *Seed of Adam and Other Plays,* pp. 65–91.

————, *The House by the Stable,* in *Seed of Adam and Other Plays,* pp. 43–63.

————, *The House of the Octopus,* London, Edinburgh House Press, 1945.

————, *Judgement at Chelmsford,* London, Oxford, 1939.

————, *The Rite of the Passion,* in *Three Plays,* pp. 139–191.

————, *Seed of Adam,* in *Seed of Adam and Other Plays,* pp. 1–24.

————, *Thomas Cranmer of Canterbury,* London, Oxford, 1936.

————, *The Witch,* in *Three Plays,* pp. 5–64.

Wright, Dorothy, *A Cradle of Willow,* London, Evan Brothers, [1952].

Index

Abercrombie, Lascelles, 281
Abraham and Isaac, 131–132
Acts of Saint Peter, The, 111, 114, 115
Adelphi Players, 255
Admirable Crichton, The, 278
After Strange Gods, 189
Agonists, The, 280
Alban of Verulamium, 289
Alcestis, 199, 200
All Hallows' Eve, 143, 146
All Things Are Possible, 289
Amazed Evangelist, The, 283
Androcles and the Lion, 25, 57, 58, 70–71, 79
Anouilh, Jean, 220
Apple Cart, The, 75
Arlett, Vera I., 116–117 289, 291
Armageddon, 30
Arms and the Man, 59
Arnold, Matthew, 3
As Good as Gold, 125
Ascent of F6, The, 21
Ashwell, Lena, 26
At the Well of Bethlehem, 288
Athenaeum, The, 25
Auden, W. H., 21, 23, 224–225, 242
Aylmer's Secret, 46–47

Bacchae, 95
Back to Methuselah, 55, 60, 61, 63, 71–72, 74, 78–79
Bad Samaritan, The, 254
Baikie Charivari, The, 80, 86, 88–90
Bainbridge-Bell, Kathleen, 112, 277
Bannister, Winifred, 79
Barker, Granville, 14, 31, 35, 51, 53–54, 95, 278, 280
Barley, Joseph Wayne, 40, 94

Barrett, Wilson, 13, 14, 24–27, 28, 32, 37, 70
Barrie, James M., 34, 35–36, 44–45, 46, 155, 278, 280, 282
Bax, Clifford, 103, 286
Baxter, K. M., 292
Becket, 29, 108
Beerbohm, Max, 99
Beginning of the Way, The, 120
Bell, George K. A. (Dean of Canterbury, 1924–29; Bishop of Chichester, 1929–58), 93, 96, 106, 107, 108, 110, 112, 266, 268, 269
Ben Hur, 27
Benefit of the Doubt, The, 12, 13
Ben-My-Chree, 14
Bennett, Arnold, 33, 136, 185
Bennett, Rodney, 290, 291
Benson, F. R., 97, 110–111
Benson, Robert Hugh, 103, 286, 287
Bergner, Elizabeth, 36
Bergson, Henri, 60
Berry, S. M., 110
Berton, Paul M., 27
Besier, Rudolf, 15–16
Bethlehem (Boughton), 97
Bethlehem (Housman), 93, 98, 101, 103, 122, 123–124
Better Life, The, 45
Bill of Divorcement, A, 282
Binyon, Laurence, 108, 288
Birds of a Feather, 282
Bishop's Son, The, 280
Bit O' Love, A, 52–53
Black Girl in Search of God, The, 58, 60–61
Blackwood, Algernon, 282
Blind Witness, The, 291
Blindness of Virtue, The, 281

Boadicea, 288
Boethius, 144
Boland, Bridget, 253, 274
Bonaventure, 285
Bondman Play, The, 279
Bost, Pierre, 247
Bottomley Gordon, 111, 114, 115, 120
Boucicault, Dion, 10
Boughton, Rutland, 97, 125
Boulter, B. C., 103–104; 121, 287
Boy David, The, 35–36, 44–45, 115
Boy with a Cart, The, 115, 207, 208–210
Bradbrook, M. C., 187
Bradlaugh, Charles, 5, 55
Bradley, G. G. (Dean of Westminster, 1881–1902), 95
Brand, 51
Bridges, Robert, 30
Bridie, James, xii, xiii, 79–90, 115, 118, 120, 275, 283, 284, 285
British Drama League, 104, 111, 117
Britten, Benjamin, 235
Brontës, The, 283
Brook, Peter, 206 *fn*
"Brother Lustig," 230–232
Brown, Robert McAfee, 143, 144, 145, 146, 184
Browne, E. Martin, xiii, 84, 93, 97, 104, 107, 109, 110, 111, 112–113, 118–120, 187, 192, 193, 200, 202, 204–205, 206, 226–227, 269, 271, 272, 273, 289
Browne, Henzie (Mrs. E. Martin Browne), see Raeburn, Henzie
Browne, Wynyard, 253–254, 274, 275
Buckton, A. M., 93, 98–100, 206, 255, 276
Bunyan, John, 291
Burden of Nineveh, The, 132–133
Burn, Michael, 291

Burning Glass, The, 11, 249–252
Burnt Norton, 193
Busman's Holiday, 165
Butler, Samuel, 5
Byrne, M. St. Clare, 165

Caesar and Cleopatra, 62–63
Caesar's Friend, 36–37
Cain, 227
Caine, Hall, xii, 13–15, 279, 280, 281, 282
Calmour, Alfred C., 27
Campden Wonder, The, 134
Candida, 278
Cannan, Dennis, 247
Canterbury Festival, 93, 96, 106, 107–110, 113, 114, 115, 121, 137, 139, 150, 165, 177, 178, 189, 192, 193, 213, 241, 272, 293
Captain Brassbound's Conversion, 278
Cardinal, The, 28
Cardinal's Learning, The, 292
Cards of Identity, 247–248, 249
Carr, J. Comyns, 30
Cary, Falkland L., 286
Catalogue of Selected Plays, A, 112, 277
Catalyst, The, 238–239
Catholic Tales and Christian Songs, 165
Caxton, William, 114
Cenci, The, 32
"Censorship Muddle and a Way Out of It, The," 27
Centurion, The, 117
Century Theatre, 255
Change, 17–18
Change for the Worse, A, 84–85, 120
Charity That Began at Home, The, 16
Charlady and the Angel, The, 289
Chaste Wanton, The, 148, 149
Chester cycle, 96, 97
Chesterton, Mrs. Cecil, 283
Chesterton, G. K., 42–44, 55 283

Chichester Diocesan Players, 97, 113
Child Born at the Plough, The, 140–141
Child in Flanders, The, 287
Choephori, 186, 195
Chorus Angelorum, 289
Chosen People, 290
Christ Crucified, 111, 115–116
Christ in the Concrete City, The, 262–263, 267
Christian, The, 14
Christian Drama, 105, 111, 112, 255, 270
Christian King, The, 27
Christmas Gifts, 292
Christmas Morality Play, A, 286
Christmas Pie, 120
Christ's Comet, 109, 110, 177–178
Clarion, The, 25
Claudel, Paul, 113
Claudian, 24
Claye, Charles A., 105
Clerical Error, A, 24, 277
Cloudbreak, 288
Cocktail Party, The, 121, 183, 196, 197–200, 202, 203, 206, 229 *fn,* 275
Coghill, Nevill, 115, 236, 270, 275
Coleby, Wilfred T., 279
Collins, Freda, 117, 268, 291, 292
Collins, Wilkie, 6
Comedy of Good and Evil, A, 40–41, 50
Coming of Christ, The, 93, 107, 134, 137–138, 139, 149
Complaisant Lover, The, 247
Confidential Clerk, The, 183, 184, 200–203, 204, 270
Conversion of England, The, 94
Corelli, Marie, 13, 27
Cost of a Crown, The, 286
Cotton, Stéphanie, 288
Council for the Encouragement of Music and the Arts, (CEMA), 119, 120

Coward, Noel, 283, 284
Cradle of Willow, A, 263, 264
Graig, Gordon, 98
Crashaw, Richard, 114
Creagh-Henry, M., 105–106, 121, 287, 288, 289
Cresswell, Henry, 94
Criterion, 185
Cropper, Margaret, 105, 111, 115–116, 287, 288, 289
Crusaders, The, 277
"Cutler's Play, The," 88
Cyprian, 292

Daily Mirror (London), 20
Dame Julian's Window, 287
Dance of Death, The, 21
Dancing Girl, The, 8–9, 11
Dandy Dick, 277
Dane, Clemence, 33, 135, 282, 283
Dangerous Corner, 47
Dante, 72
Dark Is Light Enough, The, 208, 220–222, 274
Dark Summer, 253
Darlington, W. A., 252
Daughters of Babylon, The, 26
Davey, F. N., 268, 270
David, 34–35, 120
Davidson, John, 279
Daviot, Gordon, 284, 285
Deacon, The, 277
Dead End, 291
Dear Brutus, 46
Dearmer, Mabel, 100–103, 265
Dearmer, Percy, 99, 100, 103, 111
Death of Good Fortune, The, 120, 156–157, 164
Death of Satan, The, 237–238, 274
Deemster, The, 14, 280
DeMille, Cecil B., 37
Dennis, Nigel, 243, 247–249

Descent of the Dove, The, 144, 145, 146, 160, 163
Desert Fathers, The, 84
Desert Highway, 49–50
Destiny of Man, The, 255, 257–258, 259, 260, 261
Devil, The, 41–42
Devil Passes, The, see *Devil, The*
Devil to Pay, The, 109, 110, 169–170
Devil's Disciple, The, 62, 64, 79
Devil's Dyke, 178
Devil's in the News, The, 284
Difficult Way, The, 100
Disarm!, 288
Disher, M. Willson, 6, 24, 26
Dixon, Campbell, 36, 283
Dobrée, Bonamy, 239
Dog beneath the Skin, The, 21, 224, 225, 235
Dolly Reforming Herself, 279
Don, 15–16
Don Juan, 237–238
Don Quixote, 100
Door Was Closed, The, 289
Doyle, Arthur Conan, 280
Dr. Faustus, 95, 108
Dragon and the Dove, The, 84, 120
Dramatic Society at University College (University of London), 105
Dreamer, The, 101–102
Drinkwater, John, 282, 284, 287
Dry Salvages, The, 193
Dull Ass's Hoof, The, 234
Duncan, Ronald, 23, 223, 226, 227, 233–239, 242, 265, 274, 276
Duncannon, Viscount, 292
Dunne, J. W., 47
Dwelly, F. W., 110

Eager Heart, 93, 97–100, 103, 206, 255, 270
East Coker, 186

East Lynne, 8, 24
Easter, 137, 138, 139
Eastman, Fred, 106, 134, 138
Eastward in Eden, 289
Edinburgh Festival, 86, 210
Elder Statesman, The, 203
Eldest Son, The, 280
Eliot, T. S., xi, 37, 50, 93, 108, 109, 110, 113, 115, 120, 142, 143, 144, 149, 176, 177, 183–206, 207, 209, 210, 222, 223, 229, 233, 239, 242, 243, 252, 254, 255, 256, 265, 267, 272, 273, 274, 275, 276
Elizabethan Stage Society, 95
Emmanuel, 292
Emperor Constantine, The, 176
English Drama Society, 96
Englishwoman's Love-Letters, An, 98
Ervine, St. John, xii, 17, 18–19, 22, 281, 282
Escape, 283
Essay on Going to Church, An, 55, 56
Eternal City, The, 280
Euripides, 95, 200
Evangelist, The, see *Galilean's Victory, The*
Everyman, xi, xiii, 93, 94, 95–96, 97, 108, 115, 121, 255
Experiment with Time, 47

Fairclough, Alan, 177
Fairy's Dilemma, The, 279
Family Reunion, The, 183, 185, 186, 187, 194–197, 200, 203, 206
Fanny's First Play, 281
Farrar, Frederic William, 95
Faust, 30
Faust in Hell, 259–260
Festival of Britain (1951), 215
Fifth Gospel, The, 291

Figure on the Cross, The, 255, 258–259, 261
Fires of Fate, The, 280
First Corinthians, 290
First Franciscans, The, 94, 96
Firstborn, The, 208, 210–213
Flashing Stream, The, 249, 251
Fleming, Tom, 263, 264, 265
Fletcher, Giles, 114
Flies, The, 196
Fogerty, Elsie, 105
"*Foolishness of God . . ., The,*" 117
Foote, G. W., 25
For Lancelot Andrewes, 185
For the Time Being, 224
Forsyth, James, 292
Fortieth Man, The, 117
Four Quartets, 200, 205
Francis, J. O., xii, 17–18, 282
Frohman, Charles, 96
From the Manger to the Cross, 32, 37
From the Nursery of Heaven, 113–114
Fry, Christopher, xi, 37, 93, 113, 115, 142, 183–185, 206–224, 226, 242, 243, 254, 264, 265, 272, 274, 275, 276

Galilean's Victory, The, 9–10
Galsworthy, John, 16–17, 46 51, 52–53, 54, 280, 281, 283
Gardner, The (Arlett), 116
Gardner, The (Creagh-Henry), 288
Gassner, John, 183
Gatch, Katherine Haynes, 75 *fn*
Gate of Vision, The, 287
Geneva, 75
George, Henry, 59
Getting Married, 280
Ghéon, Henri, 113, 256
Gilbert, W. S., 279
Giraudoux, Jean, 220
Gittings, Robert, 215 *fn,* 241, 242
Glastonbury Festival, 97, 105, 111

Go Down Moses, 261, 262
God of Quiet, The, 287
Gods Whom Men Love Die Old, The, 131
Goethe, Johann Wolfgang von, 30
Golden Legend, The, 114
Gomme, Allan, 95
Good Friday, 134, 135–136, 138, 139
Gott, John (Bishop of Truro, 1891–1906), 25
Grab and Grace, 120, 156, 159
Granite, 283
Grant, Neil, 290
Great and Mighty Wonder, A, 116
"*Greater Love Hath No Man,*" 288
Green Bay Tree, The, 284
Greene, Graham, 8, 10, 243–247, 252, 253, 274
Greet, Ben, 96, 97, 100
Gregory, Lady, 103
Grimm, The Brothers, 230–232
Guthrie, Tyrone, 285
Gwynne, Stephen, 100, 101, 102

Hale, Lionel, 283
Hall-marked, 281
Halverson, Marvin, 224
Hamilton, Cicely, 287
Hamilton, Clayton, 11
Hamilton, Cosmo, 281
Hankin, St. John, 16, 279
Harrying of the Dove, The, 105
Hassall, Christopher, 109, 177–179, 275
Hastings, Basil Macdonald, 281
Hastings, Charlotte, 285
Hay, Ian, 282
He that Should Come, 118, 167–169, 170, 176
Heart of the Matter, The, 245
Heartbreak House, 74, 78
Heath, Frank, 129

Heine, Heinrich, 8
Henry Bly, 229, 230–232
Henry V, 179
Herbert, Percy Mark (Bishop of Norwich, 1942–59), 96
Herman, Henry, 24
Herod, 29
Hewlett, Maurice, 280
High Ground, see *Bonaventure*
His Eminence of England, 293
Hitler, Adolf, 75
Hoellering, George, 193
Hole, S. Reynolds, 25
Hole, W. G., 31
Holly and the Ivy, The, 253, 275
Holst, Gustav, 107
Holy Family, 255–256, 262
Holy Isle, 85–86
Holyest Erth, 290
Home, William Douglas, 253, 254, 285
Homer, 87
Hopkins, Gerard Manley, 149
Horne, Kenneth, 284
Hougham, E. R., 263–264, 291
Hour Glass, The, 103
House by the Stable, The, 120, 156, 157–159, 164
House of the Octopus, The, 159–162
Housman, Laurence, 37, 93, 98, 101, 103, 104–105, 110, 112, 114, 122–134, 140, 165, 287
Howson, Vincent, 187
Huckleberry Finn, 132
Hughes, Richard, xii, 40–41, 42
Huxley, Aldous, 21, 23, 283
Hypocrites, The, 9, 280

I Have Been Here Before, 48–49, 50
I Will Arise!, 290
Idea of a Christian Society, The, 189
Iliad, 86

Importance of Being Ernest, The, 278
"*In Good King Charles's Golden Days,*" 59, 75, 77–78
In Him Is Life, 290
In His Steps, 45
In This Sign Conquer, 131
Indifferent Shepherd, The, 285
Inspector Calls, An, 50
Interlude of Youth, The, 96, 97
Invisible One, The, 290
Irving, Henry, 28, 29
Isherwood, Christopher, 21, 23, 242

Jack Straw, 279
Jackson, Barry, 110
Jacob and Esau, 96
Jacob's Ladder, 132
Jane Clegg, 281
Jerome, Jerome K., 38–39, 42
Jerusalem, 289
Jevons, Stanley, 59
John Bull's Other Island, 65
John Ferguson, 18–19, 22
John Knox, 85, 86
John of the Cross, St., 183 *fn,* 186
Johnson Over Jordan, 50
Jonah and the Whale, 82–83
Jonah 3, 83
Jones, Doris Arthur, 5, 19 *fn*
Jones, Henry Arthur, xi, 3–11, 13, 14, 15, 16, 19, 21, 22, 23, 24, 26, 27–28, 29, 51–52, 206, 253, 266, 274, 275, 276, 277, 279, 280, 282
Joseph and His Brethren, 31–33
Journey, The, 292
Journey's End, 19
Joyous Pageant of the Holy Nativity, The, 105
Judah, 6
Judas Iscariot, 36
Judgement at Chelmsford, 145, 146, 153–156, 157, 159, 161, 163, 164

Judgement of Adam, The, 258 *fn*
Judgment of Pharaoh, The, 27
Judith (Abercrombie), 281
Judith (Bennett), 33
Just Vengeance, The, 175–176, 177
Justice, 52, 53

Kallman, Chester, 224
Karma, 282
Kate Kennedy, 120
Kay, J. Alan, 271
Kaye-Smith, Sheila, 140–141
Keily, Pamela, 119, 267, 271
Kelly, Edgar Stillman, 27
Kennedy, Charles Rann, 39–40, 287
King, Philip, 286
King's Daughter, A, 135

Lady's Not for Burning, The, 208, 212,
    218–219, 220, 223, 274
Lamarck, Jean, 60
Lamb, Philip, J., 261–262, 263
Last Days of Pompeii, The, 24
Last Man In, The, 116
Last of the De Mullins, The, 279
Last Trump, The, 284
Last War, The, 290
Lawrence, D. H., 34–35, 120
Lee, Laurie, 109
Legend of Baboushka, The, 288
Legend of St. Christopher, The, 288
Lehman, Leo, 292
Lehmann, John, 189
Letters from a Field Hospital, 100
Levy, Benn W., 41–42, 285
Liberties of the Mind, 249
Like Stars Appearing, 292
Linklater, Eric, 284
Little Dream, The, 46, 52
Little Dry Thorn, The, 285
Little Land, The, 126

Little Man, The, 16–17, 52
Little Minister, The, 278
Little Plays of St. Francis, 122, 125,
    127–131, 134
Living Room, The, 243–246, 247, 275
Living Water, 291
Loaves and Fishes, 20
*London Quarterly and Holborn Review,
    The,* 271
London Stone, 290
Long Strike, The, 10
Lord of the Harvest, The, 125
Love All, 165
Love—and What Then?, 281
"Love Song of J. Alfred Prufrock,
    The," 205
Loyalties, 52
Ludus Coventriae, 96, 97
Lyttleton, Edith, 103, 286, 287

Maeterlinck, Maurice, 328
Magic, 42–43, 50
Maid of Orleans, The, 287
Major Barbara, 59, 61, 65–69, 74, 77,
    78
Makers of Violence, The, 241
Making of Moo, The, 248–249
Man and Superman, 63–64, 65, 74, 79
Man Born to be King, The, 118, 165,
    166, 170–175, 269
Man of Destiny, 278
Man Who Was Thursday, The, 283
Man Who Wouldn't Go to Heaven, The,
    290
Man's Estate, 241
Man's House, A, 284
Manxman, The (novel), 13, 14, 279
Manxman, The (play), 13, 14
Mariners 283
Marlowe, Christopher, 95, 169
Marriage Is No Joke, 284
Marriage of the Soul, The, 286

Marrying of Ann Leete, The, 278
Marten, D., 105
Marx, Karl, 59
Mary, Mary, Quite Contrary, 282
Mary Rose, 282
Masefield, John, 37, 93, 105, 107, 108, 109, 122, 134–140, 149
Mask, The, 229–230
Match for the Devil, A, 240
Maugham, W. Somerset, 17, 19–21, 279, 280
Mavor, Osborne H., *see* Bridie, James
McCarthy, Lillah, 33
McChesney, Dora Greenwell, 286
McCormick, Pat, 105
McGinley, Phyllis, 203
McLachlan, Laurentia, *see* Stanbrook, Abbess of
Melloney Holtspur, 135
Methodist Drama Society, 267
Michael and His Lost Angel, 3, 6–8, 24
Midsummer Night's Dream, A, 279
Milne, A. A., 284
Milton, John, 95
"Mind Control," 249
Miracle, The, 32
Miracle at Midnight, 263, 264, 265
Missing Bridegroom, The, 229, 232–233
Mitchell, Yvonne, 286
Mixed Marriage, 18
Mob, The, 281
Mocking of Christ, The, 165–166
Modern Everyman, The, 291
Monck, Nugent, 96–97, 108, 109, 112
Morality Play Society, The, 100, 103, 111
Morgan, Charles, 11, 243, 249–252, 253, 274
Morrah, Dermot, 36, 289
Morris, T. B., 290, 291

Mountain, The, 282
Mr. Bolfry, 80–81
Mr. Gillie, 285
Mrs. Dane's Defense, 10
Mrs. Harrison, 134
Mrs. Warren's Profession, 278
Munro, C. K., 282
Murder in the Cathedral, 105, 108, 109, 110, 120, 121, 183, 188, 189–194, 198, 203, 206, 209, 226, 235, 256, 273
Murder in the Cathedral (film), 193–194
Murray, Gilbert, 53, 95
Mussolini, Benito, 75, 234
Mystery of the Epiphany, The, 103
Mystery of the Passion, The, 104
Mystery Play in Honour of the Nativity of Our Lord, A, 103
Mystical Players, 105–106
Myth of Shakespeare, The, 147

Naboth's Vineyard, 33, 135
Nan Pilgrim, 100
Nativity with Angels, The, 116
Nazareth, 125
Neale, Ralph, 283
Nero, 30
New Hangman, The, 131
New Magdalen, The, 6
New Model of the Universe, A, 48
"New Orpheus, The," 126
New Pilgrim Players, 112
Next Religion, The, 281
Next-Door House, The, 287
Nicholson, Norman, 183, 184, 223, 226, 233, 239–240, 242, 276
Napier, Frank, 110
Newman, John Henry, 7
Noah's Flood, 115
Norwich Players, 96, 108
Notorious Mrs. Ebbsmith, The, 12

"Novel, The," 34
"*Now Barabbas* . . . ," 285
Nunc Dimittis, 122, 131

O'Casey, Sean, xii, 75, 204
Oedipus Rex, 32
Ohad's Woman, 290
Old Bottles, 131
Old Friends, 280
Old Man of the Mountains, The, 226, 239
Old Testament Plays, 122
Oliver Cromwell, 282
Olivia, 4
Olivier, Laurence, 219
"On Power Over Nature," 249
On the Frontier, 21
On the Rocks, 57, 75
Open Door, 115, 208
Ora Pro Nobis, 234
Oresteia, 194, 195
Other People's Lives, 284
Our Lady's Tumbler, 237
Ouspensky, P. D., 48, 50
Out of the Whirlwind, 178-179
Outcasts, The, 106
Outside the Gates, 286
Outward Bound, 45-46, 50
Overture, 45-46
Ox and the Ass, The, 292
Oxford Recitations, 134

Pageant of Peace, The, 289
Pageant of Saint Alban, The, 289
Paolo and Francesca, 30
Paradise Enow, 284
Parker, Louis N., 28, 31-33, 279
Parsifal, 51
Parson Herrick's Parishioners, 241
Passing of the Third Floor Back, The, 38-39, 40, 45, 50

Paul, a Bond Slave, 291
Paul and Silas, 287
Paull, H. M., 125, 287
Pavlov, Ivan, 60
Peareth, Vera, 113, 291
Pearn, Violet, 282
Pearson, Hesketh, 13, 15
Peasant's Priest, 109
Pedlar's Progress, 289
Pepler, H. D. C., 288, 289, 292
Pete, 279
Peter's Chance, 287
Petronius, 217
Philip the King, 134-135
Phillips, Stephen, 28-31, 46-47
Phillpotts, Eden, 282
Phoenix Too Frequent, A, 208, 217-218, 226
Physician, The, 9, 11
Pigeon, The, 16, 52
Pilgrim Pie, 120
Pilgrim Players, The, 84, 113, 118-120, 156, 226
Pilgrim Players (Birmingham), 97
Pilgrim's Progress, The, 291
Pimp, Skunk and Profiteer, 234
Pinero, Arthur Wing, 11-13, 277, 280, 281
Play of Mary the Mother, The, 97
Play of St. George, The, 139
Play of the Maid Mary, The, 97
Poel, William, xi, xiii, 93, 94-96, 97, 121, 255
Point Counter Point, 283
Possession, 287
"Possibility of a Poetic Drama, The," 185, 187
Post Mortem, 283
Potter, Phyllis M., 113-114
Potting Shed, The, 10-11, 246-247
Pound, Ezra, 233, 234
Powell, Jessie, 112, 277, 290, 291, 292

Power and the Glory, The, 247
"Preface on the Prospects of Christianity," 57
Preserving Mr. Panmure, 281
Priestley, J. B., 46–50, 284
Prince of Peace, The, 291
Prisoner, The, 253
Prodigal Son, The (Caine), 15
Prodigal Son, The (Ward), 259, 260,
    261
Prophesy to the Wind, 239–240
"Prophets, Ancient and Modern,"
    126
Pull Devil—Pull Baker, 292
Purdom, C. B., 54
Purvis, J. S., 97
Pusey, Edward, 7

Queen Elizabeth, 285
Queen's Comedy, The, 80, 86–88
Quintessence of Ibsenism, The, 56
Quo Vadis (play adaptations), 26
Quo Vadis? (Italian film, 1913), 37

Raeburn, Henzie, 119 *fn,* 120, 288
Rahab of Jericho, 290
Rake's Progress, The, 224–225
Ramoth Gilead, 132
Rape of Lucretia, The, 235–236
Ratcliff, Nora, 289
Rawkins Jeffers, I. P., 289
Real St. George, The, 290
Redemption, 268–269
Redford, G. A., 98
Reinhardt, Max, 32
"Religion and Literature," 267
"Religion and the Stage," 4
*Religious Advance Toward Rationalism,
    The,* 123
Religious Drama (Browne), xiii, 107
Religious Drama I (Halverson, ed.),
    224

Religious Drama Society, 93, 106,
    107, 110–112, 113, 119, 121, 123,
    215, 272, 273
Return, The, 253
Return of the Prodigal, The, 279
Return to Tyassi, 285
Ridler, Anne, 143, 147, 149, 226,
    227–233, 242, 276
Rise of Dick Halward, The, 38
Rite of the Passion, The, 147, 148–149,
    153, 163
River Line, The, 249, 251–252
Robert's Wife, 22
Roberts, A. O., 288
Rock, The, 109, 115, 187–189
Rock Theatre Company, 119
Rococo, 280
Romeo and Juliet, 127
Rosary, The, 288
Ross Williamson, Hugh, 267, 285,
    291, 292, 293
Rubinstein, H. F., 289, 290, 291
Rutherford and Son, 281

Sacred Wood, The, 185
Sacrifice of Isaac, The, 95, 97
Sailor, Beware, 286
Saint Alban, 291
Saint Chad of the Seven Wells, 292
St. Francis Poverello, 125, 126
St. George and the Dragons, 282
Saint Joan, 72–74, 78, 192
St. Martin Players, The, 104
St. Martin's Pageant, 105, 114, 124,
    125
St. Silas Players, The, 103–104
Saint's Day, 286
Saints and Sinners, xi, xiii, 3–4, 5 *fn,* 6
    19, 206, 275
Salomé, 277
Same Sky, The, 286
Samson Agonistes, 95, 115

Samuel, Herbert, 32
Samuel the Kingmaker, 133
Sandals of Rama, The, 292
Sangster, Alfred, 283
Sanity of Art, The, 74
Sara, 285
Sartre, Jean-Paul, 196
Saturday Review, The, 94
Sayers, Dorothy L., 43, 109, 110, 118, 142, 164–177, 252, 259, 268, 269, 271, 273, 275
"Science of Drama, The," 51
Scofield, Paul, 206 *fn*
Scott, Lesbia, 117–118, 291, 292, 293
Sea and the Mirror, The, 224
Seaver, George, 106
Second Mrs. Tanqueray, The, 12
Second Shepherd's Play, 124
Seed of Adam, The, 114, 143, 151–153, 162, 163
Sensation on Budleigh Beacon, 263–264
Serial Universe, The, 47
Serious Charge, 286
Servant in the House, The, 39–40
Shadow Factory, The, 226, 227, 228–229
Shairp, Mordaunt, 284
Shakespeare, William, 46, 114
Shaw, Bernard, xii, xiii, 6, 7, 8, 12, 13, 14, 25, 26, 27, 32, 38, 51, 54–79, 81, 85, 90, 94, 120, 206, 207, 223, 275, 278, 280, 281
Shaw, Gilbert, 268–269, 270, 271
Shaw, Martin, 101, 111, 188
She Passed Through Lorraine, 283
She Shall Have Music, 208
Sheldon, Charles, 45
Shepherd of Lattenden, The, 140–141
Sheppard, H. R. L., 104–105
Sheppey, 17, 20
Sherriff, R. C., 19
Shewing-up of Blanco Posnet, The, 32, 69–70

Shipp, Horace, 289
Shirley, Arthur, 45
"Shooting of His Dear," 229
Sienkiewicz, Henryk, 26
Sign of the Cross, The, 24–26, 28
Sign of the Cross, A Candid Criticism of Mr. Wilson Barrett's Play, The, 25–26
Sign of the Prophet Jonah, The, 83
Silver King, The, 14, 24, 26
Simpleton of the Unexpected Isles, The, 76–77
Sin of David, 30
Sirocco, 283
Sister Beatrice, 32
Sladen-Smith, F., 83, 290
Sleep of Prisoners, A, 207, 208, 210, 215–217
Sleeping Clergyman, A, 80
Society for Promoting Christian Knowledge, 268
Sons of Adam, 261–262
Sorrows of Satan, The, 27
Soul of Nicholas Snyders, The, 39
Soul of the World, The, 100, 101–102
Sowerby, Githa, 281
Spalding, Ruth, 118, 156
Speaight, Robert, 94, 95, 109, 110, 113, 226–227
Spender, Stephen, 223
Stage Society, The, 135, 136
Stanbrook, Abbess of, 56, 58
Stanford, Derek, 115, 207
Star, The, 288
Stars Bow Down, The, 284
Stations of the Cross, The, 289
Steerman, Harding, 93
Stevenson, Olive, 110
Story of Christmas in Mime, The, 289
Story of Jacob, The, see *Jacob's Ladder*
Story without an End, The, 291
Strange, Stanislaus, 26
Stratton, 236–237

Stravinsky, Igor, 224
Stray Sheep, The, 288
Strife, 52, 53
Sunlight Sonata, The, 80, 81
Surprise, The, 43–44
Susannah and the Elders, 84
Swann, Mona, 288, 289, 290
Sweeney Agonistes, 183 *fn,* 185–187, 194

Taliessin through Logres, 160 *fn*
"Taliessin's Song of Byzantion," 147
"Taliessin's Song of Logres," 147
"Taliessin's Song of the King's Crowning," 147
"Taliessin's Song of the Setting of Galahad in the King's Bed," 147–148
Tartuffe, 20
Taylor, Jeremy, 217
Temptation of Agnes, The, see *First Franciscans, The*
Tempter, The, 10, 29
Ten Commandments, The, 37
Tennyson, Alfred, 29, 108
Tenth Man, The, 280
Terrible Meek, The, 287
Terror of Light, 162
Tewkesbury Festival, 113, 114–115, 208
That Fell Arrest, 117–118
Theatrocrat, The, 279
Then Will She Return, 291
They Came to a City, 50
This Is the Gate, 116–117
This Way to Paradise, 283
This Way to the Tomb, 226, 234–235
Thomas, Cyril J., 267, 270, 271
Thomas Cranmer of Canterbury, 109, 110, 149–151, 154, 156, 159, 160, 161, 233
Thor, with Angels, 208, 213–215

Thorndike, Eileen, 108, 111
Thorndike, Russell, 108
Thorndike, Sybil, 74, 110
Three Plays (Charles Williams), 147–148, 149
Three Temptations, The, 162
Three Time-Plays, 49
Thunderbolt, The, 280
Thurber, James, 199
Thursday's Child, 208
Thurston, E. Temple, 36, 282
Tilly of Bloomsbury, 282
Time and the Conways, 48
Time-Servers, The, 131
Times, The (London), 14, 15, 26, 27, 30, 31, 33, 93, 95, 99, 100, 104, 107, 115, 237, 240
Tobias and the Angel, 82, 115, 118, 119
Tolstoy, Leo, 60, 281
Too True to Be Good, 59, 75–76
Top of the Ladder, 285
"Towards a Christian Aesthetic," 164
Tower, The, 115, 208
Tragedy of Good Intentions, The, 285
Tragedy of Nan, The, 134
Travelling Man, The, 103
Tree, Beerbohm, 28, 29, 30, 31
Tree, Violet, 20
Trewin, J. C., 210
Trial of Jesus, The, 105, 134, 136–137, 138
Trial of Thomas Cranmer, The, 233
Triumph of the Philistines, The, 9
Truants, The, 279
Turner, Philip W., 261, 262–263, 267–268, 270
Two Sides of the Door, 288

Unburied Dead, The, 233
Unknown, The, 19–21
Unknown Star, The, 125
Upper Room, The, 287

Use of Poetry and the Use of Criticism, The, 186
Ustinov, Peter, 285

Vale, Terence, 105
Vane, Sutton, 45–46
Venus Observed, 208, 219–220
Verschoyle, Derek, 187
Vicar of Wakefield, The, 4
Victoria Regina, 131
Village Wooing, 120, 207
Vision, The, 287
Vollmoeller, Karl, 32
Voltaire, 60
Voysey Inheritance, The, 53–54

Waddell, Helen, 84
Waiting-Room, The, 131
Wakefield, Henry Russell (Bishop of Birmingham, 1911–24), 20
Wallace, Lew, 27
Wandering Jew, The (novel), 24
Wandering Jew, The (play), 282
War God, The, 281
Ward, A. W., 95
Ward, R. H., 162–164, 255–261, 262, 263, 265, 270–271, 272–273
Waste, 53–54
Waste Land, The, 185
Water Party, 289
Webb-Odell, R., 187
Well-Remembered Voice, A, 44
Wells Repertory Players, 207
"*What* Cocktail Party?," 199
"What Do We Believe?," 165
"What Is Christian Drama?," 267
When We Are Married, 284
Wherefore This Waste?, 293
White Horseman, The, 291
Whiting, John, 286
Widower's Houses, 278
Wilde, Oscar, 277, 278
Wilkinson, Oliver M., 292

William Poel and the Elizabethan Revival, 94
Williams, Charles, 93, 103, 109, 110, 111, 114, 120, 142–164, 175, 177, 184, 192, 204, 230 *fn,* 233, 242, 255, 261, 265, 272, 274, 275
Williams, Emlyn, 285
Williams, Harcourt, 110
Williams, William Carlos, 204
Wills, W. G., 4, 24
Wilson, Edmund, 177
Wind of Heaven, The, 285
Window, The, 292
"Winking Providence, A," 123
Winnington-Ingram, Arthur Foley (Bishop of London, 1901–39), 104
Wise and the Foolish Virgins, The, 260
Witch, The, 148, 149
Woodgate, Herbert, 27
Woods, Frank Theodore (Bishop of Winchester, 1924–32), 112
Woodward, Clifford Salisbury (Bishop of Bristol, 1933–46), 113
World of Light, The, 21
Wright, Dorothy, 263, 264
Wrong Door, The, 131

Ye Fearful Saints!, 131
Yeats, W. B., xii, 103
Yellow Book, The, 100
Yes and No, 284
York cycle, The, 88, 97
York Festival, 97
York Nativity Play, The, 97
Young, William, 27
Young King, The, 108
Younghusband, Francis, 106, 110, 111
Youth and the Peregrines, 207

Zangwill, Israel, 73–74, 281, 282
Zeal of Thy House, The, 109, 110, 165, 166–167, 273